RACE AND RUMORS OF RACE

RACE AND RUMORS OF RACE

The American South in the Early Forties

by

HOWARD W. ODUM

With a New Introduction by

BRYANT SIMON

THE JOHNS HOPKINS UNIVERSITY PRESS

BALTIMORE AND LONDON

Originally published as a hardcover edition in 1943 by The University of North
Carolina Press.
Johns Hopkins Paperbacks edition, 1997
06 05 04 03 02 01 00 99 98 97   5 4 3 2 1

The Johns Hopkins University Press
2715 North Charles Street
Baltimore, Maryland 21218-4319
The Johns Hopkins Press Ltd., London

Library of Congress Cataloging-in-Publication Data

Odum, Howard Washington, 1884–1954.
   Race and rumors of race : the American South in the early forties / by Howard
W. Odum.—Johns Hopkins paperbacks ed.
      p.   cm.
   Originally published: Chapel Hill : University of North Carolina Press, 1943.
With a new introd. by Bryant Simon.
   Includes bibliographical references.
   ISBN 0-8018-5757-0 (acid-free paper)
   1. Southern States—Race relations.   2. Afro-Americans—Southern States—
Social conditions.   3. Whites—Southern States—Attitudes—History—20th
century.   4. Southern States—Social conditions—1865–1945.   I. Title.
E185.61.O33   1997
305.8´00975—dc21   97-14450
                                                                         CIP

A catalog record for this book is available from the British Library.

CONTENTS

PART III

THE WAY ON

PART IV

QUESTIONS AND ANSWERS

INTRODUCTION TO THE 1997 EDITION

by Bryant Simon

When Howard Odum sat down to write *Race and Rumors of Race* in the early years of World War II, terrifying stories of bloody race wars and domestic insurgencies were circulating through the white South. White Southerners told each other that African Americans in Charleston, South Carolina, were stockpiling ice picks. In Memphis, Tennessee, they were said to be ordering cartons of pistols and rifles from the Sears and Roebuck Company catalog. From there the rumors multiplied: Training under a local man who spent a couple of years up North, African American farmers were supposedly drilling outside of New Orleans. Across the South, domestic workers were allegedly quitting their posts, saying they would not work for white women any more. Those who stayed on the job secretly joined "Eleanor Clubs," named after the liberal first lady. When their white employers were not looking, these club members whispered among themselves and plotted insurrection. By the next Christmas, they said, they would be living in the big house, eating roast beef and fresh asparagus cooked and served by their ex-bosses. As white soldiers pulled out of town near Valdosta, Georgia, and headed for basic training, it was rumored that a few grinning African American men waved and told them not to worry, they would take care of their mothers, wives, and sisters. And then there was the one about a group of white men who slaughtered twenty-seven African Americans because they had dared to act "white," then left their bodies to rot at the bottom of a putrid lake. These are some of the stories that white Southerners invented and spread during World War II.

While saving ration coupons, planting victory gardens, clapping at war bond rallies, and listening to Edward R. Murrow's radio reports from London, many Southern white people talked about race, but not always directly. They spread fearsome, violent rumors, accusations based on slivers of truth, wild embellishment, and hearsay. All the rumors had a similar plot line, and they sounded quite similar to rumors of slave insurrections told in the antebellum period and stories about threatened Christmas riots that were repeated just after the Civil War.[1] In each of the World War II–era narratives, once-docile African Americans, under the nefarious influences of first lady Eleanor Roosevelt, liberals, New Dealers, "bad niggers," and Yankees, would rise up against white rule, usually by the time of the next Christmas. Once empowered, they would humiliate, mock, and sexually exploit whites. Virile, well-armed white men would then turn the tables back on devious, dishonest African Americans, restoring the "Southern way of life." Everything would return to normal. White men would be back on top, just where they thought they belonged.

Rumors are a special form of speech. More structured than gossip but less carefully crafted than political rhetoric, rumors, as the historian Steven Hahn explains, are an important means of cultural expression. They allow people to establish identity and give meaning to ambiguous information and actions. Cloaked in secrecy, rumors serve further, in the words of the political scientist and ethnographer James Scott, as a "vehicle for anxieties and aspirations that may not be openly expressed."[2] By repeating rumors, frightened white Southerners in the 1940s created space to speak about things that they felt uncomfortable talking about out in the open. Still, rumors, in this case and most others, are not the whole story; they are instead a rough map of social and psychological pressure points.

"Rumor," psychologists Gordon W. Allport and Leo Postman observed, "is most frenzied when the public is expecting a momentous event to occur." On the homefront of the American South, World War II was one of these frenzied moments.[3] Historian Morton Sosna suggested that the Second World War may have had a more profound and lasting impact on the South than the Civil War. Whether or not this is true is difficult, if not impossible, to figure out. Yet without a doubt the war reconfigured the economic and social landscape of the South.[4] Massive government spending and the huge defense buildup ripped the South out its deep, dark depression doldrums, transforming it from the nation's number one economic problem into a land of opportunity. As German soldiers poured across Western Europe and the United States geared up to enter the battle, thousands of new jobs appeared in the South, especially in the cities. (The war also led to unprecedented urbanization in the South.) At the same time, the draft and military service siphoned off millions of potential workers. The result was an acute labor shortage. As economic spaces opened up, thousands of African Americans left farms and low-paying service jobs to enter industries that had historically been organized along racial lines. Now, black men and black women were doing white men's work. Other African Americans, meanwhile, were drafted into the army. In the South, the nation's military training center, the sight of black men in neatly pressed uniform marching in tight formation with rifles slung over their right shoulders unsettled many white men.

With African Americans serving in the armed forces and gaining greater economic power and higher standards of living, whites feared they would no longer stay in their place. Even before Japanese bombers attacked Pearl Harbor, many Southern whites noticed that the black population had already started to stir. More than a decade before the *Brown v. Board of Education* decision and the Montgomery bus boycott—the usual textbook starting points of the modern Civil Rights movement—African Americans began to mobilize for a no-holds-barred offensive against Jim Crow. Between 1940 and 1945, NAACP membership, itself a badge of opposition to Jim Crow, climbed from just over 50,000 in 1940 to more than 450,000 in 1946. In South Carolina alone over 15,000 people joined the NAACP during the war years. Liberals in Washington, meanwhile, led by first lady Eleanor Roosevelt and African American leaders like A. Phillip Randolph, insisted that unless democracy was renewed at home—meaning an end to segregation—it was hardly worth fighting abroad. Taking matters into their own hands on street corners and buses, African Americans simultaneously launched a series of seemingly uncoordinated assaults on Jim Crow. Throughout the war years, in thousands of subtle and dramatic ways, black people stopped playing their parts in the public theater of segregation. They refused to tip their hats to whites, make room for white pedestrians on jammed sidewalks, or give up their seats on crowded buses.[5]

Liberal political pressure, black economic advances and military service, and similar challenges to Jim Crow alarmed whites, but few discussed their uneasiness in public. Such talk would make African American agency clear and expose white supremacy's shaky foundations. Instead, whites invented stories and rumors that, in the tense climate of the 1940s, allowed them to voice their fears about black progress and at the same time assure themselves that they were still on top.

Fascinated and alarmed by the wild, fragmentary tales he heard swirling around him in the summer of 1942, Howard

Washington Odum, a well-known and well-regarded professor at the University of North Carolina at Chapel Hill, set out
to collect and catalog these wartime rumors of race. He
wrote to sociologists, philosophers, and an assortment of
other academics around the South asking them to find out if
their students had heard the stories about ice picks, sexual
assaults, and Eleanor Clubs. Many had. Odum received
thousands of reports of race rumors from every corner of the
region—mostly from cities and towns, but also from rural
hamlets and tiny railroad junctions, as well as a few African
American communities and a spattering of places above the
Mason-Dixon line and west of the Mississippi River. These
accounts formed the basis of *Race and Rumors of Race*, first
published in 1943 by the University of North Carolina Press.

More than fifty years later, Odum's book remains the single best and most comprehensive catalog of wartime rumors. If Odum had not collected these stories, they might
have faded from memory and eventually disappeared.
Equally important, Odum's work contextualized the wartime
rumors. Confirming reports by the Federal Bureau of Investigation and other police sources, Odum determined that the
rumors were not true, that African Americans were not
stockpiling weapons and domestics were not organizing
Eleanor Clubs.[6] Still, he understood that the rumors were
windows into the minds of the South. He stared through
these panes of glass to see and hear the origins of the rumors:
where they came from, when they started, and why people
believed them. In so doing, Odum presents a snapshot, fo-
cused in some places, blurry in others, of racial attitudes in
the South, especially white ones, during the turbulent era of
World War II. He explains in this book how white Southerners looked at African Americans and how African Americans
saw whites, as well as how non-Southerners viewed the South
during this crucial intersection in American history. Finally,

like all books, *Race and Rumors of Race* reveals something about the ideology, sympathies, and contradictions of the author himself.

Howard W. Odum was born in 1884 in Bethlehem, Georgia, a small community tucked off the road between burgeoning Atlanta and the then sleepy college town of Athens. His family owned their own home and farm, but they were neither rich nor poor, sharecroppers nor planters. Like people around them, Odum's parents worked hard and prayed hard, and hoped to pass the benefits of their labor on to the next generation. When Odum was thirteen his family moved to Oxford, Georgia. An average high school student, Odum went to nearby Emory College, at the time an average school with an average reputation. He graduated from the Methodist-affiliated institution in 1904 with a degree in classics and no other distinctions. Unable at first to find a teaching position on his own, he eventually secured a post in Tuccapola, Mississippi, with the help of an agent. Perhaps the best thing about Tuccapola was that it was close to Oxford and the University of Mississippi. Legend has it that Odum commuted to graduate classes on a mule. However he got to school, by 1906 Odum had earned a master's degree in classics.

Despite the apparent continuity between his undergraduate and graduate studies, Odum discovered a whole new field of study at "Ole Miss"—the emerging disciplines of the social sciences. The social sciences quickly became more than an academic specialty for Odum; they served almost as a new religion. According to Odum's biographer Daniel J. Singal, the young scholar saw the social sciences as a "source of salvation rather a research technique." Following in the footsteps of one of his University of Mississippi professors, the newly converted Odum headed north to Clarke University, in Worcester, Massachusetts, to study "character formation" with the cutting-edge psychologist, J. Stanley Hall. Odum was awarded a Ph.D. degree in psychology in 1909. The next year he earned a second Ph.D, this one in sociology, from Columbia University.[7]

Odum left Columbia as a man virtually handcuffed to the intellectual currents of his time. It was 1910, the heyday of the Progressive Era, and the newly minted doctor of psychology and sociology was a budding Progressive intellectual. Like John R. Commons, John Dewey, and other leading scholars of the day, Odum saw no lines of separation dividing the university from society, scholarship from policy. Sharing the ethos of the moment, he believed that the world was flawed but that it was also perfectible. He believed in the singularity of truth and maintained that the truth could be uncovered. However, finding the truth—and thereby solutions to social ills—first required objective scientific study. An unbiased, thorough examination of social maladies, Odum insisted, would lay bare problems and point to obvious remedies. Then it would be up to policymakers to do the right thing. Here, then, was the path to making the world better: it was a path laid down brick by brick through objective, rational, scientific research.

Unable to obtain a teaching position in the unusually tight academic job market (difficult even for someone with two Ph.Ds), Odum spent two years working for the city of Philadelphia, studying African American life there. Finally, he landed a position at the University of Georgia, just down the road from where he grew up. From 1913 to 1919, he taught in the Department of Education there. Combining his faith in the social sciences with his commitment to reform, Odum fervently advocated agricultural diversification. Preaching this gospel of change, he pushed for the development of a Southern dairy industry and showed his students the latest techniques for breeding Jersey cows. In 1919,

Odum left Athens and returned to his alma mater, Emory College, to become dean. Shortly after starting his new job, Odum bumped heads with the college's conservative chancellor, who bristled at the young administrator's attempts to turn the school into an instrument for social change. When officials at the University of North Carolina at Chapel Hill offered Odum a position as chair of the Sociology Department and dean of the School of Public Welfare in 1924, he jumped at the opportunity.

The leadership of the University of North Carolina, beginning at the top with President Harry Woodburn Chase, shared Odum's commitment to the Progressive Era ideal of engaged scholarship. They wanted the school to play a part in making the state a better place. Taking advantage of the highly charged academic atmosphere, Odum and his talented colleagues in the social sciences, most notably Rupert B. Vance, Arthur F. Raper, and Guy B. Johnson, recruited like-minded associates and graduate students. Rejecting the mindless bravado of New South boosters, Odum and his allies pointed to the painful limits of economic development in the region. True to their Progressive creed, however, they were not a gloomy bunch of pessimists. They felt certain, that intensive study would point to progress. Perhaps the truest believer of them all, Odum turned his faith in the social sciences into a highly effective fund-raising pitch. He persuaded, cajoled, and, when necessary, begged state and federal agencies as well as Northern philanthropic groups to fund his detailed studies of Southern life.

With the money, Odum hired additional faculty, assembled a crew of able research assistants, founded the prestigious *Journal of Social Forces*, and established the widely respected Institute for Research in Social Sciences. Almost single-handedly, he transformed the University of North Carolina from a country club training ground for the state's mercantile elite into a vibrant, nationally recognized intellectual center. Arriving in Chapel Hill in 1934 to enter graduate school, C. Vann Woodward, who would go on to become the most influential historian of the South of the twentieth century, called the constellation of journals, institutes, and departments revolving around Odum "the most thriving academic empire in the South at the time."[8]

For his part, Odum thrived in Chapel Hill both as a scholar and what we might today call a public intellectual. By the time he retired in the 1950s, he had published more than twenty books and some one hundred fifty articles. According to one observer, he became the "South's best known social scientist in the first half of the 20th century." After Odum's death, in 1954, the *Washington Post* eulogized him, calling him the "Eli Whitney of the Modern South." "Certainly," the paper added, "there was no one—unless it was Franklin Roosevelt—whose influence was greater than Odum's on the development of the region below the Potomac."[9] Even though social science jargon bogged down some of his work with thick layers of nearly impenetrable prose, much of his writing reached beyond tightly drawn academic circles, finding its way onto the desks of politicians and policymakers, New York book reviewers, and Atlanta reformers. So wide was his readership that one of his books, *Southern Regions of the United States,* was banned in his native Georgia. Usually only those who matter are censored.[10]

Throughout Odum's productive career, four main intellectual streams ran through his writings. First of all, Odum was intrigued by the distinctly unscientific discipline of folklore and what is often called folk culture. His earliest writings concentrated on African American folk songs and folk traditions.[11] Reflecting the influences of his graduate school mentor, Hall, and borrowing ideas about folkways from the pathbreaking sociologist William Graham Sumner, Odum suggested that folk cultures rose organically out of the common experiences and shared pasts of ordinary people. Rarely, however, did these people put down their ideas and values—what he would call their culture—in systematic, easy-to-grab forms. Instead, they encoded their culture in oral traditions that could be reconstructed only through painstaking, scientific research into nonliterate sources such as songs and stories handed down from one generation to the next. Folkways, Odum argued, took centuries to develop. The Progressive in him insisted that such habits and beliefs could be changed, but he warned that change would take time. Nothing could be accomplished overnight.

Second, always an aggressive empiricist, Odum advocated methodical, extensive research in preparation for change. He branded his social science methodology "descriptive studies," and even more commonly called it "portraiture." One his biographers said that he presented his findings as "word paintings."[12] To Odum, portraiture meant giving the reader a detailed, wide-angle picture of whatever subject he set out to describe. Interpretation was to be left out or shuffled off to the margins. Odum's books and articles were typically filled with numerous stories, seemingly endless pages of charts and tables, and long lists of open-ended questions. Often the tables repeated what the stories said, and the charts documented what the tables reported. Obviously, there was a point to this method of portraiture. Odum seemed to think that the more evidence he heaped on, the more readers would believe him and think the picture he painted was true. Why use only one example, when you had collected two, three, four, or more? At times the style could be almost numbing, but it also revealed, like a portfolio of Dorothea Lange photographs, the painful realities of, southern poverty and underdevelopment, topics that were the foci of most of Odum's work by the 1930s.

Regionalism was the third and probably the most widely recognized component of Odum's thought. Of course, regionalism, or what some have called sectionalism, was not new to the twentieth-century South. Since before the Civil War, white Southerners have continually argued that the region's climate, Anglo-Saxon heritage, or culture produced a distinct people below the Mason-Dixon line, a people markedly different from—and better than—their Yankee compatriots. Selectively reconstructing the past, many celebrated the Old South as a noble age of gentility, respectability, and aristocratic order. When it came to the postbellum era, sectional loyalists presented simple pictures of a vibrant and harmonious South. Injured millhands and beleaguered tenants were left out of these sketches.

During the late 1920s and early 1930s, regionalism flourished in every section of the nation, but again, nowhere more so than in the South. Writing at least partly in response to H. L. Mencken's barbed attacks on Dixie—the Baltimore journalist once called the region the "Sahara of the Bozarts"—Southerners rose up to defend their homeland. Many answered these insults with tired and insipid paeans to the South's glorious past and its prosperous, hard-won present. Others, such as the "Southern Agrarians," fashioned more thoughtful responses. Based in Nashville around Vanderbilt University, the eclectic band of poets and writers who made up the Agrarians lashed out at the modern world. In their famous 1930 manifesto, "I'll Take My Stand," they decried the factories, the cities, the centralized state, and the amoralism and gaudiness of mass culture. Against the steel beams and bulldozers of Gotham, they held up the yeomanry and the small-scale agricultural South, not the planters and the plantations of the Old South, as models of simplicity and tradition and as a cultural ideal superior to the crass materialism of industrial society.

Odum and his coterie of Chapel Hill social scientists outlined a different kind of "regionalism." Indeed, no one was more closely associated with the term than was Odum. His brand of sociology, in fact, often went by the name regionalism. Like their contemporaries, the Agrarians, Odum and his cohorts rejected the romanticism of the lost cause and the hollow promises of prosperity embedded in New South mythology. But they also laid aside the backward-looking antimodernism of the Nashville crowd. What's more, they zeroed in on economic issues rather than cultural or social ones.

Armed with data marshaled from scores of scientifically drawn portraits of the region, Odum argued that the South was different from other parts of the nation. In fact, he said that it was a separate, unique region, but he saw little to applaud or celebrate in this uniqueness. What made the South distinct from the rest of the country was its people's shared history of poverty and backwardness. This was what molded the area below the Mason-Dixon line into a *region;* in the words of historians David Carlton and Peter Coclanis, "a geographically defined unit whose characteristics were interrelated, and the destinies of whose people where intertwined."[13] To Odum, then, regionalism was a specific project. It represented the close, scientific, empirical study of the measurable demographic differences between distinct parts of the country and the rest of the nation. Odum's regionalism featured another, not so rational component. Despite his faith in empiricism, Odum remained a devoted Southerner. He loved virtually without limit the poor and middling white Southerners of small town Bethlehem, Georgia. He wanted above all to find a way to make their lives and those of their families better in the long run.

Perhaps more than any of his books, Odum's *Southern Regions of the United States*, published by the University of

North Carolina Press in 1936, epitomized his commitment to regionalism.[14] Sprawling and unwieldy, much like the place he set out to depict, *Southern Regions* is filled with chapter after table after chart after map, displaying everything from income per capita to bathrooms and physicians per thousand to radios per family to newspaper readership to infant morality. When added up, the various points of data, each like a brush stroke, document that the states of the Old Confederacy had more of what was worse in America and less of what was good. The shaded maps and carefully arranged tables also said—they almost cried out—that something needed to be done to address the South's problems.

Odum's ideas about regionalism point to the fourth and final strain of his thinking. When it came to politics, Odum was a gradualist. Eschewing radical ideologies of any sort, he maintained that the system—that is, representative democracy and industrial capitalism—could be fixed and that it was worth saving. To this end, he pushed for modest reforms, ways of tinkering with the economy and adjusting the bureaucracy that would slowly change things for the better. Odum's sense of folk culture gave shape to his sense of gradualism. The sociologist believed that people's thoughts and values had been forged over long periods of time, almost as if they were rock formations. Altering these views would therefore not be easy. He endlessly worried about pushing people too far, too fast.

Nowhere was Odum's gradualism clearer than on the race question. Strangely, considering the tight focus of his regionalism on the Jim Crow South, Odum rarely talked about race directly. To be sure, he looked into poverty, literacy, birthrates, and even radio ownership, but race was almost never used as the dependent variable. When race did slip into his discussions, it was framed as a natural category, not a social construction. Race was a thing, not an idea. Region remained the key factor in his sociological studies. Yet despite erasing race from his examinations, Odum remained concerned, indeed troubled, by Southern race relations. By the late 1920s, Odum was widely known as a Southern liberal, someone who believed that the Jim Crow system was wrong and that someday it would have to be replaced. Although he vociferously denounced lynching and for a time headed both the Commission on Interracial Cooperation and the Southern Regional Council, Odum refused to work with the NAACP, an organization he regarded, according to Morton Sosna, as a "well-meaning but unscientific agitation agency that did more harm than good."[15] He feared that if the leaders of the NAACP had their way, they would push for reforms that would alienate the good white people of the South, leading them into a perilous alliance with reactionaries. The region, he repeatedly observed, was not ready for radical change or ready to have outsiders tell it what to do. Something had to be done about the race problem, Odum readily acknowledged, but he insisted just as emphatically that it was a Southern problem and that Yankees should step back and let white Southerners take care of it.

Odum's four key intellectual concerns—portraiture, folk culture, regionalism, and gradualism—permeate *Race and Rumors of Race*. The easiest to see is the method of portraiture. In the later sections of the book, for instance, Odum reprints verbatim, without commentary, long, informative reports on race relations. Meanwhile, in the book's middle chapters—titled Part Two, "Race and Rumors of Race"—he inventories wartime race rumors. Dividing them into five separate categories, he relates story after story, example after example of strange racial tales, mostly from the South but also from as far away as Detroit and Harlem. He recounts as many as twenty different versions of the Eleanor Club rumor, explaining that these imaginary organizations went by many names: "Eleanor Clubs," "The Daughters of Eleanor," "The Eleanor Angel Clubs," "The Sisters of Eleanor," and "The Royal House of Eleanor." By repeating multiple variations of each kind of rumor, literally one after another from every corner of the South, Odum is painting with words. He seems to be saying to his readers that since he has uncovered all these examples of rumors, something must be going on. The method of portraiture, in this case sheer repetition, is meant to drive home the point that the rumors were so pervasive that they had to be taken seriously.

Race and Rumors of Race, however, represents more than a catalog of wartime stories and half-truths. Odum digs for the roots of the stories, uncovering the outlines of wartime racial tensions. In the opening sections of the book, aptly titled "A Crisis in the Making," he explains where the rumors came from. He documents shifts in employment patterns, municipal transportation, and increased racial interaction on busy city streets triggered by wartime mobilization. Each of these developments, Odum writes, exacerbated racial tensions. Yet he maintains that the Jim Crow system and white resistance to even the slightest adjustment to white supremacy remained the deeper sources of the rumors. As the war broke out, Odum notes, African Americans, rallying around the banner of "Double V"—Victory Abroad Against Fascism and Victory at Home Against Jim Crow—started to organize to bring an end to segregation. Black women and men, particularly the younger generation, demanded equal treatment, the integration of the armed forces, fair wages, and the right to vote. White Southerners reacted with rage, furor, and (mostly during 1942 and 1943) by telling weird, wild stories.

In order to understand why white Southerners told these tales and why they believed them, Odum explains, it is first necessary to understand what he calls the "Southern credo" with regard to race. Always the social scientist, Odum lays out the specifics of this credo, or what he labels "white folk culture," in other places in the book, point by point—twenty-one points in all. Basically, the folk culture of the white South boils down to two rather pungent main ingredients: White Southerners did not believe that African Americans were really human and they definitely would not subscribe to racial equality. They could not even imagine a world in which whites and blacks were equal. Dedicated to the method of portraiture and wedded to rather static notions about folk culture, Odum chronicled the "Southern credo" from a distance. Claiming scientific objectivity, he refused to condemn this pernicious mix of ideas outright.

As in Odum's other works, the politics of regionalism was also an important component of *Race and Rumors of Race*.[16] From a moral perspective, Odum's regionalism was built on a strong sense of place and caring about the South and its position in the nation. Throughout the book, Odum emphasizes his loyalty to the region, even when its actions, like spreading the wildest of the Eleanor Club rumors, embarrassed him somewhat. Still, Odum would not and could not give up on his homeland. He wrote *Race and Rumors of Race* not as modern scholars might have, to explore the tangled intersections of race, class, and gender in Southern thought, but to help the war effort. Rumors and race tensions, he feared, were hindering the fight against fascism. He also wanted to ring a warning bell for the people he loved and respected. By putting some of the exaggerated stories flying around the region in print for all to see, he wanted to jar the good people of the white South out of their slumber, to wake them up before the smoldering dangers of extremism that fueled the rumors caught fire. Fabricated tales about insurgencies and impending doom, he concluded, sprung from the poisoned soil of Dixie's oppressive racial order. If nothing was done to alter relations between black and white, the murderous edge to the rumors could come true, leaving the region awash in blood. The violence in Odum's language about the problem of the rumors did not, however, translate into an equally urgent call for action.[17]

Dedicated to gradualism, Odum searched for ways to ease the South's transition from the violence of segregation to peaceful integration. Perhaps more than anything else, a commitment to slow, orderly change infuses *Race and Rumors of Race*. In Part Three, "The Way On," Odum searches for solutions, but he repeatedly holds back. Playing the role of the objective social scientist, he poses question after question about the problem, more than a hundred in all. Ever cautious, he steadfastly refuses to answer any of his own queries. What Odum does propose in the book is a conference bringing together "responsible" leaders of both races to "strike," in the words of one commentator, "a golden mean between the heedless urging of pro-democratic reforms regardless of the folkways and state-ways of the southern people and the philistine resistance to any constructive program characteristic of those who want to be left alone—in a position of dominance."[18]

According to Odum, the crisis in the South was aggravated by the presence of three distinct groups operating at cross purposes: the new generation of better educated African Americans committed to gaining their full political and economic rights; northern liberals dedicated to bringing an end to Jim Crow; and white Southerners unwilling to relinquish their power and determined to keep African Americans down. Though admitting that the position of the "white South" was the "least right," Odum nonetheless assails African American political leaders and newspaper editors of both races for stirring up the masses. Contradicting himself

somewhat, he implies here that the problem was not segregation, as he had suggested elsewhere, but radical agitation. If
"they" would just stop yelling so loudly for change, Odum
seems to be saying, everything would be all right. His position is much like the one taken by white religious leaders in
Birmingham during the Civil Rights movement, who were
also worried about outside influences. Wait, Odum contended, for the good people of the South to catch up; then
we will go forward together. Gradualists like Odum never
quite seemed to understand what Frederick Douglass never
forgot: "Power concedes nothing without demand. It never
did and it never will."[19]

Along with the four persistent themes in Odum's work,
Race and Rumors of Race also exposed a new, emerging, yet
still cloudy element in the Chapel Hill sociologist's scholarship. According to Daniel Rodgers, by the late 1940s Odum's
earlier Progressive Era faith had been shaken, but not broken. All of the books, articles, and carefully planned examinations had done little to change the South. Once a true believer, Odum began to doubt whether scientific study, no
matter how diligently undertaken, could uncover problems
and point to solutions. Sounding a bit like one of those fussy
old Agrarians, or maybe just like a curmudgeon, he criticized
mass culture and technology. About two-thirds of the way
through *Race and Rumors of Race*, Odum begins, almost
without warning, to rail against the unnaturalness of technology. In this section he blames the spread of rumors not so
much on southern anxieties or poisonous race relations, but
on the irresponsible media, which refused to filter its own
stories. Fittingly, this is perhaps the weakest and worst-orga-
nized chapter in the book. Somehow, it seems to speak to
Odum's own confusion, his tentative move away from absolute faith in the social sciences to a yet undetermined intellectual place.

As the UNC Press prepared to release *Race and Rumors of Race* in the spring of 1943, Odum seemed worried. After Harry F. Comer of the YMCA read a draft of the book, Odum nervously asked: "Do these rumors seem exaggerated to you? Have you heard most of them? Is the Credo of the South too hard on southerners? Have we emphasized the new behavior of the young Negro enough?" "Many people," he speculated in another letter to another reader, "will criticize us for making it and for letting it out."[20] Odum gauged the response correctly. Fellow Southern liberal Virginus Dabney, for instance, feared that "some people may think that you are passing along rumors and gossip as truth."[21]

Certainly not everyone was critical of the book. "I think the whole thing is damn good!" exclaimed Odum's colleague Guy B. Johnson.[22] Sociologist H. C. Dixon praised Odum, saying that the author wrote with "a combination of balance, warmth, and liveliness." The *Springfield Republican*, meanwhile, tagged the book a "careful collection of rumors . . . as valuable as it is tragic." "Even more valuable," the paper added, "is the accompanying commentary and discussion by Dr. Odum, noted sociologist and authority of southern regional problems." Applauding Odum's handling of the white "mythology of race," an anthropologist added, "I think this is probably the best book for its purpose ever written." Others were more guarded. A. W. Taylor of the *Christian Century* called the book "splendid in presenting the issue." "Not so much," he wrote, however, could "be said for its dealing with ways and means to meet the issue."

African Americans were especially critical of *Race and Rumors of Race*. The left-leaning New York intellectual Alain Locke blasted Odum's politics. "This study's approach, though representing southern liberalism at its best," Locke contended in the *Survey Graphic*, "also clearly defines its limitations—a lack of courage to come to grips with the real reasons . . . behind the folkways." Then he added in a caustic voice: "Counter-arguments against race prejudice merely on the level of public opinion chops off these social weeds only at the ground line, leaving their vital roots unexposed and relatively safe and intact."[23] Writing in the *Nation*, E. Franklin Frazier, one of the nation's foremost African American sociologists, welcomed the book's coverage of rumors and its analysis of the source of the crisis, but showed little patience for Odum's gradualism. Attacking "outside agitators," Odum, however fair-minded and liberal, became in Fraizer's mind little more than an apologist for Southern racism.[24] Carter Woodson, a prominent African American historian, reviewed the book as well. He, too, praised Odum's reporting of the rumors, but he questioned the sociologist's caution. "If Odum's order have any hope for an amicable adjustment" of race relations, he argued, "they are not acquainted with the history of mankind." Ending on an angry note, he concluded, "We have had many riots in this country, and we shall have many more before Jim Crow can be killed."[25]

Strangely, no one criticized Odum's sources. Writing to his friends and colleagues at colleges and universities across the region, he asked them to see if their students had heard any of the rumors he was hearing in Chapel Hill. Indeed, many had heard discussions of Eleanor Clubs and impending race riots. Yet these reports came from a rather limited section of the South. Very few people except the sons and a few of the daughters of the region's agricultural and mercantile elite attended institutions of higher learning in the 1940s. This skewed Odum's evidence and might explain why he heard so many stories about rebellious African American domestics and so few accounts of job competition or housing shortages. Odum's portrait of the South, therefore, is really a portrait of the wealthiest parts of the South.

In the end, *Race and Rumors of Race* remains exactly

what it is: a document of the times and a window into
Howard Odum's mind. As well as any text, this book reminds
us that the war was never the simple morality play, pitting
innocent Americans against evil Germans, that has been
depicted by deep-voiced gray-suited narrators on the History Channel. The homefront itself vibrated with conflict,
and Odum's short volume captures the volatility of the moment. He points out the wide racial fissures in the South at
the outbreak of war, at a time when the region stood at
the historic divide between the end of the Jim Crow era and
the start of the modern Civil Rights movement. His book of-
fers a glimpse at the academic world and how sociologists in
the 1940s thought about and addressed social problems.
Without setting out to do so, Odum's book also exposes the
limits of Southern liberalism, the timidity that ultimately
placed it not on the side of change but, on the side of the
status quo. Finally, *Race and Rumors of Race* reveals the
absurdity of racism. Story after wild story shows what
strange, odd, evil products come from making fact out of the
fiction of race. When a society is based on a lie, anything is
believable.

But perhaps there is another way to look at the wartime
race rumors. As Locke, Frazier, and Woodson suggest, Odum
delivers his findings from a white perspective, a white gaze,
in the modern parlance. To be sure, he does include a short
five-and a half page chapter on wartime rumors in the
African American community. There were, he reports, stories about white soldiers killing black servicemen and white
MPs gunning down black women. Nonetheless, for Odum,
the wartime rumors point most clearly to white frenzy. Still,
there is perhaps another way to look at the stories that white
people and African Americans told one another during the
war. There may be a way to piece together another perspective from Odum's rumors. Perhaps some of the rumors were

true or at least began with a grain of truth. Once the racism
of the white storytellers is wiped away, the sketchy outlines of
another story can begin to emerge.

Historian and cultural critic Robin Kelley has pointed to
an alternative way to look at African American politics in the
era of Jim Crow, one that downplays victimization and high-
lights agency.[26] He has shown that the ordinary, the odd, and
the submerged might actually be about politics, about the
distribution of public power. When African Americans
shouted on buses, occupied white seats, or dressed to kill on
a Saturday night, they were reclaiming their bodies, the same
bodies that the Jim Crow order sought to possess. White
Southerners clearly picked up on this clash of wills. They understood that gestures could be, and often were, a form a
protest. By talking about these actions, by telling each other
rumors, white Southerners were recognizing African American behavior for what it was—an attack on Jim Crow. Perhaps by using rumors rather than formal means to talk about
African American behavior, white people communicated
their uneasiness about African American protest, but they
did so in a way that attempted to delegitimize that protest. In
a rather complicated twist, rumors, by their nature, suggest a
kind of exaggeration that turns what might be real into make-
believe. They trivialize events and behavior while simultaneously calling attention to them.

Whatever was actually going on, the wartime rumors constituted a text more complicated and more multivocal than
Odum realized or was willing to admit. They provide vivid
evidence of the tangled and tortured world of the last days of
Jim Crow's reign. They are a shadow play of the civil rights
drama of black protest and white resistance that would take
place in the South a few years later. While Odum imagined a
world in which race would not matter, he could not figure
out how to get there. To see the rumors as real was perhaps

too painful. That would have made him confront the gap between his vision of tomorrow and his everyday politics of waiting until the time was right to act.

NOTES

1. Stephen Nissenbaum, "An Insurrection That Never Happened: The 'Christmas Riots' of 1865," in *True Stories From the American Past, Vol. 2, Since 1865,* ed. William Graebner (New York, 1997), 1–17.

2. Remarks from James Scott and Steven Hahn, in Hahn, "'Extravagant Expectations' of Freedom: Rumor, Political Struggle, and the Christmas Insurrection Scare of 1865 in the American South," *Past and Present* (forthcoming), For more on rumors see Luise White, "Between Gluckman and Foucault: Historizing Rumor and Gossip," *Social Dynamics* 20 (Winter 1994): 75–92; Patricia A. Turner, *I Heard It Through the Grapevine: Rumor in African American Culture* (Berkeley, 1993).

3. Gordon W. Allport and Leo Postman, *The Psychology of Rumor* (New York, 1947), 33–47.

4. Morton Sosna, "More Important Than the Civil War? The Impact of World War II on the South," in *Perspectives on the American South: An Annual Review of Society, Politics, and Culture,* ed. James C. Cobb and Charles R. Wilson (New York, 1987), 145–61.

5. For more on World War II in the South see ibid., 151–55; Pete Daniel, *Standing at the Crossroads: Southern Life in the Twentieth Century* (Baltimore, 1996); George B. Tindall, *The Emergence of the New South, 1913–1945* (Baton Rouge, 1967), 687–731. On liberals in the 1940s see Doris Kearns Goodwin, *No Ordinary Time: Franklin and Eleanor Roosevelt: The Home Front in World War II* (New York, 1994), 10; and Patricia Sullivan, *Days of Hope: Race and Democracy in the New Deal Era* (Chapel Hill, 1996). For some suggestions on African American behavior, see Robin D. G. Kelley, "'We Are Not What We Seem': Rethinking Black Working-Class Opposition in the Jim Crow South," *Journal of American History* (June 1993), especially 86, 103–104.

6. The results of the FBI's investigations are reported in the *New York Times,* September 23, 1942. See also the Richard Manning Jeffries Papers, Folders 50–52, Race Relations, April 1942–September 1942, South Caroliniana Library, Columbia, SC. Jeffries checked with law officers across the state seeking information about Eleanor Clubs.

7. On Odum's background, see Daniel Joseph Singal, *The War Within: From Victorian to Modernist Thought in the South, 1919–1945* (Chapel Hill, 1982), 117–19; and George B. Tindall, "The Significance of Howard W. Odum to Southern History: A Preliminary Estimate," *Journal of Southern History* 24 (August 1958), 286.

8. C. Vann Woodward, *Thinking Back: The Perils of Writing History* (Baton Rouge, 1986), 20.

9. Wayne D. Brazil, "Howard W. Odum," in *Encyclopedia of Southern Culture*, ed. Charles Reagan Wilson and William Ferris (Chapel Hill, 1989), 296. The *Washington Post* article is quoted by Tindall, "The Significance of Howard W. Odum," 285.

10. See Brazil, "Howard W. Odum." On the banning of Southern Regions, see Daniel Rodgers, "Regionalism and the Burdens of Progress," in *Region, Race, and Reconstruction: Essays in Honor of C. Vann Woodward* ed. J. Morgan Kousser and James M. McPherson (New York, 1982), 11.

11. See for example, Odum, *Social and Mental Traits of the Negro: Research into the Condition of the Negro Race in Southern Towns* (New York, 1910); Odum and Guy B. Johnson, *The Negro and His Songs: A Study of Typical Negro Songs in the South* (Chapel Hill, 1925); and Odum and Guy B. Johnson, *Negro Workaday Songs* (Chapel Hill, 1926).

12. Singal, *The War Within,* 131.

13. For this quote, along with more about the mission of regionalism, see David L. Carlton and Peter A. Coclanis, *Confronting Southern Poverty in the Great Depression: The Report on Economic Conditions of the South with Related Documents* (Boston, 1996), 5–6.

14. Other important regionalist works by Odum include, *An American Epoch: Southern Portraiture in the National Picture* (New York, 1930); and Odum and Harry E. Moore, *American Regionalism: A Cultural-Historical Approach to National Integration* (New York, 1938).

15. Morton Sosna, *In Search of the Silent South: Southern Liberals and the Race Question* (New York, 1977), 51–52.

16. While the historian Daniel Rodgers, in his study of Odum, maintains that the Chapel Hill sociologist was edging away from regionalism in the late 1930s, regionalism seems to have indeed, still mattered to Odum. See Rodgers, "Regionalism and the Burdens of Progress," 14–15.

17. For example, see Odum to H. N. Massey, Milledgeville, Ga., April 16, 1943, Odum Papers, Box 58, Folder—Rumor—Letters—Misc. 1942–1943, Southern Historical Collection, Chapel Hill, N.C.

18. Gwynne Nettler, review of Odum's *Race and Rumors of Race*, *The American Journal of Sociology* 5 (March 1944), 548.

19. Frederick Douglass quoted by William H. Chafe, *Civilities and Civil Rights: Greensboro, North Carolina and the Black Struggle for Freedom* (New York, 1980), 2.

20. Odum to Mr. Harry F. Comer, YMCA, May 5, 1943, and Odum to A. A. Alexander at the Cosmos Club, Washington D.C., April 10, 1943, Odum Papers, Box 58, Folder—Rumor—Letters—Misc. 1942–1943.

21. Virginus Dabney is quoted by Odum in a letter to W. T. Couch the head of the UNC Press. Odum to Couch, August 20, 1943, UNC Press Records, Sub-Group 4 (Author/Title Publication Records), Odum, Howard W., *Race and Rumors of Race*, Southern Historical Collection, University of North Carolina, Chapel Hill.

22. Ibid, comment by Guy B. Johnson on *Race and Rumors of Race*, n.d.

23. These last three reviews come from the always useful *Book Review Digest* (New York, 1944), 619; and RR Digest (New York, 1945), 570.

24. E. Franklin Frazier, "The South and the Negro," *Nation,* April, 15, 1944, 453–54.

25. Carter Woodson, review of *Race and Rumors of Race, Journal of Negro History* 29 (January 1944), 93–94.

26. Kelley, "'We Are Not What We Seem.'"

PREFACE

The time covered by this story of race and rumors of race was the short span of one year from July to July 1942–1943, a cross section of American time, place, and behavior which demanded a new inventory. This little volume tries to set down observations and recordings of what happened during that year of yesterday but with the understanding that an essential part of the drama was grounded in the backgrounds upon which that year's chronicles were based. So, too, a part of its importance was reflected in the ever-sobering questions as to what yesterday's behavior and trends would mean to the day after, and to all the tomorrows after that.

The stage setting and the chief actors were primarily in the southern regions of the United States, although inseparable from the rest of the Nation and the world, from which the South could no longer be isolated. What the South had called "the North" had become the larger Nation, Northeast and Middle States, Northwest and Far West, in all their regional interrelations. So, too, the South had become, through its millions of youth throughout the allied nations, a new part of a new world. Yet in the story of the Negro and of race tensions, the southern regions still appeared in bold contrast to the other regions of the Nation and to much of the newly stated philosophy of global democracy.

Thus the problem, while essentially of the South with many of its issues painfully simple to most of the southern people, in reality was also essentially complex and American, set in the revolutionary stirrings of a new world. The total story reflected something timeless, yet full of the quality of time in the here and now; spaceless, yet of the essence of the region and its folk; universal, yet of the stuff of America, and more specifically of the epic and epoch of its southern biracial culture

Without sensing the realism of the situation or understanding the total problem, it might have seemed relatively easy to exhort that America and the South ought to be capable of rising to the occasion and making quick adaptation to the ideals of the new freedoms of folk everywhere. Yet the essential heart of the story was the fact that it reflected the most difficult of all problems for the very reason that it was set in a special time and place and culture in conflict with other times, other places, other cultures. The very telling of the story or the recording of things that happened illustrated the fact that here was problem and planning which demanded their own peculiar and distinctive specifications commensurate with the organic nature of the situation and the qualities of particular crisis.

There were qualities in the Walt Whitman democracy which appeared adequate for both the specific and the universal. If he proclaimed the universal equality of all men, so also he pictured his "O Magnet South" in all affection and understanding.

O magnet South! O glittering perfumed South! My South!
O quick mettle, rich blood, impulse and love! good and evil!
O all dear to me!

Yet always the Walt Whitman universal pointed back to the great principles of the folk, of nature, of democracy, assuming somehow that there would be planning and human will to take each step in its order.

I speak the password primeval, I give the sign of democracy,
By God, I will accept nothing which all cannot have their
    counterpart of on the same terms.

Since this story is part and parcel of the folk themselves,
there is no inconsistency in combining affection for the
people and their region with the conclusion that some of
their heritage of the past may be terribly wrong. It must be
clear, therefore, from this introductory approach that the
story is not merely one of description but also of purpose.
One purpose would be to attain a sense of objectivity and
of looking at the scenes of yesterday in such ways as would
transcend the old emotional bitterness and would declare a
moratorium on tempers and violence, on name-calling and
race politics, and on smartness and irresponsibility, for such
duration as would win the greater cause for all. In this
search for objectivity, thère are many questions asked. One
preview question might very well be, "What shall it profit
to gain a world of argumentative points and lose the soul
of the people and of America?"

The dynamic Franklin Henry Giddings had a way of saying that the educated person was one who had found out
most of the more important ways in which human beings
have made fools of themselves and had thought about them
long and seriously enough to have acquired an aversion for
them. This volume, then, in that sense is an appeal for genuinely realistic education rather than revolutionary action,
yet always sensing the new role of education in setting the
stage for orderly change commensurate with the stated
ideals of the best that men can do.

Three special considerations are urged. One is that it is
not possible to sense the total meaning of this story without
reading all of the different parts; nor is it possible to understand the different parts without knowing the total. A second is that the story is grounded in several thousand

itemized rumors authentically gathered. It is of the essence
of the story that it be checked with such details, references,
sources, and acknowledgments as are presented in Part IV,
Chapter XXIII. A third is the fact that the story, having
closed, is presented in the past tense with the understanding
that its readers will be constantly checking and asking:
Were the observations accurately made? Were they well
reported? Were the conclusions justified? Were the facts as
stated? Were their meanings well interpreted? Was the crisis
as serious as indicated? What can be done about it? Is there
any more important story that needs telling in the Nation
than this?

From this story we know what the situation is, how it
came to be as it is, and what is needed. We know the truth,
but we do not know the way. It is, therefore, literally an
affectionate appeal to all the people of the Nation and a
challenge to its leadership for wisdom and maturity, bottomed in the facing of truth wherever found; in the asking
of essential questions; in the search for correct answers. The
eager quest for a new covenant through scientific and cooperative endeavor on new high levels leaves no place for
bitterness and hate, for name-calling and blame, for flight
from that reality which is America's heritage and opportunity.

H. W. O.

Chapel Hill, N. C.
August 1943

PART I

CRISIS IN THE MAKING

I

Crisis in the Making

This is part of the story of the crisis of the South and of
the Negro in the United States of America in the early 1940's
—years of war tension and of another prospective post-war
tragic era. It is a part of the story, therefore, of a national
crisis as well. It is called *Race and Rumors of Race* because
the measure and nature of the extraordinary crisis were reflected with such vividness in the mass of race rumors that
swept, flood-like, upon us in the major areas of white and
Negro relationships in the South, and thence as reflected in
the rising tide of rumors and tensions in the hinterlands.
They flooded even such cosmopolitan centers as the Nation's
capital like flood waters suddenly released by a bomber's
blast.

It is, moreover, part of the story of two great regional folk
cultures caught up in the midst of transition between the
powerful heritage of the past and the mighty pull of the
future. For here was the white South, a great people often
doing little things and a good people often doing bad things.
And here was the Negro South, caught as always between
the upper and nether millstones of conflicting forces and also
paying the price of extraordinary transition from level to
level of cultural achievement and needing plenty of sympathy and guidance. And here was the white South inexorably conditioned in cultural complexes, suffering terribly
and needing sympathy and help as few peoples ever needed
it in the annals of man. And, even more important, the two,
white South and black South, were part and parcel of a great

3

national culture whose dynamics, scarcely less than the two regional cultures, needed the sense of time and wisdom, of organic regional perspective, and of the essence of cosmopolitan, global culture.

And the story, like the reality itself, must be told in the language of the folk, not over-mindful of the sensitiveness of those who get too far away from the people. The story is of the crude stuff of which realism is made and needs the hand of a double Walt Whitman, one whose sense of nature and organic unity can portray crudeness, diversity, and conflict in terms of esteem and affection, and one who senses the democracy of the folk and the spirit of America.

For abundant evidence in the catalogue of rumors, tensions, conflicts, and trends justified the conclusion that the South and the Negro, in the early 1940's, faced their greatest crisis since the days of the reconstruction and that many of the same symbols of conflict and tragedy that were manifest in the 1840's were evident again a hundred years later.

It will be the purpose of this work to try to present a vivid picture of the southern scene as it was primarily reflected through a catalogue and analysis of race rumors and tensions; with an analysis of the general historical and evolutionary background, with special reference to the war situation, to the total national picture, and to the future development of a great region of the Nation in the midst of such titanic conflict as to test the enduring quality of American institutions. It was already clear that the regional portraiture could not be isolated from the national picture.

The total picture comprehended a brief preview of the backgrounds and conditioning of the southern cultural development; a glimpse of the southern credo on the Negro, with its variations, in contrast to the newer demands that were made upon the South; and this in contrast again to a symbolic northern credo. And it included an analysis of the conflicting attitudes and groups and the resulting folk regional and national reaction to the whole situation. But most of all it comprehended the long and vivid catalogue of rumors and tensions, of conflict and hatred rising to floodtide. There was also inherent in the situation the need for careful study of fact versus rumor and of their meanings and implications throughout the whole range of regional and national life. And, finally, there was need to focus upon the challenge of what was to be done about it if tragedy were to be avoided and crisis passed successfully.

Throughout the telling of this story of racial crisis three levels of approach were fundamental. The first was the attempt to present facts and conclusions as completely and objectively as possible, as free as possible from mere opinion and minimizing conclusions of "good" or "bad," "right" or "wrong," and yet to present the picture strongly, vividly, alike for all aspects, white, Negro, South, Nation. For everywhere two conclusions seemed justified. There was extraordinary ignorance of the total picture, on the part of the South and the Nation, both white and Negro. The picture was rarely ever seen as a whole or free from emotional fog and bitterness of unreasoning dogmatism.

The second approach was always to ask: "Now was this true?" "Was it a fact?" "In the reading of the story, could emotional reactions and quick denials framed in anger be avoided?" After all the evidence was in, "was this about the way the situation stood?" For all to see the picture as it was, the South, the Nation, white people, Negro people, all—this was the first essential. No matter how much "it hurt" or how surprising or unbelievable, South, Nation, white, Negro— "was this the way it was?" Repeat and repeat and repeat: "Was it true?"

And in the third place: How would the telling of this story, if it was true portraiture, look a long time hence in the years to come? How mature could the people make their observations and their reporting? How would southern and American behavior appear in historical perspective? Could the American people, and the South in particular, sense the time quality of the drama?

Yet from the beginning and throughout the story there was contradiction and paradox. While many people sensed the dangers ahead and sought ways and means of quick adjustment, many others were unaware of impending crisis or at least of the size of it. And many were strongly of the opinion that emphasis upon crisis would increase the tensions. "Let the situation alone," they would insist. The situation was always complex, with never a simple "yes" or "no" answer to the main questions.

Perhaps the two questions most commonly asked were: First, was there a real crisis, so pregnant with tragic possibilities as was assumed in the portraiture of a cross section of regional and racial rumors and tensions? And, second, why the sudden flare-up the accelerated tensions, increasing conflict, and growing fear that threatened to sweep the Nation, from California to New York, Beaumont to Detroit, Mobile to Washington? First, what evidences could be catalogued to indicate crisis? Were the startling assertions summarized into the catalogue of counts true? In answer to the first question, did the following assumptions appear evidence of crisis?

1. An almost universal assumption on the part of the rest of the Nation that "something must be done about" the South's treatment of the Negro. "What," they kept asking, "can we do about the South?" "And do it now?"

2. A general pressure movement to force the hand of the South to eliminate segregation in its technical and legal arrangements, and an almost universal southern movement to resist.

3. A surprisingly large number of the ablest and best Negro leaders who concluded sadly that it might be necessary "to fight it out." "We hope not, we pray not, but we don't know."

4. A surprisingly large number of the intelligentsia in the Nation who saw Federal coercion as the next and necessary step. "In matters of race, State sovereignty is a myth."

5. A surprisingly large number of representative southern leaders who stood to resist at any cost and to subordinate all other issues to that of race. "The passing of laws," they said, "and the increase of coercive pressure will not and cannot change the South's conventions and traditions."

6. A demonstrable tendency in both the "South" and the "North" to sacrifice war efforts and endanger national unity in a stubborn determination to resist or to agitate. In the press, in congress, and in politics, the costs were hardly ever counted.

7. A growing hatred on the part of many Negroes for the whites: an increasing satire and bitterness on the part of many individuals in the Nation at large against the southern whites and their biracial culture.

8. Relative retrogression in the South in both attitudes and action in emergency racial matters, as compared with what appeared to be unusual progress a few years earlier. There appeared to be a new pro-South tempo, a solid South again highly motivated for self-defense.

9. An unmeasurable and unbridgeable distance between the white South and the reasonable expectation of the Negro. The fact that both were inevitable and logical products of what had gone before and was to come did not change the situation.

10. Widespread rumors of an extraordinary number, range, and variety, all pointing toward increasing tensions, threatened violence, and tormenting fear, in the major fields

of race relations—work, sex, travel, education, politics, military services, freedom, and equality of opportunity.

11. Widespread violence of an extraordinary number, range, and variety of incidents, from police brutalities to violence on bus, streetcar, and in work places, resulting in interracial homicides, riots, and threats of coming reprisals.

12. A new and logical behavior pattern of Negro youth to experiment with all possible ways of achieving equality in all aspects of life. That this was a logical and normal product of education and progress did not alter the case.

13. A new and logical Negro labor pattern for both men and women in relation to work for white folks and a consequent breakdown of the southern way of workaday life.

14. Over against this were the unchanged attitudes and ways of doing things on the part of the whites, with the exception of minority individuals among the youth. This appeared to accentuate rather than relieve the tensions.

15. And there was the almost universal assumption of the great body of southern folk that nothing could be done about it. And the assumption by the majority that nothing should be done about it except to stop outside agitation to break down the South's biracial culture.

16. That this was a technical crisis was evidenced by the fact that southern governors took formal cognizance of outside agitation and promised the public they would do what they could to stop it.

17. That it was again a technical crisis was reflected in the verdict of southern youth in the armed services who protested that, while they would gladly give their lives for America's freedom to govern herself, they did not want, in their absence, their most precious heritage, the southern way of life, taken away without their consent.

18. And there were thousands of other soldiers and sailors, aviators and marines who protested that, while they

would gladly give their lives for American freedom, they did not want to fight for world freedom which Americans would not give the Negro.

There were ample specific illustrations and interpretations of the above evidences of crisis and other evidence of like kind to be added. Such a catalogue reflected that elemental meaning of crisis which assumes the usual dictionary definition as a time when there are concrete dangerous situations or desperate movements or when there is a period of suspense, or when the hope is eternal that the turning point may be made without disaster or tragedy.

But inherent in most of the situations were other and more profound implications of crisis. Thus, to utilize the medical analogy, there was undoubtedly in the South at that time a striking change of symptoms as reflected in interracial behavior, which was accompanied by equally striking outward manifestations. And, furthermore, the South was facing the question as to whether it could survive, in any reasonable living success, unless it could make adjustments to meet the demands of the present and post-war conditions with reference to the Negro. There was an increasing uneasiness on the part of many leaders that the South might be "wrong," but that there was no way out of the dilemma at that time.

This was, of course, a supreme test, and the challenge was again to repeat and repeat and repeat: "Was it true?" "What changes ought the South to make?" "What changes could the South make?" "What changes would the South make?" "Was there any doubt that the South had come to the turning of the ways?" "How could the South be made to realize the crisis, crisis even more for the spiritual welfare of the South than for dangers of mere physical conflict?"

Then there was another implication of crisis in the sense that the South had reached a point in time to ask whether it was to be the only major region of the world which made discrimination and segregation its major cultural issue. Was the South forever to be on the defensive, subordinating all other issues to its segregation principles and practices? Had the South come to the point where it must be decided whether it would go on as in the past; would change its patterns or modify its behavior and laws to what extent? How this was an indication of crisis was reflected in the fact that even to raise the question was signal of danger.

Then there was another basis for crisis in the Nation. Again, repeat and repeat and repeat: Was it true that there were minority leaders and agitators in the Nation of both races, North and South, who were willing to set the Nation in racial revolution, with all its resultant death and carnage, in order to seek immediate ends which according to all scientific and historical evidence could not be attained at once? Were there insincere leaders in politics who unthinkingly played the game, in the North, of wasting time and statesmanship on minor issues, and in the South, of filibustering away the chances of winning war and peace? This, too, was a crisis, very similar to the crisis of a hundred years earlier in the 1840's, which did not pass without tragedy.

Still, again, there was crisis for the Negro. Had the time come when the test might well be whether literally and figuratively he would survive or perish? The crisis was, of course, part crisis of the whites, but also the test was whether Negro leadership and Negro youth could face the realities of organic inheritance, cultural conditioning, racial and religious facts, limitations of equipment and training, and so organize and develop their great program for freedom as to attain it instead of being satisfied with mere revolution. Rarely had a people of such great personality and wisdom been challenged to maturity and increasing wisdom.

And, again, there was a symbol of crisis in the challenge

to the South to do something big in meeting a situation in which not only a regional but a national and world problem was involved. In the military demands of a global war the youth of the southern states had led all others in their enlistment. The South had expressed itself vigorously for all-out war effort; and in many ways and in many times the South had shown remarkable stamina, endurance, high motivation, and courage. Yet when it came to the question of the Negro all standards as applied to other issues seemed to go by default. Was it possible for the South now to envisage this problem in terms of tomorrow as well as of today? And nothing short of bigness could make increasingly satisfactory adjustments in an area where no satisfactory solution was possible.

Finally, the outcome of this crisis of race would have very important bearing upon the other two major problem-situations that faced post-war America, namely, the problem of labor groups and the problem of conflict in government and economic life. In each of these, both in philosophy and in action, race would be heavily involved and might be a balance of power.

That it was a crisis, capable of a better turning, was evident from the fact that there were many leaders and common men in the South who sought the best possible solutions. There were thousands of deeds of courtesy and justice to Negroes as everyday happenings in contrast to those other tragic happenings so often recorded. The Negro, as a race, alongside his many mistakes, reflected a magnificent example of trying his level best to do the right thing. And there were millions of other people in the rest of the Nation trying their level best to do what was right. Moreover, most of the millions of folk, North, East, and West, did not approve of advocacy of the extremes of force and violence. There was everywhere evidence that resources and the will were available for a new "better ordering of our society." This evidence was a part of the total picture of what was happening and of what was being done about it; as was to be recorded in many a later chronicle.

Here, for instance, was a college president of a church school telling his church that it would reflect grave discredit if they "sit supinely by and allow situations which are still remediable to develop in our communities." "Is it not true," he continued, "that many of us have protested that we like the Negro in his place, meanwhile doing our best to guarantee that his place would continue to be toiling in our kitchen, often at wages which would scarcely provide a decent living?"

Another distinguished administrator in another of the largest church denominations expressed the feeling that in all his life and work, what he had tried to do in race relations appeared as the most important of all and that now there must be greater unified effort to do more.

There was the unusual phenomenon of many chamber of commerce officials and members seeking in alarm and earnestness to find out what was the best they could do.

And there were literally thousands of individuals all over the land writing letters, forming committees, making suggestions, offering their services.

So great, however, was this catalogue of efforts that it would require a separate chapter in the telling of "What was being done."

II

The Rising Tide of Tension

One of the first tasks was to explain why the crisis had developed so rapidly; why there was such sudden flare-up of emotions, tensions, and conflicts; and why, in both the South and the rest of the Nation, it so quickly assumed major proportions in the early war years. An understanding of the backgrounds and the immediate incidence of change and of the speed of change was essential to a preview of the crisis and what might be done about it. For, repeat and repeat, it was never a simple regional problem. And because it was a southern problem, an American problem, and because it was of the essence of world progress, it was therefore more difficult and would neither be isolated by the South nor "solved" by the Nation.

There had been, of course, a number of events, situations, and incidents which had accelerated the sweep of rumors and tensions, chiefest of which was the incidence of war with its attendant demands and opportunities and its philosophy of global democracy. These had all been logical and inevitable products of the time, reflecting the cumulative power and sweep of a logical long-time evolutionary process. While an adequate cataloguing and understanding of the mass of war episodes and influences constituted a first step, it was the portraiture of the reaction of the South and the explanation of the folk psychology involved that were essential, first, to understanding the situation and, second, to directing next steps. And by the same token the folk psy-

13

chology of the rest of the Nation and of the Negro was part
and parcel of the total picture.

A major element in the crisis was found in the South's
vivid reaction to the total situation. More specifically was
the role of reaction to outside criticism and war efforts to
force her hand in making radical change of policies. Over
against the outside verdict of denunciation, the South was
thinking all along that it had made great progress toward
better race relations; that it had attained a good deal of
unity; and that perhaps it was finally on its way toward such
interracial cooperation as would lead to the best possible
adjustment.

There was, for instance, great pride in the Negro leaders
and educators of distinction whose fellowship and participation in regional development were so highly valued. There
were common gatherings and conferences between leaders of
both races. There were meetings between the white and
Negro college youth. Many things were being done, as a
matter of fact, in racial fellowship which a short time ago
would not have been considered. There was less and less
violence and more and more inclination to increase the Negro's participation in all matters economic and cultural.

Furthermore, there were increases in appropriations for
Negro education, often as much as fifty to one hundred percent. Teachers' salaries were more and more being equalized
and special efforts were being made to develop Negro institutions of higher learning and to give the Negro increasingly
greater opportunities in professional equipment. There had
been such great strides in the reduction of lynching and mob
action that already the hope was being expressed that a new
era was in the making.

Then, suddenly, as it appeared to the South, there was a
flood of criticism, denunciation, demand. Prospective measures of coercion were proposed which seemed to assume

that the South was doing something new and quite bad in its whole pattern of biracial culture. It was as if there came the assumption that the South was initiating backward policies in which it boldly challenged the rest of the world in new reaches of injustice and discrimination. Instead, therefore, in the light of a normal and logical period of development, of being credited with substantial measures of progress, the South found itself, in wartimes, reflecting, relatively, retrogression in comparison with what was demanded and in comparison with the commitments of the American people to global democracy. And the South, hoping to achieve some measure of united patriotism, felt that the war crisis was no time to split the Nation again and to foment bitterness and violence.

Once again, it was as if the rest of the Nation, in particular the publicists, the intelligentsia, and the youth of other regions had suddenly discovered the structure of the South's biracial culture. They kept saying, "What is this new thing the South is doing to the Negro? What are we going to do about the South's treatment of the Negro?" Yet, it is not surprising that the new generation of the Nation, largely ignorant of the earlier backgrounds of national development, should know little or nothing of the tragedies of the South. There grew up quickly, therefore, a remarkable concern to save the South, to free the South, to take the occasion of war to purify American democracy. It was one of the most dramatic episodes in the long history of America's idealism.

What the South had done was, of course, nothing new. It was an old story except that the South was of the impression that it had actually made many concessions and had grown in stature through certain logical, advancing stages of development. The South was assuming, as it always had, a continuation of the economy and culture of a biracial caste culture and therefore appraised its progress as new gains. Who

ever thought the South would abandon segregation anyhow?
Hadn't the issue been settled over and over again? Was
there not a powerful heritage of trial and error to make this
sure? Had not every community or group of communities in
the old days lived in the shadow of fear and in the relative
disgrace of some racial tragedy? Was this to be done over
again?

Yet because of the war and the revitalizing of America's
ideology of democracy and freedom in global war, and because of the new discovery of the South by the Nation and
consequently a new level of irresponsible agitation, even with
the progress that the South had made, its culture economy reflected to its critics glaring inequalities that appeared neither
right nor necessary. And even though there would be no inclination on the part of many southerners to deny the great
distance between what the South was doing and what needed
to be done, nevertheless the psychology of the sudden impact of criticism and accusation, when the South had thought
it was going forward, was the key to the speed and intensity
of reaction. The South, too, needed sympathy and understanding, the people thought, instead of denunciation and
misunderstanding.

And here the South was following its standard folkways
of resentment of outside criticism and Federal coercion.
They were back again in united defense against outside aggression. "If outsiders," they began to react again, "would
let us alone, we would work out our problem." "Mrs. Roosevelt and the New Deal," they would say, "are trying to make
us discard the pattern of segregation." From the governors
to the common man the refrain was that the southern people were quite capable of running their own government
and would continue to do so. In the light of American experience, this was, of course, nothing new. Yet the South
might very well have replied, "Well, of course, the rest of

the Nation is still trying to make the South over; who said they were not? What of it? From their viewpoint, why wouldn't they? That, too, is an old story and we will not let it get us excited again." But that was not the way of the South, and so here again was basic soil for the multiplied rumors and rifts of a threatening crisis.

And then the Negro portion of the biracial culture was proceeding to assume attitudes and to initiate action in accordance with this new and radical freedom, whereas the white part of the South was not only not acquiescing but was finding a new unity in resisting, to the end that they went to extremes reminiscent of the old days of reconstruction. They did things and talked and listened to rumors that to the outsider could not be interpreted in terms of any logical and reasonable explanation. And because the rest of the Nation did not understand and because their verdict was primarily a "group" judgment, they advocated partial and unrealistic solutions, often advocating action without estimating the costs that might follow.

One of the first tasks, therefore, essential to the understanding of the situation and preliminary to the cataloguing and interpretation of what happened was to sense the realistic, living credo of the South with reference to the Negro and its relation to what might be called a symbolic credo of the rest of the Nation at large. The understanding of a folk psychology, which was committed to the defense of this credo at any cost, by the same token, was a first essential.

For, against this well-nigh universal southern credo came assumptions and demands that appeared to the South to be about as near the complete opposite as it would be possible to find. In substance, here was a sudden demand for the South, long conditioned in the Negro complex and southern loyalties, bottomed in the long heritage of race prejudice and cultural evolution, to change its whole structure of race relations overnight. And, equally vivid, from the outside regions was reflected what seemed an unreasonableness of the South in not being willing to conform to the larger American credo of democracy and the American dream of equality.

Now the bare statement of an organic credo, which would startle even most southerners, appeared crude and harsh. So, here again, it was important to repeat and repeat the question: Was it true that the South believed these things about the Negro? Or, if not, now that it was put down in black and white as the composite feeling and folkways of the South, what part of it was *not* true? Of course, no southerner ever wrote such a credo for himself and no one ever heard a southerner parading his credo as such. Yet, tested and checked in private life, in religious attitudes, in politics and law, and in the defense mechanisms of the region, in the great body of common folk, was this the South's credo and was it the heart of the whole drama?

Without an understanding of the South's organic feelings and beliefs it was not possible to explain such violent reactions to episodes and experiences which appeared to outsiders as mere commonplace behavior. Keeping in mind the variations of a composite credo and ratio of different groups of southerners who might dissent, and also the possible comparison with what people in the other regions held, it seemed important to ask again and again whether the white South would face the issue of its beliefs. Here, again, as always, there were paradox and contrast. While one group of leaders would protest the unfairness to the South of the presentation of such a credo, another large group would seem to say, "Sure, of course, that's what we believe. Why mention it? Everybody knows the Negro is just a Negro." Yet it was in many ways a startling credo that seemed to be the heart of the crisis. It seemed possible to count a score of units in the total and to ask again, Was it true that the South believed:

1. That the Negro was a Negro and always would be that and nothing more.

2. That, being a Negro, and different from the white man he therefore could not be expected ever to measure up to the white man's standards of character and achievement.

3. That, not being capable of full achievement and being of an inferior race, it was logical that he should be kept in an inferior place, which is "his place."

4. It followed that this was a white man's country, and that therefore the white man would dominate in about whatever way he chose. Laws and resolutions only made matters worse.

5. Political equality and equal educational opportunities, if given to the Negro, would lead to social equality and the mixture of races, which was contrary to all the major premises of the southern way of life.

6. Furthermore, political and social equality would lead to the domination of the white South by the Negroes and their northern supporters.

7. Discrimination and segregation, therefore, were necessary to keep the Negro in his place and protect the interests and integrity of the whites.

8. It was assumed, from this point on, by the best of the South, that the Negro, when kept within his rightful sphere, should not be treated unkindly or unjustly.

9. That he should be given fair trials and protected by law.

10. That he should be paid a living wage. Since, however, his standards of living were lower, he could live on less than a white man could.

11. That if given too much pay, he would waste the

money and get out of bounds to his own harm as well as to the detriment of the South.

12. That the Negro was by nature inclined to criminal behavior, partly because of his animal nature and partly because of his irresponsibility and immorality.

13. Moreover, the Negro was better off in the South where he was "understood" and where his best friends were.

14. That, while as a race the Negro was inferior and generally untrustworthy, as an individual he was often honest, loyal, lovable, capable, and even talented and distinguished. Yet this was the exception.

15. That his music, his carefree, patient disposition, his homely philosophy added interest and color and richness to the culture of the South.

16. That recognition should be given to the Negro for having made outstanding progress in many fields since being freed from slavery.

17. Yet the Negro in general was not capable of taking great responsibility or of assuming leadership.

18. That no self-respecting southerner would work under Negro supervision.

19. That if the New Dealers, northerners, and reformers would let the South and the Negro alone, peaceful adjustments of the race problem could be made.

20. That those who were inviting the Negro to discontent and trying to force his participation in industry and politics on an equal basis were fomenting race riots which would hurt both whites and Negroes and the total Nation in the long run.

21. And that, finally, this was not a debatable issue.

There were, of course, various self-evident facts with reference to such a credo. In the first place, there were some variations from the norm as indicated in this credo. Yet, for all practical purposes this made little difference, since it was the mode of southern attitude and folkways which gave rise to points of tension, conflict, and the like. This credo was presented, not because there was anything new in it, but rather in order to highlight and make more vivid the folkways of the South concerning the Negro. Such a bold and bald statement of a credo was so vivid that it was perhaps surprising to southerners and, therefore, might go a long way toward explaining why the other regions of the Nation have rediscovered a level of their own national life with which they were either not acquainted or which they had forgot. The credo was in such complete contradistinction to the urgings and demands that were being made on the South in the name of war and freedom and Americanism that the resulting tension and conflict were easily explainable. It had to be repeated often that the understanding of the realistic folkways of the South was necessary also to explain the reaction of so many people from other regions to what seemed to them arbitrary, unreasonable, and entirely unfair attitudes and procedures in the South with reference to the simplest, most common, everyday, reasonable expectations of the Negro for life, liberty, and the pursuit of happiness.

That is, unless the full meaning of the southern folkways concerning the Negro was clearly understood, most of the incidents, stories, and happenings that had been basic to recent race tension and conflict would themselves be unreasonable and unexplainable. On the contrary, to the South, sensing its concept of the biracial society, what had happened seemed so simple and logical as to need no other explanation than that it had happened.

III

The Heart of the Southern Dilemma

Now the heart of the southern credo was manifest in the central theme—"the Negro is a Negro, and nothing more." It was difficult for many southern leaders to agree that this was the central theme of the southern folkways of race. Yet the measure of this appraisal appeared everywhere to be abundant. And because this, together with the power of caste, was at the bottom of the southern culture complex and explained so easily what had happened, it was of the utmost importance that southerners face the plain assumption that they did not appraise the Negro as the same sort of human being as they themselves were. This was no revival, either, of the old southern scriptural argument that the Negro was created to be the hewer of wood and drawer of water. That had long been relegated to a past level of cultural and religious heritage. This central theme, through the tensions of the early 1940's, made articulate something more realistic, and it had appeared to be organic in the structure and function of the southern culture. If this was true, what evidence was available to indicate that it was true, and, if not, what evidence could be cited?

Perhaps the first exhibit submitted to indicate the fact that the Negro was not human was the almost universal refrain that "the Negro thinks he can act like white folks; well, he can't do it down here." "These niggers coming back South try to do like white folks. But it don't take us long to put them in their place." "A smart nigger knows better than to try to act like white folks." And here was a common refrain offered by religious youth, defending their appeals for better treatment of the Negro: "I know the Negro is just a Negro and must be kept in his place, but he is just as dear in the sight of God as a white person."

The South professed to be the most Christian and religious of all the regions. In professed Christianity the "Fatherhood of God" and the "brotherhood of man" had been basic planks in the total religious platform; preaching at home, missionary work abroad. "But the Negro, that is different. You don't understand. He is the Negro. No, we can't worship with him, work with him, vote with him, associate with him. Don't you understand? It just isn't done. It just can't be done."

Why was southern conduct, then, so contrary to all preaching and principles which, without a peradventure of doubt, were sincere? Why didn't the tenets of fellowship and Christian religion hold here? The only answer was that the Negro did not come within the framework of human brotherhood.

In devout missionary meetings of church women, to take a sample, there were uniform evidences to the same effect. Papers were read, devotionals held, talks made on the duty of Christians to all the folk of the world—the caste-ridden people of India, the ignorant of Africa, the handicapped of China. But, "Now I believe in Christian fellowship and feel it is our duty to help the Negro, but if I have to sit by him in church, well, you can have my church. . . . Did you hear about what the Negro girl said to 'Eleanor' when she went visiting the Negroes in the slums?" The explanation again: The application of Christianity to the present case just didn't register. This was the Negro.

This has been written in no sense to criticize many of the very excellent results of the women's work of the churches. Perhaps they did more to focus the attention of the public against lynching than any other group except the Commission on Interracial Cooperation, under whose leadership they often worked. So, too, many churchmen of the Episcopal following and leaders from the larger denominations were active in many ameliorative efforts. The point of emphasis was, however, that even so, from the viewpoint of the Negro, the efforts were always on a different level—whether right or wrong was not the issue.

Once again, among the traditions of the South that of chivalry towards women stood high. Yet, white men, irked and irritated by the "new" behavior of Negro girls and women, resorted to physical violence, a pattern of behavior which would be inconceivable if directed towards white women. The answer again was that the Negro woman was a Negro. A part of this was a heritage from the old aristocracy, where, in the midst of the very flowering of chivalry of the gentleman and the lady, the mistress of the big house overlooked slave relationships between the master and Negro women. The answer was that the Negro was not a human being but a slave or a Negro; or else the whole edifice of the pure womanhood and the chivalry of the southern gentleman would have tottered to the ground.

So, too, women in high places, in civic life, in church life, in social life, feeling often a genuine interest in their helpers, and having as their cooks, maids, and laundry women fine specimens of middle-class Negroes, were among the severest critics of the Negro women trying to get along in the world. With a relatively large family, and clothing them and educating them in fine fashion, such women were abused for wanting more than $20.00 or $30.00 a month to maintain such a family and standard of living. The first answer to this was, of course, southern tradition and thoughtlessness; but the question was raised as to whether the real answer was that the Negro woman was, after all, just a Negro and her children just Negroes. Such evidence could be added up and multiplied literally into the thousands of instances. Was it true or wasn't it?

In women's groups in the highest brackets of southern society and in home parties and dinners, when it came to a discussion of the Negro and Mrs. Roosevelt, the most sordid rumors were repeated and laughed at with no thought of its reflecting upon southern chivalry. The answer was, again, the Negro, without any seeming awareness of this terrible breach of southern etiquette and chivalry.

Another test was applied in the case of Negro college youth. Physical violence and abuse were often heaped upon the heads of Negro youth for no other reason than that they were assuming a part of the standard and rights of college men and women, such as they had been taught not only to expect but to demand. Violence in answer to these logical and normal expectations could apparently be explained by a Christian, democratic South only on the assumption that the young Negro was just a Negro and not a college man or woman guaranteed the rights, privileges, and appurtenances commonly vouchsafed by the higher degrees.

Here was another exhibit: Negro college graduates marching in academic procession, in fine form and dignity, proud of the day when sacrifices and hard work had been rewarded, and looking eagerly ahead to their new promised heritage. The South, if consistent, would have been proud of them. On the contrary, they were "uppity" and trying to do like white folks. The explanation again was that they were just Negroes.

The explanation of the southerners' cold-hearted torture of Negroes, of lynching, of burning, and of dragging the body, which was an old pattern of southern violence, on the southerners' basis of being a Christian, kindly generous folk was apparent only on the basis that the Negro was not a human. The Christian religion and the human heart do not permit the murder of human beings. How else, therefore, could this sort of thing be justified, except in the case of nonhumans? And it had been justified over and over again. "Negroes who want to work, we give 'em work. Those who don't we put on the chain gang, or shoot 'em."

There was another common evidence which appeared in the expressed fear of the Negro by the whites. It was part of the old pattern being renewed, when women were afraid to live in isolated places or to move about alone. This was a terrible shadow, an unjust implication of the Negro's animal nature which had well-nigh been relegated to the past. Its renewal was a challenge to the South's self-examination of its credo.

It was natural that vigorous questioning of such credo and its defense be made, and that there should be protests against the placing of all southerners in the same category with reference to beliefs, attitudes, and behavior about the Negro. The task of differentiation was a difficult one, and here again there was need to check and check in as many ways as possible with as many people as possible to ascertain whether estimates of variation were realistic and accurate. It was, however, important to present as vividly as possible the mode or majority credo in order to explain what had happened and why it happened, as well as to challenge the region to check and check its credo. Nevertheless, important alongside the mode of behavior and attitudes, and fundamental in any consideration of the future trend would be an analysis of the variations. Of particular importance, of course, would be the viewpoint of minorities and professional leaders who tried their level best to do the best job possible. Yet, these variations and exceptions themselves were part and parcel of the explanation of the total culture complex.

In order to estimate the possibilities of broad considera-

tion of the problems as well as to attempt an accurate diag-
nosis, the following variations seemed valid. A very small
ratio, certainly not more than five percent of the people of
the South, might hold that the Negro should have equal political, economic, educational, and social opportunity with
the white race and would be willing to take steps immediately to provide such equality of opportunity. Some college
youth, both men and women, would appear willing to set up
the premise of complete equality. But even with this small
minority only the smallest fraction would appear to surrender the old level of attitude in the case of social equality
which implied sex and marriage relationships. Even "social
equality" did not contemplate that.

There was a second relatively small ratio of the white
people of the South who appeared to believe that the Negro
had been sinned against from the beginning. Always he had
been discriminated against unjustly, and always was between the upper and nether millstones of oppression. He
ought, therefore, to have equal opportunity to prove that he
is not inherently inferior. Such a group appeared to be willing to provide equal educational opportunities, privileges of
voting, an increasingly approximate measure of economic
opportunity, but they were afraid of and violently opposed
to "social equality."

The largest ratio of the white people of the South, perhaps between two-thirds and three-fourths, thought little
about the subject until stirred by the new revivification of
the old trouble. Their reactions were those of feeling and
conditioned inheritance based on loyalty and religion, and
they assumed as a matter of fact that any matters of pure
equality were out of the question, and that matters of race
relationships had been settled in line with the credo of the
great mass of people. In so far as they were *for* the Negro,
they felt proud that he had been given as much opportunity

as he had in education and training and work. They were, as a simple matter of fact, opposed to having the Negro participate in political, educational, community, and social activities on the level of equality. Any such demands simply did not register, until later when they interpreted the demands as "social equality." They felt and said: "We may be wrong, but we will not *live* with social equality; we may die, but we won't have that."

Perhaps a final minority of the southern white people, less generous than any of the above, constituted the nucleus of conflict. Perhaps also it was not possible to diagnose accurately their total attitude. Many observers felt that there was growing up between this group and the younger Negroes something pretty close to hate. Many factors, such as complexes of various sorts, were involved. There was the force of frustration and aggression. There was the inferiority complex. There was confusion and ignorance. The net result was the determination to keep the Negro in his place at any cost.

There was, then, of course, a relatively large number, but small ratio, of southern white leaders who, in their professional work in church, school, social work, and community leadership, sought ways and means of integrating the Negro in American life in such ways as to give him as complete opportunity as was possible. Yet such individuals and groups, almost without exception, appeared to the Negro so far from the realistic attainment and practical advocacy of these ends that they did not have the complete confidence of Negro leadership or of the white intellectual leadership from the other regions of the Nation. More and more these so-called liberal leaders were inclined to be discouraged because of attacks made upon them by the extremists among the Negroes.

As one index of the uniformity in the midst of variety and

of the complexity of the situation, it seemed apparent that there were no southerners, white or Negro, who were intellectually free in the sense that their attitudes and behavior were not powerfully influenced by what the white South would think and do about it. Nor were there any southerners, as judged from a consensus of studies and opinions, who did not agree with the much-quoted statement that there were not enough armed forces in the world to force the South to abandon its principles and practice of segregation.

Now the sheer reality and power of this situation, in its conditioning of the South and the resulting action, had little to do with what might be right or wrong or what might be in the future or might have been under other circumstances. The facts were as they were, and the deeper and more "organic" the cultural conditioning, the more impossible it was to ignore it as a part of the scientific and humanistic picture. It seemed clear that any student of cultural anthropology or of race or religion might have known that such a culture complex was the product of the long-time process together with the sanctioning of the folkways, to which there were added the stateways of law and institutions.

There was, therefore, an urgent task awaiting the South. It was much more important frankly to understand, than to talk loftily, to satirize, and argue about wrongness. For in America race conflict was grounded in two organic backgrounds. The one, of course, was the age-long tragedy of errors of all men, everywhere reflected in the exploitation of one race by another, and race persecution through economic, religious, and other avenues. The other was an even more organic situation as reflected in the southern United States of America, in which the race problem came, after the Civil War and reconstruction, to symbolize the old slogan of what men live and die for: for God, for home, and for country.

Thus, in the separation of the northern and southern churches, the religious factors involved allegiance to the southern way of worship, so that the issue came to be one of God. In the folkway of race purity, it became a question of the home and family. In the loyalties of the southern people to their region and to the different states against the North, it came to be "for country." Now, manifestly, people grounded in the loyalties of these three noble motivations and having had no possible opportunity to sense any other attitude cannot be bad people simply because they work on these motivations. On the contrary, they are good people. There was, therefore, another basis of conflict in the ideals and concepts of what was considered "good" and what was considered "bad." To the South the biracial economy was good—all good; to the rest of the Nation it was bad.

Whether this situation was one of impending crisis or an inevitable and logical development toward a more complete integration of the southern regions in the national picture remained to be seen. Was it possible that the era represented the powerful growing pains of a changing people? The situations and attitudes, it must be remembered, were strongly reinforced by an inexorable caste system which, although it reflected cumulative racial and economic heritage of the South, was primarily one of sex. Most of the liberal college youth who advocated complete freedom and equality of the Negro often paled at the very thought of men and women relationships on the more personal levels of social life. The understanding of this was necessary to the understanding of what so often appeared to outsiders as illogical and unreasonable emotional reaction on the part of southerners. On the other hand, to the South, the greater unreasonableness appeared to be limitations of intellectuals "who ought to know better." This caste factor also was one which accentuated the element of crisis rather than logical development and evolution. If it were not for the sex-caste foundation it might have been possible to make adjustments. This powerful factor of caste also explained the prevalence of so many rumors of particular sorts and made clear both the individual psychology and the folk psychology underlying many of the rumors and propaganda.

IV

The New Negro Generation

Over against and in the midst of this accelerated tension and conflict, little of which was new except in specific manifestations, there was, however, a level of southern cultural dynamics which in many respects was new. This was a new Negro behavior on several levels, primarily of Negro leaders, Negro youth, Negro women workers, Negro labor in general. This new behavior explained many of the concrete incidents of conflict.

First, there was the vigorous, lusty enthusiasm and aggressive attitude and action of a whole new generation of Negro youth, much of which was as spontaneous and inevitable as would be the growth of the youth of any people and the increasing education and experience of a race in the midst of a region and a Nation that were going forward rapidly. A part of this enthusiastic aggressive attitude and action of the young Negroes was due, of course, to the new education and to the leadership and agitation of many of the Negro educational leaders North and South. But even if this had not been a great influence, this changing reaction and responsibility of Negro youth would have become an inevitable product of any evolutionary development. To this extent the situation in the South might be one of growing pains and evolutionary development rather than of impending crisis, provided there were made available regional-national arrangements adequate to take care of the situation.

To those who would face reality, this relatively new and vigorous aggressiveness of the young Negroes appeared to be something quite natural. Why, therefore, should that which was so natural and logical be the cause of impending crisis? The answer was being sought and interpreted as one means of turning the situation into an evolutionary development instead of a revolution. In general, the young Negro was portrayed as wanting to experiment and to demand his rights. In substance, this was what they appeared to feel. They might have said:

"We naturally want equal opportunity to live in this the best land in the world. Well, why not?"

"We naturally want a chance to do the best work and to get the best pay. Well, why not?"

"We naturally want to express ourselves fully, and as youth in a youthful race perhaps we are considerably bumptious and noisy. Well, that's natural, isn't it?"

"We naturally want the right to travel, to trade, to work without embarrassing segregation laws and custom, and we would like to live anywhere in the community whenever we can make the grade. That is natural, too, isn't it?"

"In more specific instances and cases, we like to go into the drug stores, in the markets, and into other public places as a matter of fact just as other people do; perhaps we want this more because we have not had it, and we are a little immature and naive about it. This is natural, too."

"And we like to dream of unreasonable things to be done and ideals to be attained, and we want to do this even as other people do without being considered presumptuous. This is a good old human failing."

"In the long life line of human beings waiting their turn for service, achievement, privilege, obligation, we want to take our place regularly and not be always slipping back to the end of the line and giving way always to someone else. Is this wrong?"

"We are in a transitional stage, boisterous, vocal, unreasonable, and we don't give a damn if we are; we will be heard."

"And don't blame us if even the best of us talk big about what we are going to do when and if we do get what we want, and if we don't get it."

"And don't blame us permanently if in this stage of new transition and learning some of us do lose our balance and if we lose our patience and run amuck. We are eager, ambitious, and we get hypnotized with the feeling within ourselves."

For, in addition to the more mature and formal discussions of Negro college youth, not much of which was articulate in the mass rumors and tensions, much of the new behavior of Negro youth, as reported in the stories and rumors so abundantly reported, was reflected in the tendency to boast and talk big among themselves. It was apparently true that this big talk ran just about the whole range of experience, and that most anything could be heard and quoted as reported, out of its setting. To illustrate with one of the common rumors that Negroes were wishing for Axis victory, of which there were many variations, here was one. A young Negro girl, talking on the street with two other girls and a Negro man, was entertaining them with such effect as to have them shouting with glee. Said the young Negro girl, complaining of not getting the meat she wanted on her ration card, "I told that g—d—s—b—m—b white man I hoped to God both the Germans and Japs would get him." It seemed more likely that what the girl said to the white man was "I'm sorry" and went mumbling out.

One of the most common of the minor rumors was constantly reporting Negro boys as trying to "hold hands" when they paid the white girls for purchases in the 5-10 cent stores. Here was a sample of what did and *didn't* happen. Three young Negro boys had purchased some small articles from a drug store. Their conduct as they paid the young white woman cashier was a model of good behavior. As they passed on to the street, however, "I'm s'prised at you," said one of them to one of the others, "tryin' to hold hands with that white girl." And they laughed their way on. And on up the street a way, another group were bantering each other and wagering that they couldn't go in the drug store and be served just like white folks. They all appeared to be having a grand time.

A young Negro, coming to a back room of a hotel where the bell boys and others were wont to congregate, was told by the head boy that a new ruling had been made. They could no longer congregate or wait around until the women workers were off. "Nothin' doin'," said this young fellow, "these white folks knows me. I told them blankety-blank white folks where to get off. They knows me and what I wants to do I does. They knows if they don't want me to, I got here what it takes." From the next room one of the hotel employees came quietly through a swinging door and said, "John, don't you reckon you are exaggerating a little?" "Haw! haw! I reckon I wus," laughed the boy and went on out.

Yet incidents of this sort, when behavior of participants might be different or when exaggerated in the telling, often formed the basis for rumors and conflicts such as are recorded in the long catalogues of this book. And the persistent demand on the part of young Negroes for service at drug store fountains had been a contributing cause for more than one to close its fountain to avoid embarrassments. Yet to the distinguished northern visitor who happened to hear the complaint of one drug store that Negroes were insisting on being served at the fountain, the objection seemed unreasonable, unjust, and rather scornfully preposterous.

He just couldn't understand it at all. To him, of course, the Negroes were right. But more of this later.

There was another major field in which the behavior of Negroes was new as compared with the older southern patterns of work relationships. It was not only that Negroes could earn more money and insisted on more pay and larger participation in work of all kinds, with shorter hours and more specialized division of labor. For here the Negro was following the new pattern everywhere. He felt strongly that his employer "needing it less" and himself "needing it more" must find new arrangements or else he would not work. And, there being opportunity for other work, the Negro simply followed the natural trend. But there was, even among Negroes who had worked long and faithfully in the same fields, a tendency suddenly to change their attitudes and modes of work behavior. Sometimes they didn't say much about it. They just changed. And sometimes they grumbled and just refused to work in the old way at the old pay. And even though they followed the natural trend, the point of emphasis was that it became a critical point of conflict, upsetting the traditional southern economy of white-Negro work relations and started the flood of talk, stories, rumors, and violence.

Even more radically changing the whole southern way of life was the new behavior of Negro women who for generations had been "servants" to the white women of the South. The net result was that for all practical purposes, for the great average white family the Negro servant was a thing of the past. It was not important in the explanation of the rumors and conflict to know that the Negro women were following a natural, logical, and fair cause in demanding more money and less work; in accepting work where they could get more money and have more time at home; or in not working at all, in view of the more nearly adequate pay of their husbands or sons. It was all logical, as was also their explanation to the white women who sought their help. "Your husband gets good money and you don't have to work out; my husband gets good money, and I don't have to work out." This illustrated the basis of the deep resentment by the white South so long conditioned to Negro help for little pay. It might even add to the resentment of the unthinking multitudes of white southerners that the Negro spoke the truth when she said she had been a slave for the white folks long enough. Here, as was to be seen subsequently, was the basis for the Eleanor Club stories and all the picturesque rumors about Negro women and their refusal to work for white women. "It is time now," the Negro felt, "for the tide to turn." What she often said was not so formal. "I'm looking for a cook myself," or "I'll work for you now if you'll help me get some help next week." "I been workin' for the white folks long enough."

Finally, of course, there were the extremists among the new Negro intellectuals whose method was so different from anything the South or the Nation had experienced that it caught them all off balance and in such complete surprise as to preëmpt much calm intelligent reaction. To these new leaders most southerners were ignorant crackers; no white man was worthy of trust; everything, literally everything, including southern Negro leadership, was wrong. The big newspapers were impossible. The textbooks in schools were all wrong. Industrial magnates were against the Negroes as were the commercial houses of business. The books, the landlords, the novelists, the films, the government, the radio —all were bad.

And there was no person or institution beyond the easy, sure denunciation of the new Negro intelligentsia. For instance, the scholars and university professors had appeared to be the one group constantly striving for progress, as con-

tinuously considered "radical." Yet the Negro minority new
intellectuals challenged "the scholars and publicists with
their shoddy statistics, their pseudoscience, their learned
lectures, and their published papers."

Now again, this exhibit has not been presented primarily
for any merit of right or wrong, true or false, but for the
phenomenon of a new type of behavior. And the technical
skill and "collegiate" approach of many of these new ones
were superb! Of course there was truth in what they said.
It was self-evident anywhere that the Negro was Negro and
that under the American tradition he was a minority group
losing more by default than by intention, but losing nevertheless. That was old stuff; the *new* was in the behavior of
protest. The South and the Nation manifestly had to get
accustomed to it; but for the time being it went mighty hard
with them.

V

The New Generation Outside the South

Now it must be clear that most of these new patterns of behavior were the inevitable results of trends in all phases of American and world conditions, and in particular of the current war situation, demands, and opportunities. Yet in the explanation of the South's accelerated tensions and conflict, the attitudes and action of the rest of the Nation commonly termed the "North" were of prime importance, as was constantly being pointed out. In the first place, without an understanding of the South, the Nation just simply couldn't understand what it was all about. In the second place, however, and more important in explaining the psychology of the situation, the South held the Nation responsible for a great deal of its trouble with the Negroes. This blame extended all the way back to the slave trade and extended through the Civil War, the reconstruction period, and then on to the 1940's with what they often called the new invasion. And the South complained that the credo of the Nation showed insincerity and unreasonableness in the dominant agitation of white leaders who joined with the Negro "radical" groups. They seemed to the South to assume that the main thing to do was to pass a few Federal laws, organize a few national movements, stir up the Negroes, and all would be well.

A part of the southern pattern of reaction had been not only the appeal to be let alone, but the assertion that the Nation, in all regions, also had discriminated against the Negro. No one, white or Negro, denied this. Yet there was

a difference which was a major one: that discrimination outside the South was not compulsory or universal or incorporated in the technical, legal institutions or in the organic
philosophy of white-Negro-caste culture. This was, of
course, fundamental, since, in theory at least, the Negro had
the possibilities within the framework of American institutions to attain complete equal opportunity. Where equality
was denied it was withheld on the basis of the individual's
failure to achieve status and not because he belonged to a
race to which equal opportunity was automatically denied.
At its worst the national credo held that, being a Negro, his
chances as an individual were limited and his individual personality was affected by his racial environment. In reality,
in many parts of the Nation for limited periods of time, on
specific occasions, and in many single experiences, many
Negroes had been accorded the fullest measure of equality
and opportunity. Perhaps there was no tendency to deny
this, although the white South felt that the rest of the Nation
was becoming increasingly race-minded and the Negroes
often complained that the North was becoming "south-
ernized."

Now, it was pointed out again and again, that the need
for looking at the credo of the Nation at large was not at
all essentially a matter of criticism or of mere accusation of
"You, too." For the new Negro leadership was itself stating
the basis upon which the total national credo was discrimi-
nating against the Negro. Thus, the composite verdict of the
latest accusation which the Negro had made of the Nation
was that "There is in America a belief on the part of great
groups of people, in every stratum of social, political, and
business life that the Negro must not be permitted to share
as a citizen on an equality with other citizens." And again,
"The result has been a deeply planted conviction that the
Negro American is a person apart, that he does not deserve

and must not be given the treatment accorded other Americans."

As a part, therefore, of the psychological reaction, there was need that, if a southern credo was presented in some composite form, so also there should be some sort of a national credo attempted. Indeed, some northern and western students, as well as many southern observers, often affirmed that the credo of the Nation, at bottom, was not very much different from the South's; that the difference of status was one of technical representation. Indeed one special student of race and an acclaimed "liberal" young southern white wrote from his swing around the country, "As I see it, there is literally no part of the Nation which stands in opposition to the southern racial policy."

All of this was of the utmost importance, not only in explaining this transitional crisis, but in looking to the future development of all regions of the Nation. Thus, it was of considerable importance that the credo of the Nation outside the South needed to be portrayed in two major divisions. One was a sincere belief in the importance for every American to proclaim and to legislate equal opportunity for the Negro on all occasions. The other was a personal credo of actual relationships. This was of the greatest significance in practical planning for the future. But it was significant, too, that many of the rumors and folkways of Negroes at work and in conflict prevalent in other regions, were practically identical with many of those in the South. Yet in most aspects of attitude and discrimination the rest of the Nation was more mature, subtle, and less crude and less frank about it than the South.

It seemed important, then, as a part of the picture, in so far as it was possible, to state a credo for the Nation, as synthesized by students and observers North, East, South, West. Perhaps such a credo at best would be symbolic rather than completely accurate. Yet the rising crescendo of race tensions and conflict in all parts of the country accentuated the need for a full consideration of some such itemized viewpoints as reflected the elemental credo of America's millions outside the South:

1. That it was the duty of America to proclaim equal opportunity for all peoples of the United States and in particular for the Negro whose major American heritage had left him primarily discrimination and segregation.

2. That the Nation, having freed the Negro and having set itself to the task of giving him justice, must not turn back.

3. That the problem, however, was primarily a southern problem and that national efforts must be primarily in the role of seeing that the South did a better job of it than had been true in the past.

4. That the approach to the desired ends was a relatively simple matter of passing some laws, such as those of anti-lynching, or anti-poll tax, or of organizing national groups and agencies, and of promoting effective education and propaganda.

5. But that individually, people from other regions, living in or visiting the South, did not believe in violating the folkways and race etiquette of the region, no matter how much they talked.

6. From this point on, the Nation believed in equal opportunity, but upon the invitation of the white man and not on the initiative of the Negro.

7. That the Negro should have the same opportunities and privileges as the white man as long as he was not competing with the white man.

8. That the Negro should have equal economic opportunities with the white man, provided no individual must be expected to employ a Negro except as a domestic or un-

skilled laborer, where he might be preferable to a white man.

9. That the Negro should have equal educational opportunities with the white man and should be permitted to attend the same schools and colleges provided he did not associate with white children in fraternities.

10. That the Negro had a right to marry a white person so long as he did not marry into "my family" or the families of friends or relatives.

11. That the Negro had a right to hold political office when he was representing his own race.

12. That the Negro should be permitted to buy or rent property and live in any neighborhood that he wished, provided it was not in a neighborhood where he was not wanted.

13. That the Negro had a right to stay in the same hotel, eat in the same dining room, frequent the same night clubs, etc., with the whites, provided he did not go to those most commonly used by the whites.

14. Nevertheless, the Nation had to be generous, so what? Of course, the Negro was here and he was the Negro and we always have had and always must have the problem. It would work out some way, at some time and place afar off.

Here, again, it was clear that an estimated composite credo for so complex a Nation, many of whose people were not conscious of the Negro at all, was more of a symbol than actuality. In a later picture of the role of outside agitation, something more than this was added. The chief significance of interpreting the out-of-the-South credo at this point was found in the fact that issues in the South were often raised primarily by great national groups and reinforced by the new ideologies of world democracy and of newer ideals of race opportunity and participation.

It was not possible, therefore, for the South to settle its

own problems alone in an abiding way, since the South could no longer be an isolationist region segregated from the rest of the Nation or the rest of the world. It was, therefore, not only that the outside criticisms accelerated the southern tensions, but that in general there was a new generation of Americans, many of whom were more concerned with the reform of the South than with work in their own regions. In this respect the South came to classify the new Negro leadership and the Nation at large together as militantly advocating a radical and revolutionary change in the southern way of life.

The range and variety of attitudes and movements could be sensed in another way by looking at several groups or segments of the American people who were most directly articulate in the problem of race. In general, of course, these groups were divided into two major categories, namely, the white South and all others. The Negro, of course, was aligned, in symbol at least, against the South. Among the Negroes there appeared to be three major groups that were becoming more articulate and on the march.

The first of the Negro group was the great body of the Negro's best leaders who asked that America give them the rights and privileges which the Constitution guaranteed and which they had been told would accrue to them as soon as they had proved themselves worthy as American citizens. This group was articulate throughout the Nation and among relatively all classes of Negroes. They appealed to the southern white leaders for confidence so as not to be compelled to find their leadership outside of the South.

There was then a smaller group of Negro leaders, articulate outside the South, but many of them southern Negroes with residence in other regions who were militant in the demand for "all or nothing." This was primarily the group that constituted the aggressive bloc pictured in the new behavior. Some of them were frank to say they were not so much interested in the great mass of Negro people as they were in winning a cause for complete equality. It was symptomatic of what was to come that, to President and Mrs. Roosevelt, who had done more than all other White House occupants combined, who had shown courage and initiative, who had alienated the South—that to them the "March on Washington" leadership chorused "words, words, words." That is, in so formidable a movement as "The March on Washington" and in the special brochure characterizing race segregation in the armed forces as America's greatest disgrace, the President was assailed as primarily a maker of words, rather than a doer of deeds, because he did not by presidential edict order all segregation abolished.

There was, then, the younger group of Negroes, many of them college youth but not all, who were committed to experimenting with every possible opportunity for equal rights with the whites in whatever fields of endeavor they might be. They were realistic, searching, and persistent. This group was considered in the South as following "northern" leadership.

That the great body of Negroes in the South were, as usual, being pressed between the upper and nether millstones and becoming increasingly restless, was a natural product of the new generations in the Nation. They were urged to attain more status, to demand better work and wages, better opportunities for education, and more specifically at that time to take advantage of the war situation to gain more work and more privileges. They reflected the life of a troubled people tending gradually to turn against the South.

There was no tendency to deny that in the midst of all of this the younger Negroes, with the urging of their radical leaders outside the South, reflected the difficulties, problems, and behavior of the transitional stage, and many of the common folks among the Negroes, through rumors and talks, acquired unrealistic attitudes that added to the complexity of the situation. The new demands made upon the Negro for his race and the ideals which had been preached to him from without often conflicted with the reasonable standards of work, and with his chances of obtaining the bare necessities of life. It made harder and harder the reasonable services of workaday occupations and good relations with the whites. It thus happened, for instance, that courtesies were then interpreted as subservience; good manners as reflecting the character of the "white folks' nigger," or "Uncle Toms." Always there was complaint of discrimination and never mention of opportunity and obligation.

In all of these situations there was always a large measure of the Negro folkways and folk culture hidden from the whites and constituting a powerful reserve, which was matched to some degree by a similar unspoken and hidden reserve folk conflict among the whites in the South and by a powerful and cautious reserve in the North. Here was one of the most interesting of all the culture complexes which contributed to the difficulties involved.

VI

Three Militant Fronts

There was special need in this crisis for a recognition of
the extent to which all of the groups, white and Negro, in
the South and in the rest of the Nation, were "right" in their
representation. A part of the crisis was found in the inflexibil-
ity of viewpoints and in the task of making adjustments
where no yielding was possible on any one of the three main
fronts. For there were, in general, three such groups, all
of which were militantly "right." What was to be done,
therefore, and what was to happen when three major groups
met head on with completely conflicting philosophies and
inflexible leadership?

Of the three groups, the Negroes appeared organically
and from the viewpoint of the good society, of democracy,
and Christianity "most right." That is, they not only had the
right and knew they had the right of better opportunity, but
they had been led to believe that this right would be forthcoming. More specifically, they had been urged and ex-
horted to demand all rights, and they had done a good job
of it. On the basis of abstract theory and in accordance with
the philosophy of the American Dream there could be no
refutation of the Negro's claim for his equal place in the
Nation.

The second great group, the rest of the Nation, often generally called "The North," and reflecting primarily the white
race, included folk from all the regions, North, East, West.
They were "right" in that they knew that America was committed to the doctrine of equal opportunity. They knew,

too, that in the good society there must be no such discrimination as had been made against the Negro. Since this discrimination, both quantitatively and qualitatively, was worse in the South, where most of the Negroes were, that was the great field, of course, for reform efforts. Nevertheless, it was much easier to talk about the government's coercing another region than it was to achieve voluntaristic fairness in other regions where discrimination was increasing rapidly.

This group was the second "most right," from the same viewpoint of the good society and American democracy, as was the case with the Negroes. For, citing the guarantees of the American Constitution and the American Dream, they felt greatly embarrassed that the Nation in times of world conflict for democracy should have entire regions in which there was little semblance of equality of opportunity. This group included not only the general urban and educational leaders but a majority of the New Deal, who represented what might be termed, in the better sense of the word, the reform group. Although admitting discrimination in other regions, they accurately made the point that discrimination was not in the organic or constitutional set-up of the Nation, whereas in the South it was.

The third group was the "White South" as portrayed. It was least "right" from the same viewpoints as were applied to the other groups. On these premises, there could be no conclusion except that the South was "wrong." Nevertheless, any physical scientist or cultural anthropologist or student of history would know what the power of centuries and then later generations of conditioning with reference to race had wrought. Any individual who used any sort of intelligence would know that nowhere in the organic world could such a situation be changed within a day or a week or a year or a decade. The South was "right" in that it was reflecting its natural evolutionary pattern.

The South was "right" again under the system of American democratic government, in which the States had been made the sovereign units of a federation of States as opposed to centralized federalism. Under the provisions of such a government the South had made its folkways and stateways coincide. This was the basis of the much-quoted statement, referred to above, that not all the forces of the world, including all the Axis powers, could make the South suddenly and at one step give up its pattern of racial segregation. Anyone who knew history or social science or psychology or the South knew that this was true.

Now, manifestly there was no solution for these three conflicts except in the type of behavior which the American groups, all three, and the total Nation, which was greater than the three, might develop. It was to be shown later that there was no time and place for the immature calling of names, the placing of blame, and the stubborn willfulness that settles differences only by combat.

There was need for each of the three groups to see and understand all the particulars of all the groups and of all the total complex situation. Could they do this? Could the South, after the manner of its revivalists' preaching, come to a certain sense of guilt and repentance through the facing of facts and the realization of impending danger? Could the South admit for once that, along with its rightness and righteousness, it was wrong? Could the other two major forces sense the enormity of the situation and dedicate themselves to the task of understanding as well as of reform, to the end that they might approximate the largest number of adjustments to the largest number of solutions with the least number of conflicts and dangers of revolution? Could they ask such questions as: Can this thing of the elimination of segregation be accomplished at once? If it was universally agreed that such a program would take time, then just what was to be gained by attempting what was known to be impossible? Was the desired purpose the successful achievement of ends or was it revolution? Was it to help the Negro or to destroy him? Was it to help the Nation win the war or was it to divide and weaken it?

Those questions would be repeated often: first in the approach to the portraiture of the mass of rumors and stories, then in the testing of the South's and the Nation's sense of humor, of fairness, and of perspective, and in the final questions as to what was to be done about it. Would the cataloguing of rumors, their classification and analysis, and a frank look at their absurdities and yet their power to stampede a Nation—would all this lead to a new era that was to dedicate itself to the rebuilding of a greater America and to the cooperative participation in global democracy?

PART II

RACE AND RUMORS OF RACE

VII

Race and Rumors of Race

There was constantly being reflected in the crisis of the early war years of the 1940's a number of insistent questions: Could the three great folk groups most concerned look upon the sweep of racial rumors, stories, and conflict as powerful drama in the making? Could they sense the logical realism of the several acts, recognize the traditional form of the rising action, sense the essential comedy and tragedy in such a cultured epoch, forthwith accept the drama as powerful teaching and influence for the better ordering of race relationships?

Could the people react with poise, maturity, humor? "Sure, we have heard these rumors; we know all about them; we expect to hear more; what of it? We understand how many of them have risen, we know how they spread, and we know that some of them have some incidental basis of fact. So what? We understand the changing conditions which have given rise to stress and tension, and we know that they will demand of us new wisdom, new courage, new concessions. Well, who said they wouldn't? From this point on, what is the best thing to do?

"And we know, too, that most of the stories are rumors and not facts and that is why they are so damaging. We know in time of war that these rumors and stories, if part truth, flood the country, and we will not let them bring tragedy to us."

If these desired reactions could come to be the major mode of behavior, there would be promise of a happy ending in which wisdom and understanding might develop new ways and new inventions as the proverbial children of necessity.

How the flood of rumors and stories reflected the whole drama of regional and racial crisis might be indicated in a number of ways. In the first place, nearly the entire catalogue tended to recapitulate the historical points of tensions and experience of the South since the Civil War. So, too, they reflected the fundamental folkways, stateways, and institutions of the present South as they have grown up through the processes of struggle, adaptation, and sanction. And they reflected again points of tension in which changing time and technology were demanding changing adaptations and new ways of meeting needs.

The catalogue of rumors and stories and their backgrounds showed clearly how they recaptured the tensions of the past and featured the very old threefold heart of the southern biracial culture. First, the Negro must be kept in his place as a Negro and all experience and all policies were geared to this determination. By the same token, movements of the Negroes or of others to change the culture economy became the basis for all possible extremes and for an attempt to discredit the Negro. Thus, the rumors that "the Negro will take over" the affairs of the white man reflected the ancient reconstruction fear and complex. They swept down with renewed power as did the rumors that the whites would some day work for the Negroes. There was a powerful contradiction in the white insistence that more Negroes be drafted, lest they be left so numerous as to terrify the families at home; and the universal rumor appraisal that Negroes could not become soldiers, that they would not obey, that they would run before the battle, and that they would shoot their officers. These rumors were bottomed then in the third complicating fear, namely, that when the Negro soldier returned he would be dangerous both in his aspirations and in his training as a fighter.

The second basic powerful group of folkways, often inseparable from the first, was grounded in the sex-caste culture, the preservation of which was worth more than all other life, liberty, and the pursuit of happiness. In the pictures of the rumors, this category was perhaps catalogued first and foremost among them all. Here were the rumors and stories of the Negroes taking over white women and of such variations of this theme as to indicate the bold intention to achieve the hated "social equality." In these rumors were revivified the heritage of a million woman-fear episodes, the basis of which, without reflection on the race at all, was so realistic that fear and terror stalked again through every rural area and in many urban centers as well.

The third major category was also very old. This included the great number and variety of rumors of riots and uprisings, of the purchase of ice picks, knives, and guns by the Negroes. These rumors were rife in the past World War and many of them followed the same patterns again. They, too, grew out of the old, old fears that followed reconstruction days, when it was often assumed that unless the Negro was kept down he would rise up to rule the white man, as he was aided to some extent by the Federal Government during reconstruction.

There was another general level of rumor, which was more difficult to classify since it was characterized more by its origin and purpose than by its content, which was likely to be varied. This was the rumor that appeared to be planted and utilized for various purposes of conflict, discussion, sabotage, or other special ends. No one was able to identify such rumors with exactness and in some instances investigating committees reported positively that some of the riots were not the product of Axis stories. Yet, here was a field which was real and was being investigated by the proper authorities.

Perhaps the category that came nearer to inflaming the folk was the series, the focus of which was upon the caste conflict as it related to Negro men and white women. It was important to cite a relatively large number of individual cases, very much alike in general tone and import, but varying in certain details and in wording. One object of citing so many was to indicate the nature and range of the folk psychology here as well as the power of the folkways. The greater number of rumors and the greater amount of talk in this area might be classified into two main divisions. First, the common rumor that, when the white men had gone to the Army and the Negroes had been left behind, the Negro men would then take care of the white women. The second large group in this field had to do with young Negro boys and men undertaking to "date" white girls. Two types of examples of the first category were presented: one in which the mere statement of the rumor was presented and the other in which those rumors reported the tragic consequences to the Negro. In these instances, as in many others, there were symptoms of very realistic folk psychology, some of which followed the tone of the Negro's folklore and folksong and some of which, of course, followed the level of the South's folkways on social equality.

The first category of rumors and stories about Negro men and white women followed from the assumption that a larger number of white men were being drafted than Negroes. The Negro men would, so the stories went, as soon as the whites were gone, take over, protect, or "have a good time with" the white women. This series reflected the points of tension and caste folk-psychology already described as the set-up of the folkways of protection for white women.

It was emphasized over and over again that those **were**

rumors and irresponsible talk and that their recording in such number and variety was itself testimony as to the nature of their power. Yet, it was always hard to destroy their influence. Said one prominent socialite, "The very fact that there are so many rumors is sure evidence that the Negroes do intend to do as is reported."

Now for rumor samplings. From South Carolina came a rumor that "when white men go to the Army, the Negro men will have the white women." And from North Carolina that "Negro men were all planning to have white wives, and that when all the white men have gone to war, the white women will be left for the Negro men." So, too, "every Negro man will have a white girl when the white boys go off to war." Also, from North Carolina, it was reported that two Negro men followed two white girls along the street talking about the good times they would have when the white men were all gone. And in Virginia, "a Negro made the remark that he had his white girl 'picked out' just as soon as the Negroes take over."

From Georgia it was reported that one fight between whites and Negroes was supposedly caused by a Negro saying to another Negro who was a soldier, "Aren't we going to have a time with these white women, when all these white men go off to war!" And from the same State, some young Negroes said to a young white couple, "You'd better be necking now because after the war we'll be doing the necking." And in South Carolina it was said that "after the war Negroes will marry white girls and run the country."

In Louisiana, two Negro men were overheard talking. One, it was said, told the other that he would be glad when all the white men had left for the Army, then he was going to find himself a white woman for company. In Alabama, at a country club, a golfer was reported to have overheard his Negro caddie talking with other caddies about what they would do when all of the white men went off to war. "They said that they would really have a good time with the white women. There are about ten Negroes to every white person around the section." And in the same State a Negro retorted to an offended white girl: "You'll be glad to have us Negroes love you when the white folks are gone."

Four samplings again from Georgia were symbolic: rumors they were, *not* facts, except as reported stories were facts of influence. One Negro was overheard to say to another, "See that white woman over there? She's the one I'm going to have when all the white men are away." A Negro, ordered to leave, turned around and said, "That's all right, white lady, but befo' this war is over us Negro men will be protecting and living with a lot of white women." Also, one night a Negro boy walking down the street behind a white girl offered to carry her bag and walk home with her to see that she got there safely. When she refused the Negro boy replied, "You can refuse now, but after the war is over a lot of us Negro boys will be taking care of you white girls."

Again in Virginia, "the Negroes told each other to pick their white women now," while members of a Negro club in Louisiana stated that "if white men, being mostly in the armed forces, could not take care of their white women, the Negro men could." In South Carolina, a Negro man, who was being reprimanded by an elderly white lady, allegedly made the following remark to her: "You white women just wait until these white men folks are drafted—that's when we are going to take over." And from South Carolina came the reported wisecrack: "When you come back from the Army, I'll be your brother-in-law."

In many of the rumors that were reported the seriousness of the offense was indicated by the action which followed. Samplings from some of those just cited: "They ran the Negro out of town." "They had the Negro arrested."

"Neither of the Negroes has been seen since." "I'm quite sure that not a single Negro will live to tell about it, if he does." "They called the police and the Negro was put in jail." The following are types of stories where the point of the story emphasized the penalty.

From South Carolina came one—a case in which Negroes told white boys who were in uniform, "We will take care of all the white girls while you are gone." The white boys, it was said, killed the Negroes. Three other South Carolina rumors were similar. One was that a man made a remark in front of a Negro "that he didn't know what was going to happen to his wife when he went to the Army; the Negro man said that he would take care of her. The white man shot him right then." Another was that "a white man was told by a Negro when he left his home town to join some branch of the service that when he returned he [the Negro] would be his brother-in-law. The white man was so angered he killed the Negro and was not punished for it."

The meat knife rumor was one of the first of the fantastic ones to spread all over the South. There were many versions with the same general pattern. In this first case recorded "a white boy of draft age was working in a meat market. A Negro came in and asked this boy when he was going to the Army. The boy asked the Negro why he wanted to know. The Negro said, 'When you white men leave we can take care of the white women.' At this the boy let a meat knife loose and cut off the Negro's head."

Then there were four other Georgia stories in which the women themselves did the killing, emphasizing the *rumor* nature rather than fact. One rumor was that "a white woman killed a Negro man because he said, 'Don't you worry, when all the white men have gone, we'll be around to take care of you.' She shot and killed him." Another reported that "a Negro walked up to a white woman storekeeper in a small town informing her that she had better enjoy being her own boss while she could because now that the white men had gone to war they, the Negro men, would be looking after them before long. The white woman then shot the Negro and killed him on the spot." Still another alleged that "a Negro man was killed by a white woman when he came into her store and said now that all the white men were in the Army the Negro men were going to 'take over.'"

There was a similar one from Florida in which it was said that "a lady was sitting on the front porch rocking her baby. The Negro man said, 'Your husband has been called to war, now who is going to love you while he is gone?' She replied, 'My baby will love me.' Then he said, 'No, I'se going to love you while your husband is gone.' She said, 'Just wait until I put the baby to bed.' When she returned, she carried a shotgun in her hands and killed him on the spot."

Still others from South Carolina: "A young married man was leaving his home to enter the Army and he was saying goodbye to his wife. A Negro man was standing near by. He told the white man that he would take care of his wife while he was gone. At these words, the white man shot the Negro and the Negro died instantly." Also in South Carolina, when a bus was pulling out from the station with a load of soldiers, "there were three Negroes on the corner and as the bus passed by one of the 'blacks' hollered, 'Take your time boys, don't hurry back, we'll take care of your women 'til you get back.' The bus stopped and the soldiers 'mopped up' the Negroes." A story of a bus racial homicide was reported from Louisiana. "A Negro man in a bus said, in front of six white soldiers, 'All the white men are going to war and us colored men can take care of the white women.' The soldiers stopped the bus and killed the Negro."

In the same general category of rumors and stories relating to Negro men and white women was another group which represented Negro youth attempting to date white girls. The same general level of tension was indicated as in the first category where the Negroes were reported to be planning to "take over." There was here a factual basis in which in certain communities the hoodlum custom had developed in which the telephone numbers of women listed as "miss" were called. Sometimes the request was for more than a date and the white women would judge from the voices and hilarious laughter that the callers were Negroes. This was, of course, a tragic circumstance in that most of the calls were certainly not by Negroes and that real fear was coupled with the rumors and stories to place the blame always upon the Negro.

From South Carolina a young white woman reported that one of the most terrible and unspeakable things that she had heard about the Negro was that some of them had been heard saying that they would be glad when all of the white boys had gone to the Army so they could date the white girls here at home. In North Carolina, Negro boys had been rumored to say, "Just you wait a few more months when all the white boys are gone and we'll be dating all these white girls," while in Alabama there were reports of a Negro being run out of town because he asked a white woman for a date.

In Louisiana a Negro soldier asked a white girl to dance. The white soldiers objected and a "free-for-all" ensued. It was alleged that a white soldier was killed. In Georgia, "they say" that "after the war white girls will be glad to go with Negro boys." An illustration was given of an attractive young woman walking down the street who passed several Negroes standing on the sidewalk. One of the Negroes gave her a long whistle and was reported to have said, "I would like to have a date with you tonight."

Slightly different was the report that a group of Negro

boys were congregating to discuss just which white girl each was going to pick out to "go with" as soon as a greater number of white men left for the Army. "One actually had a list of white girls' names." This was a South Carolina story, while from North Carolina it was reported that "a girl working in a ten-cent store was asked by a Negro man when she got off from work. She thought he said, "What time do you close?" and she told him. After he left she remembered what he had said and called the police. She was told not to worry and leave at her usual time. When she left the store, the Negro man grabbed her and the police grabbed the man."

The two next examples from Florida and South Carolina represent a type commonly repeated. First, "A Negro man 'phoned a white girl for a date. She accepted and called the police. The Negro was jailed." Next, "A Negro soldier entered a store and asked the owner's daughter for a date. The girl's father shot the man and was not prosecuted."

There were rumors that many Negro soldiers in Georgia, South Carolina, and Virginia had been calling white women to ask for dates: "One stepped up to a girl working in the dime store and asked her if she were doing anything that night. She told him that it was none of his business. He told her that he just wondered, as he wanted her to go out with him."

Differing again, but symbolic, were the hand-holding stories. From South Carolina came several. One was that "a Negro man while paying a girl in a dime store for an article tried to hold her hand. That night after the store closed the same Negro started following her down the street. The girl ran into a store and called the police. Police came and asked him what he was trying to do. He said, 'I want to go home with that girl—that's the way we do in New York.'" Another reported a Negro boy as purchasing an article at a dime store, and as the girl who waited on him returned the change, he grabbed her hand and asked her for a date. A third one reported that in a certain town a sales girl in one of the dime stores handed a Negro man change from the purchase he had made. "He caught her hand and held it for a minute."

Other stories from Georgia were similar. "A Negro man in a hotel asked a white woman for a date." "Another rumor that is in our community among the Negroes is that the white women will sometimes be glad to go with Negro men." Still another reported that "a lady was sitting on the bench waiting for the car to come. A Negro man came up and sat down on the same bench at the other end. She noticed that he kept sliding down, nearer and nearer her end of the bench. Finally, she stood up and he stood up by her. He asked for a date. She told him not to be foolish. He told her that after the war was over she would probably be eager to date him. The street car came along then and she sat towards the front; he, towards the rear."

Back to South Carolina. It was reported that "a Negro man sent a box of candy to a white girl in high school last Christmas. In a note on the inside of the box he asked her for a date the following night." Again, "Negroes tried continuously to walk with white girls and to take the place of white men. In the cafe one night a Negro man held a waitress' hand until she had to scream for help." Said another, "I heard of a Negro man asking a white waitress here in a hotel for a 'date.'" "There was a Negro who was put in jail for talking with insolence and for insulting some girl clerks in a dime store."

A third category of rumors relating to Negro men and white women was that which reflected the traditional fear and accusation that Negro men would attack white women. This was the basis of the South's great fear in the old days. There were pathos and tragedy in its revival. For scarcely an old southern family or community but had its terror story and its skeleton of Ku-Klux vengeance on Negroes, sometimes guilty, often not guilty. And millions of Negroes suffered from the results of that fear which itself perpetuated by suggestion the shadow of a great terror. There were adequate samplings from all the States.

In South Carolina, it was heard that "a white girl was attacked by a Negro last summer. He stuffed her mouth with Kleenex, and ran after the act." North Carolina reported that "the murder of a white sailor and several attacks on white girls by Negroes was part of a planned 'Reign of Terror.'" In Mississippi, it was rumored that a lady who worked in the cotton mill "was attacked by a Negro when she was going home from work one night about 10:30. She screamed and help came, but not before the Negro had taken his knife and cut her up quite a bit."

From Alabama it was rumored that "in a little town in which there is a girls' school, the Negroes wrote letters, threatening the girls," and from South Carolina they heard that "the Negro soldiers whistled at the white girls as they went down the street. They also made some vulgar remarks to them." In several places in Louisiana, it was said that students had to have chaperons to accompany them on the campus at night because of the fact that there had been a sudden outbreak of Negroes' attacking white women. So, too, special policemen reported that they had orders to shoot on sight any Negroes prowling about all girls' schools. In the same State it was reported that "rape by Negro men upon young white girls was very prevalent. That was not all rumor: they cited facts from the city hospital to show that this situation actually existed." So, too, they told of several instances when men in the neighborhood had "had to kill Negro men who had tried to enter a girls' convent at night in the same neighborhood, and on trying to escape had been given fair warning to stop or be killed." From North Carolina came the story that "a Negro shot and killed a sailor and wounded two others. A few days before that a high school girl of twelve years of age was raped. Another white woman was raped in the fall."

One of the most serious aspects of the whole rumor situation was the way in which rumors appeared to be plausible happenings, as they clustered around common folkways and traditional fears. No matter how groundless many of the fears may have been and how slight the rumors, many of the common folk really believed that much of what they heard was true. No matter how unjustified their fears and how unfair they must have been to the Negroes, the realism of these fears and the resulting action were part and parcel of the folkways that contributed to the total of tensions and hazards. It so happened, therefore, that the rumors often appeared sufficiently realistic to change the whole pattern of behavior.

This was true even in the Washington, D. C., alarms in the early summer of 1943, when practically the whole city was on the alert for hours. And it was reported from Mississippi that "it was dangerous for a colored man to appear around on the streets in the daytime and practically fatal if one was seen around at night." In North Carolina, "on occasion when feeling began to rise against Negroes, the city officials made and passed a rule that no Negroes would be allowed on the street after 7:00 o'clock, and also, they said, that when the Negro soldiers came to town it would be unsafe for white women to walk on the streets unescorted." Yet, "often these incidents have been kept out of the papers, so that it would not bring about hard feelings." In another North Carolina community, "white girls were asked not to go alone on streets at night," and in a university town in Alabama young women students were not allowed off the campus after 6:00 o'clock in the evening. In two Louisiana college communities new chaperonage rules had been reported where girls "had to walk in pairs or more to the library at night, and, if they went down town, at least three must go together." So, also, library privileges were limited at night and "girls were not allowed to go out during the day unless they went in a party of three or more."

VIII

The New Dilemma of Domestic Service

A chief complaint in the South against the New Deal had been that it demoralized Negro "help" through the high level of pay advocated and offered. There were many examples cited, with complaints of inconvenience and the Negro's irresponsibility but rarely with consideration for the Negro's better opportunity.

Reflected perhaps in as many rumors and sayings as in any other field was that of the relation between Negro women and white women in the sphere of domestic service. This series reflected in remarkably vivid ways again the powerful folkways of both races. It was, in its historical and psychological backgrounds, a part of the caste-sex conflict. Here also was the basic origin of the rumored Eleanor Clubs, themselves a favorite classification that constituted more than one dramatic chapter. A common form of story centered in the long mental and spiritual conflict between Negro women and their white employers. It was not always an idle boast that "white women will be working for us." The Negro woman sometimes succeeded in having the white woman work for her, as when she rushed to the curb market to buy the white woman's wonderful cakes or dressed chickens and favorite jellies. In the new economy of money to spend, she not only would not work for the white woman, but she saved herself work by buying what the white woman had prepared.

However, it was clear that in this field rumors were rich and rife, and for the reasons indicated. Yet again, even though the basic behavior of Negroes led to a changed economy and relationship, it was emphasized that rumors must be separated from actual facts. So many of the rumors were of a stereotyped nature that they bore little resemblance to what would have been reality. Many were humorous and many bore the earmarks of the folk-retorts so genuinely characteristic that they were reported to have "actually happened."

The stories vary little from State to State; yet it was a part of the picture to identify some as different from others. Thus in South Carolina: "White people are going to be working for the Negroes after the war." And in North Carolina: "White women will be Negro women's maids." So in South Carolina, again, the Negroes were talking about "the time when all the white men and boys had been called to fight for their country that things would certainly change. The Negroes would live in the homes of the white people and instead of their working for the white people, the white women and children would have to work for them."

And preview to the Eleanor Clubs, in Louisiana, Negro women were quitting work to "put the white woman back in the kitchen." And in South Carolina, Negro cooks were quoted as saying that most housewives would be in the kitchen cooking for themselves by Christmas of 1942. So, too, in Louisiana it had been said that the servants in homes had organized for higher wages and shorter hours, while Negro women were quitting jobs because they wanted more money or better conditions. They were more independent because of scarcity of domestic servants, and, "they said" in South Carolina that the Negro woman was going to stop working for the white woman altogether.

A story of a stereotyped nature was that "a white woman was away for a while and when she returned to her home she found her maid sitting at her dresser combing her hair with her comb." Other stories had the Negro "servants" taking baths in the white woman's bathtub during work hours. Still others represented the young Negro women as asking for the parlor to entertain their men friends. "Once when a Negro nurse was asked for a health certificate, she in turn asked her prospective employer for a health certificate." Another, typical of a later series, was that a Negro woman refused to work for a white woman because the white woman would not allow the Negro to call her by her first name.

And there were other abundant and vivid types: "The story was told that a lady asked a Negro 'wash woman' if she would do her wash that week, whereupon the woman replied, 'I'll do yours this week if you'll do mine next week.'" This was a common South Carolina story as was the next one which told about some "white ladies" seeing a Negro woman walking around during morning hours and asking the Negro if she would like to cook for someone. The Negro replied hurriedly, "I was looking for someone to cook for me."

Similar ones from Georgia reported that one colored maid, when asked if she wanted a job, said: "I'm looking for someone to work for me!" Two more from South Carolina were similar. One was that "a lady called her cook to come up and fix dinner as she was having company. The cook turned the tables and asked her mistress to come to her house by eight o'clock Sunday morning to help her since she was having company!" A similar story was also told about "a white woman asking a Negro woman to wash for her. The Negro replied that, on the contrary, she would be glad to pay the white woman to wash her clothes!"

Still another grouping featured a new behavior that greatly troubled many of the whites. The young Negro housemaids were insisting on calling the men roomers in the house by their given names. "Well, don't they call me by my given name? But if it's going to cause trouble, I'll just quit working here. White folks always calling us that way." So, too, "a Negro servant went to work one day and called the woman for whom she worked by her given name. The woman asked her why she did it. The Negro woman said: 'Well, you don't call me Mrs., so I won't call you that.'" Another story reported that both men and women servants of a prominent family refused to work any longer unless they were allowed to call their employers by their first names. Another vivid one was that "one day a cook walked into her mistress' bedroom, called her by her first name, and told her she thought it was time for her to get up for breakfast." The same sort of behavior, however, was reported from Pennsylvania and New Jersey as well as from the South.

There was humor to be found in this category of the Negro's rise to more leisure. So common had become the story of the Negro woman's repartee that it had appeared in the comic strips. For instance, there was a white woman who asked a Negro woman to do her laundry for her. The Negro woman replied, "All right, you come and wash for me one week and I'll do yours the next." And from South Carolina, "a white lady asked a Negro woman why she hadn't come back to work for her. The Negro said, 'I have a proposition to make—if you work for me a week, I'll work for you a week.'"

A Georgia story had it that "a Negro servant, who had worked for many years for a family, one morning told the woman for whom she worked that she would not be back after that day. The woman asked her if she was dissatisfied with her pay. The Negro woman said, no, it wasn't that. She said her 'society' was going to take care of her for the duration. The white woman asked her what she planned to do after the duration. The Negro woman replied, 'By then you white folks will be working for us.'"

It was, of course, not rumor but fact that many Negro women refused to work because their husbands were making "good money." The Negro women insisted that they didn't need the extra money as much as they needed "to stay at home and cook three meals a day for their working men." Why not? And when "they said" that a lot of cooks were going into war and government services for the money involved, and labor unions were being organized among the house servants, they were reporting reality and not mere hearsay. Rumors, however, grew up to the effect that domestic servants were going to demand an eight-hour day at union pay rates, and that the government would need all the men and women, so there would be no more Negro servants, and "they said" that the Negroes were going to form unions and the maids and men servants would demand a certain wage per hour. It was also often rumored that in trying their best to organize the Negroes they were also trying to stir up trouble.

The "turned table" had its abundant catalogue of sayings and rumors. "A white lady's cook asked if she might use her parlor that night as she was having a guest. When the white lady said, 'No,' and told the cook that she could leave, the cook said, 'That's all right. You white women will be working in our kitchens by Christmas.'" This from North Carolina was similar to one from South Carolina, where it was reported that "a certain Negro woman asked for a raise. The white lady could not afford it, so the Negro quit. When she left, the Negro told the white employer, 'Some day you will be working for me instead of my working for you.'" And still another one was that "one day a white woman asked a Negro worker to scrub the floor but the worker refused at first. A quarrel ensued and the Negro finally exclaimed, 'O.K. I'll do it now, but before long, you'll be scrubbing my floors, washing my clothes, and tending my babies.' "

There was, of course, a great variety of details alongside a rather uniform refrain. There was humor and there was pathos, too. "A white lady asked a Negro woman if she would work for her. The Negro said, 'I don't have time—how about you working for me?' " One story was that "a policeman stopped a Negro woman on the street and asked her if she had time to do some work for his wife. The Negro woman said, 'No, but does your wife have time to do some work for me?' " This was from North Carolina and was matched by two from South Carolina. One was that "a lady went out to get help and she saw a very neat colored girl standing in a door. The white lady asked, 'Would you like to have some work?' The Negro said, 'No indeed, my husband is working for the government making good money.' " Another told of a Negro woman who bluntly informed a man that she wasn't going to work for any white man because her husband was making just as much money as he and had told her not to work.

Still another frequent story, reflecting a bit of Negro humor and folk-banter, was the looking-glass variation. Thus, in one town a woman who had been unable to get a cook decided to go out in search of one herself. "She drove down into Negro town, went up to a house and knocked on the door. When she inquired if the woman knew where she could get a cook the Negro woman looked at her mockingly and said, 'sho—look in the mirror and you'll see your cook.' " A variation was the retort to a northern Negro who wanted help. Said the southern Negro, "Look in yo' mirror and see yo' big black cook."

IX

The Romance of the Eleanor Clubs

Perhaps the most remarkable of all the rumors were those relating to the Eleanor Clubs and to the activities and attitude of the First Lady of the Land. These rumors abounded in all their richness and variety wherever southerners abode. Not only in the South but in New York, in Los Angeles, in Chicago, vivacious southerners told the stories as they were told to them. The Eleanor Clubs struck deep at the heart of the South's whole domestic home economy. Basic causes were found in the opportunity for Negro women to work at higher wages, their organization into clubs and branches of organized labor, and the subsequent folk psychology of the South. That the Eleanor Club rumor seemed to reflect the "weakest" and most unfair perhaps of all the folkways of "servants," makes it all the more important as a chronicle of the era. The fact that the folkways of survival here were so strong as to lead the South to forget its manners was again evidence of crisis.

The slogan of the Eleanor Clubs was nearly always a variation of "A white woman in every kitchen by 1943." There were many variations of the same theme, and samplings were offered in abundance because of the richness of their details. Thus, from Mississippi it was reported that an Eleanor Club was found by the sheriff. "My cousin told me that the sheriff went down there and told those 'niggers' that they'd better get back to work, or else." In Georgia, they had heard a special version of the Eleanor Clubs as the "Royal House of Eleanor."

From Georgia it was reported that when an army camp was started "in my town and cooks were asked to cook for the soldiers, receiving as much as $15.00 a week, many housewives decided that this was a project of the Eleanor Clubs to get Negroes out of domestic service, and to give them higher pay." "Here was the way it was: 'Why, all the Negroes are getting so "uppity" they won't do a thing. I hear the cooks have organized Eleanor Clubs and their motto is: A white woman in every kitchen by Christmas.'" This was from North Carolina, where it was also heard that "all the colored maids at a hotel joined Eleanor Clubs and walked out in a body one day because their pay and hours did not suit."

Two major points of emphasis in the Eleanor Club stories were loyalty to the First Lady and her loyalty to the Negroes to the end that they would have better opportunities. Thus, a Negro girl left during the middle of a meal which she was helping to serve because one of the guests had said something she didn't like and "she had been instructed by the Eleanor Club to leave whenever she was insulted." So, too, a very common rumor was that a maid must resign whenever anyone spoke disparagingly of either the First Lady or the President. From Florida came the version that when a Negro applied for a job she first asked if the head of the house liked Eleanor Roosevelt. If not, she replied that she belonged to the Eleanor Club and couldn't work for her.

Another level of the Eleanor Club activities had to do with their influence. One story from North Carolina had it that by the time of the next presidential election the Eleanor Clubs would have enough strength and power to control the election. But always the heart of the situation was in the scarcity of help. Thus, it was said that in a community of two hundred families, who originally had cooks, but two of these families had a cook at that time. "This

Eleanor Club is spreading like wildfire all over the South and their motto is 'a white woman in every kitchen.' " And again, "Eleanor Clubs are stirring up troubles that never should have arisen. Clubs are making the Negroes discontented, making them question their status." This was from Georgia, but again the crux of the trouble was reflected in the North Carolina verdict that before the appearance of the Eleanor Club story, back in the early spring, probably in March, 1942, the community buzzed with the story that outside organizers were organizing the colored maids; that they were going to ask for a twelve dollar a week minimum in the wealthier residential section, and eight dollars a week in the middle-class residence area.

Still another type of story reflected the trend toward specialized labor. One woman's maid stopped bringing in any wood for the fire because the other maids in the neighborhood had "jumped on" her and told her that she could not belong to the Eleanor Club and bring in wood. That was not her job, and her employer would have to hire someone else to do the bringing in of the wood or she would have to do it herself. Likewise, the maids refused to wash any windows—that was a man's work—and the maids were to do only the lightest work. Again, a friend reported that "a friend had a maid who had been with them for fifteen years. She joined the Eleanor Club and told her mistress that she would have to leave as she could not work for less than a certain sum, which sum was much more than my friend was paying or could afford to pay."

That was a Florida story, and from Florida came also one telling of a woman who went to the "quarters to see why her maid had not showed up to work. She blew her horn in front of the cottage—no response. She could see there was someone in the place so went to the door. The colored woman was lying down, but said, no, she wasn't sick. When asked why she hadn't come to work, she said, 'because there had been a meeting of the Eleanor Club where they had been told to demand more wages.' The woman told her she would gladly have paid her more if wages had gone up but wanted to know why she hadn't come to tell her. That also had been forbidden. Also, the Club ruler had told them not to answer any more horn calls from a car."

The First Lady was held responsible for these developments and more, although she had appeared in very few towns. Yet a common saying was that in nearly every town in which she had occasion to speak, an Eleanor Club was formed by the Negroes soon thereafter. "They said maids walked out any time of the day with the excuse of going to an Eleanor's meeting."

A variation from South Carolina had it that "a Negro girl came in the front door of a white woman's house. The white woman asked why she came in the front door instead of the back door. The Negro's reply was that she had joined the Eleanor Club and she was supposed to come in the front door instead of the back." In Georgia, it was related that "Eleanor Clubs had drawn up a Black List of white employers and that several Negro servants had stopped working for people on this list. So, also, it was reported that Eleanor Clubs made a practice of investigating their employers and if they found a lack of sympathy for or had a dislike of Mrs. Roosevelt they quit their job and placed the employers' names on a Black List."

A Florida inquiry reported that "since the war started the Negro men had higher incomes and they could afford to have a higher standard of living. Therefore, their wives and children no longer had to cook for the whites. The Negroes had formed unions demanding higher wages and working conditions, so that it was almost impossible to find any help at all. It was thought that the First Lady had a hand in trying to organize the Negroes. It was also rumored in one community that the Eleanor Clubs intended to take an educational grievance to court and that they had money enough to 'fight it out.' It was reported that the money was given to the Eleanor Club by Mrs. Roosevelt who received it from one of her public lectures. They had, it was rumored, more money than one of the larger white high schools had for its entire budget that year."

Sometimes there was more comedy than pathos in the fantastic aspects of the Eleanor Club. A prominent business man who had visited most of the States actually professed to believe there was some relation between the Eleanor Clubs and the zoot-suit young Negroes and their doings.

And in Alabama, they said that "whenever you saw a Negro wearing a wide-brimmed hat with a feather in it, you knew he was wearing the sign of the Eleanor Club." In North Carolina there was a story going around that the number and size of feathers in the new zoot-suit hats being worn by Negroes determined their position in the Eleanor Club. The larger the feather, the greater the number, and the brighter the color were symbols of rating. It was a long way from this to the other Alabama report that the Negroes called Mrs. Roosevelt the "Great White Angel" or the "Great White Mother," and made her sponsor for their Eleanor Clubs.

The intensity of the atmosphere in which the Eleanor Club rumors had grown up was indicated by the response of a very wealthy southerner who said that he would be willing to contribute substantially to a civic fund if it would stop the Roosevelts. His chief complaint was that his large organization could no longer work Negro women on the farm! From Florida came the story that "a gentleman of considerable wealth and position made this remark during a conversation, 'Thanks to Mrs. Roosevelt and the Eleanor

Clubs, we're liable to have a race riot here in the South. Mrs. Roosevelt is poking her nose into a situation about which she knows nothing.'" A Louisiana householder reported that her cook at home had been attending meetings of the local Eleanor Club. "She said they promised the Negro to raise his standards of living as high as that of the whites as soon as the war was over. She spoke of the First Lady as Eleanor this, Eleanor that, and Eleanor the other. There were other rumors to the effect that Negroes in several places had said that they believed after the war there would not only be social equality but that the Negro would be the superior race. They believed that Eleanor Roosevelt would put them on this level."

From the mass of rumors, apparently abundant in all the southern States, it was possible to learn not only the general theme but also the "rules" of the Eleanor Clubs. When it was recalled that the rumor was prevalent in most northern cities, especially in Detroit, it was not surprising that there were variations. Nevertheless, there was generally a common thread running through most of the stories, with the exception of the reference to the zoot suit. "White women were to be in the kitchen by Christmas, 1942, or January, 1943. Negro women were to be out of the kitchen. There must be more pay, more privileges, less hours. There must be no disparaging remarks about either Mrs. Roosevelt or the President. And Negroes must have equal opportunities with whites."

It was clear, of course, that the original Eleanor Clubs were not Eleanor Clubs at all, but new ventures in organization and talk. From these efforts and the accelerated demand for workers and especially Negro women workers, it was an easy step to follow some incidental local club tribute to Mrs. Roosevelt and spread the rumor far and wide. Unfortunately, it was not possible to determine the origin of the clubs with certainty. They appeared inspired by those seeking either to cause trouble or to disparage the President and his wife. The earlier stages did not have the earmarks of the Negro folk story, although many of the later versions were genuine reflections of the folk tale. As a matter of fact, the ideals and aims of the clubs were irreproachable from the folk viewpoint, whether from the vantage point of the Negroes as genuine folk wishes and demands, or for perfect propaganda material, either for the Axis or against the Negro and the First Lady.

A few samplings indicated the range of rules and requirements as rumored. In addition to "Eleanor Clubs," the common designation, they were also called "Daughters of Eleanor," "The Eleanor Angel Clubs," "The Sisters of Eleanor," "The Royal House of Eleanor."

The clubs were, of course, named after the First Lady of the Land. The early slogan was the previously mentioned "A white woman in every kitchen by Christmas." The club's membership was made up of colored domestic workers. The members agreed not to work for less than a fixed amount a week, varying from rumor to rumor. The members agreed that if they heard any criticism whatsoever of Mrs. Roosevelt or the President they would immediately quit their jobs.

Another summary, featuring Virginia and North Carolina rumors, reported that the members of the Eleanor Clubs refused to work on Sunday. They would not serve extra people without a day's notice. They must be called "Miss" and "Mrs." and not just their first names. Servants must go to work by the front door of their employers' homes. Servants must strike for a dollar or more a day wages. Servants must take a bath in their employer's family bathtub before going home from work.

A South Carolina story reported that in an Army camp in

the South a Negro maid was employed by an officer and his wife. "One day the wife entered the dining room and saw three places set at the table. She asked the maid if her husband had called and said he'd bring a friend home for lunch. The maid said, 'no.' The wife then asked what the extra place was for. The maid replied, 'In the Eleanor Club we always sit with the people we work for.' "

A North Carolina version had it that the clubs worked through the church. "When a maid quit work she handed the name of her employer to the church group to which she belonged. The name was read from the pulpit and no person's name which was read could expect to get a maid again. Other than remarks about Mrs. Roosevelt, the maids held grievances for low wages and unfair treatment."

Another summary emphasized the fact that Negro women could work at only one job. "That is, if they were to cook, that was all they were to do. They couldn't help with the house cleaning at all. There must be a butler to put the garbage out and mop the kitchen. A woman could do only one thing, such as wash, scrub, or clean house; the Eleanor Club would not allow her to do general work. The Eleanor Club consisted of Negroes who were going to better themselves and try to be equal to the white race. They believed that the First Lady was their white god and was setting them free. There was coming into existence a 'black list' made up of white employers for whom the Negroes refused to work. It was connected with the Negro women's membership in the Eleanor Clubs and seemed to be gaining ground."

And so the Eleanor Club rumors multiplied and competed with other stories that added to the humor of the era but also reflected an unbelievable abandonment by the South of its chivalry toward women.

X

The First Lady's Heritage to the Folk Story

The Eleanor Clubs constituted a symbol of what appeared to be one of America's most vivid and entertaining chapters in folklore that had yet appeared. The rumor and subsequent stories about the First Lady were symbolic also of what Gerald Johnson had referred to as a sublime faith in the idiocy of American history, which never had proceeded in accordance with reason and logic. This episode required a second chapter for two reasons: First, because of the extraordinary spectacle of the American people, and more specifically, the southern people, excelling in the ancient art of the unwritten story as a chief mode of entertainment. And, second, because of the alleged profound influence which the First Lady had upon the epic of race relations in the United States and especially in the South.

Criticisms, while most frequently being centered on her influence in causing Negro women to quit working for the whites or to demand new arrangements, often went much further. The common talk was that "she goes around telling the Negroes they are as good as anyone else." "Wherever she has spoken the Negroes always act like they are white folks." A prominent southerner wrote that "no individual in my lifetime has created as much trouble. She preaches and practices social equality." A Mississippi editor wrote that she, more than any other person, was morally responsible for race riots.

A tremendous body of folklore had grown up around the personality and life of the First Lady. There were many

stories that had all the marks of the folk story. One collected
in North Carolina and Virginia told a Mississippi tale. "She
goes to a small Mississippi town. She enters the hotel and
registers. Then she says to the bellboy: 'Go out and get me
twenty Negro ladies, for I must have them to dinner with
me.' And the bellboy does so. When the Negro women arrive
the hotel manager says, 'I would have you know, my dear
Lady, that this is the South. You must get out.' And she
does."

On the other hand, there were exaggerated and glorified
versions of her activities which apparently stemmed from
her Nashville visit in early 1942. One version was heard
in Georgia. In the attempt to test its range and authenticity,
there was a specific checking and rechecking of notations
that "I heard it from so and so." Each person was definitely
specified and he or she had heard it from "so and so," again
specifically identified, who got it from "so and so." All of
these personalities were leading citizens and reliable persons
in the community. That is, the persons specified were not
themselves saying it happened, but they were saying that
they heard it as told in such and such ways and could prove
that it came to them authentically from such and such
people and places.

The Georgia story ran as follows: "The First Lady came
to Tennessee to a Negro convention. She came into the hotel
with two Negro teachers and proceeded to register. The
clerk says, 'Hold on, you can't register these Negroes here.'
Whereupon, she replied, 'I will just leave your hotel.' So he
says 'ok.' She goes to another hotel and a young assistant
clerk was at the desk, and when he saw her registered he
thought she was ok and would be all right. Then she goes
to her room with the two and calls for a meeting in the
lobby. Just as they were congregating, the manager of the
hotel comes in and walks over to clerk and asks, 'What's

this?' and the young clerk says that she was registered, and he thinking because it was her and he thinks so much of President Roosevelt he just did not think anything. Then the manager turns to the crowd of Negroes in lobby and says, 'You Negroes know better than this, and quick get to hell out of here.' Whereupon the First Lady appears and was also told he did not need her kind of business. Then they proceeded to trace her out and found she went out to the Negro school and spent four days and nights."

There were other rumors and stories about the First Lady which unfortunately were not so simply stated. The list was a long one and merited a special collection. Around the Nashville visit, for instance, where she conferred the year's honorary citation of the Southern Conference on Human Welfare upon one white and one Negro citizen, there grew up many other stories. In one it was reported that she registered for a room only on condition that a great Negro singer should have the suite next her. So, too, it was reported that she declined to ride in the car which the governor sent to meet her in order that she might ride with the Negroes who came to meet her.

One story from Alabama had it that when she came down, "the white people, who were among the aristocrats of the South, had planned a banquet for their guest. But when the time for it came, she said she was going to some other banquet with a certain army captain, and when he appeared he was a *big black Negro*. They added that they didn't think it was safe for her to come back."

From Virginia a "first hand" picture was reported by the daughter of a man who was in the construction business. He was building a large government housing project, and the First Lady was coming to look over the almost completed project. "All the workmen, white and colored, had everything in very good order and they waited all day. She never came. Later somebody found out that she spent the entire day at a colored settlement making speeches to the colored people there." The same informant had heard a rumor that she had invited seventy or eighty Negroes to luncheon at the White House recently and no reporters were allowed because a race riot was feared and Washington was on the verge of a race riot.

From Tennessee one wrote: "I have heard very outstanding professors and people say that she is the most dangerous individual in the United States today. I have also heard them say that they hate to see more blood shed, but if it is necessary to settle the racial problem that it will have to be." From the same State came a different version of the hotel episode. "It seemed that she had tried to reserve a dining room in a large hotel for herself and twenty Negro women. Insisting on knowing the cost in advance, she was told that it would be two million dollars—the value of the hotel."

There was a certain pathos in many of the folk stories. In North Carolina it was told that the Negroes went to reserve a room for her in the best hotel in town and wanted a room beside her for the Negro women who were to preside over the Negro convention. The manager of the hotel refused and she stayed in a private white home alone. Another story was that when she "was here last spring, no white person spoke to her."

The complaints were multiplied in Virginia, Georgia, and Tennessee. Thus, "after her talk everyone said that she had tried to make the Negroes feel equal to the whites and she had told them that they could demand higher wages and shorter hours. And again it seemed to be a rather widespread opinion that the Negroes were being encouraged to become more powerful, where the whites were concerned, by the aid they were being given by Eleanor Roosevelt. By her policies, the Negroes were likely to feel that they were less inferior and think of themselves as being on the same basis as the whites."

The pathos continued in Alabama. "After her last visit the Negroes went on strikes and demanded social equality in many instances." And from Virginia, the rumor that she was the "Negro lover of the U. S. had spread and was used as a slogan almost." And from Georgia, "A wealthy southern lady was suspicious of the First Lady's mission and motives. She wanted to know what else was included on her itinerary. When told that she would go on to a Negro college, she snorted, 'I might have known this was only a convenient stop en route to some Negro affair. She would go anywhere to be with Negroes.' She then proceeded to attribute to her responsibility for stirring up racial feeling in the South." And also, "At a club meeting at the time of her visit to England this fall, there was an excited interest among the members in the First Lady's trip. One of the club members, a prominent and well-to-do middle-aged woman, said rather abruptly, 'I wish she'd drown on the way back!'"

Another version was that she "went to Nashville, Tennessee, to address some group on behalf of the Negroes. Several Negro women were with her. They went to the leading hotel to get rooms for the night. The hotel would not let the Negroes spend the night there. A Negro college volunteered to let the colored women stay in a dormitory. She said that she would stay with them. Her secret service agents said that if she did they would not be responsible for her. She finally registered at another hotel."

Most of these stories were of the sort that made easy telling and did not involve factual evidence. They started, grew, and spread, and presently they were part and parcel of what the people talked about and what they believed or thought they believed. And they were no respecter of persons. For instance, a Woman's Missionary Society was responsible for this one. "One day when she was slumming among the Negroes she saw a picture of herself hanging on the wall of a Negro home. So she asked a Negro girl who the woman was whose picture was on the wall. The Negro girl replied that she didn't know. She insisted and wanted to know why the picture was there. The girl replied that her mama hung it there for her to see, because if she didn't behave she would grow up to look like that woman."

The collection of the rumors of Eleanor Clubs constituted an excellent exhibit of how the rumor, based on popular plausibility, was contrary to the facts. For, according to all the evidence that could be found, there were no Eleanor Clubs up to 1943. Samplings of various rumors and rules of the clubs were recorded from the several states. "Yes, we have Eleanor Clubs," they all said. And over and over again the rumored motto was the same, "A white woman in her own kitchen by Christmas," or "A white woman in every kitchen in a year," or "No Negro women in the kitchen by Christmas." Yet, in no single instance was there found measurable evidence of the existence of a club. The standard refrain was, "Yes, I know we have Eleanor Clubs, but I don't know the details," or "Yes, I have heard of Eleanor Clubs, but I have not got the facts."

Samplings of these are of the essence of the total rumor picture. Thus from South Carolina, "I asked people in my home town about Eleanor Clubs—they didn't know anything definite about them. I asked girls at school and they told things they had heard." A Georgian said that if there were no Eleanor Clubs in Georgia there were definitely some in Alabama. Again from Georgia, "I have heard nothing specific about the Eleanor Clubs except that it is thought they are being organized steadily in our section of the country." And from South Carolina, "It was said they were having

Eleanor Clubs. I asked a good many Negroes about this; they didn't know of any clubs but they had heard of them." And again "Eleanor Clubs are rumored to be existing. These rumors cannot be traced."

Some composite references from Georgia are similar. "I have heard bits about Eleanor Clubs. The only thing that I know about them is that it is a movement among Negro women to organize against the whites." Again, "I know it to be a fact that a Negro girl won't work over three days at a time. I don't know whether the Eleanor Clubs have been started or not." "The seniors interviewed ten students each in different dormitories and found that all had heard vague rumors about Eleanor Clubs but had no definite information." Finally, "Several prominent women were interviewed. None could connect any person definitely with the so-called Eleanor Clubs nor did any know of any facts that could be established concerning the clubs."

Since there were no Eleanor Clubs in reality as a foundation for the great sweep of rumors, it was clear that the basic complaint was one in which the main mode of domestic southern folkways of servant and mistress was being violated, both in the actual scarcity of help and in the revolutionary change in attitudes and status. Here, as was the case with Negro youth, even without the influence of war and outsiders, the wage level and the ethics and etiquette of Negro and white would have to change in any progressive society. It was logical that the blame was to be placed upon something or somebody. Ordinarily the blame would have fallen upon labor unions and organizers; yet in the case of race rumors and war tensions, labor troubles were not so susceptible to narration as were the folk-rumors. The First Lady had provided a dramatic way out of a situation which needed explaining and in which the blame must be placed elsewhere than on the white women. Yet the indisputable facts were that in all her talks she showed great poise and care and was especially mindful of interregional manners.

It seemed important, therefore, to go further in an effort to find out and to sense just how basic the southern Negro work situation was to the rumor growth. Sample selections, therefore, emphasized the wide range in variety of situations, the logical reasons why Negro help was not available, and the traditional servant-mistress relationship. In many, perhaps most, southern towns many families no longer expected to have help and they realized the logic of the Negro woman's new attitudes. Yet for the most part there was complaint. Thus, a prominent capitalist wrote: "I am at the head of a corporation that operates a large farming project. Either their husbands are receiving fantastic wages from government projects, or they are getting a $50 a month allotment on account of their husbands being in the Army. One of our superintendents recently spoke to a woman about not working, and her rather arrogant reply was, 'I don't have to work no more. The Government is going to take care of me.' "

Of course, Negro women were inclined to accept better opportunity. To decline would have been unusual, as was, however, the case in many individual instances. It was clear, from even a limited case study, how real the new opportunity was. Thus, "at the boarding house where I have my dinners both the cook and the waitress quit during Christmas. One of them went to her husband in Jacksonville, Florida, where he recently won a citation in the newspapers as the most expert plasterer on the defense project where he is employed. The other is enjoying her volunteer services as a military maid at the colored USO so much she has decided not to work any more. Her husband, too, is earning a good wage. Again, a housewife told of looking for a washwoman and in one interview the Negro woman informed her she did not expect to have to work as her son is in the Army and her husband on a defense job. It was reported from Georgia that Negro men refused to let their wives work in the white women's homes in this small town because the local peanut shelling plant employed whites instead of Negroes during the past season. From Alabama, a case was that of 'an Army camp which, needing laundry workers, offered as a price a wage of 40 cents an hour. This was far better than civilians could pay. And as a result all servants began to quit their jobs to work in the camp laundry.' "

XI

Men, Work, and Equality

That a special point of tension was found in the issue of higher standards and pay with fewer hours and less hardship was again reflected in the stories with reference to Negro labor in general. The illuminating feature was that stories and rumors which were spread about Negroes organizing and demanding more pay still trailed the actual facts which everybody ought to have known. Of course, the Negroes were organizing. Of course, they had clubs. Of course, they had "changed" with reference to their old easygoing acceptance of whatever was paid them. This series of mild and mixed rumors was added merely to complete a certain amount of evidence in support of the white-Negro work conflict basis of much of the present tension.

Here, again, the picture appeared full of pathos as if the South had been in almost complete isolation and mindful only of its own provincial interests. Much progress had been made in the field of labor, and many leaders in the South had apparently made progress toward both wider occupational opportunity and better pay. There was a standard level of life upon which all could agree. Discrimination here was perhaps the backlog of the Negro's complaint. When, then, war tensions began to pile up, it was natural that the Negro would extend his claim for other rights.

A few samplings were enough to illustrate a situation already made clear. Thus, "Negroes are organizing labor unions to strike for higher wages." Again, "They say the equally skilled Negro man will receive the same pay as the skilled white worker." And, "It has been rumored that the Negroes are going to form unions and work only a certain number of hours at a certain price." Finally, "Negroes are striking to gain more important jobs in factories and industries in order that they might influence Negro employment, and put more and more white men out of jobs. By such methods, the Negro is supposed to become superior to the whites economically."

Reference has often been made to a new behavior pattern of Negro youth. The heart of this behavior was possibly best described as the motivation to behave as white people behave. There was reference also to the heart of the southern white credo as being found in the essential feeling that the Negro was a Negro and must in all essential matters be different and act differently from the whites. Perhaps the most common complaint of the common man against the new Negro was somewhat as follows: "These Negroes have been up North and come back, and they think they are as good as whites." "These young Negroes think they can do like white folks." In substance, this was exactly perhaps what the Negro did expect to do. His interpretation, however, of doing like white folks was that it was natural and right for him to want to have the same opportunity and rights and privileges in all aspects of life as anybody else would have, whether white or otherwise. It did not mean, as was commonly interpreted, that every Negro must have the right in all phases of social and economic life to do the same things that the whites do in the same setting and in the same association. Nothing of this sort happened in the rest of the Nation where the Negro professedly did have opportunity. It meant, however, that in so far as the Negro had needs and opportunities and had ability and capacity that he wanted and expected to go along and be a natural human being.

It was dramatic and tragic that this relatively simple and natural expectation should be interpreted by the whites as the essential evidence of improper ambitions and of conduct and attitudes which led the Negro to "get out of his place." The series of rumors, sayings, stories, and incidents here was practically limitless and was perhaps a little more difficult to classify and analyze than some of the others. The important thing to know was the sheer conflict between these expectations and the assumptions of the white South. To the observer from other regions the demands of the Negroes seemed so logical and reasonable that he could not understand the furor that they created.

There was, for instance, the "Double Victory" emphasis. "I've heard that the Negroes have a two victory slogan. 'V' for victory abroad and another 'V' for victory at home. The colored race wants absolute equality, wants to be able to sit at the same table, go to the same dances, schools, etc." That was from North Carolina and had its South Carolina counterpart, "The Negro is going to win a 'double V.' Conditions will not be the same after the war." And from Alabama, "The Negroes declare among themselves they are fighting this war for a double victory." And from Virginia, "There was a rumor that cars had been seen with a double V sign on the license plate, one for the victorious uprising of the Negroes."

Again and again the folkways of survival, a chief means of which was to "keep the Negro in his place," were reflected in the rumors and fears of Negro equality. From Florida, "It seems to be the opinion of the people here that the Negroes will soon be demanding a place in society equal to the whites." And from Georgia, "A Negro man told a woman in South Georgia that she would learn soon that he was to be respected as much as she was and she would have to look up to him." Again, "The caste line is being broken down by this war, and after the war, the Negroes will think they are equal to whites." From Louisiana, "The Negroes will demand a definite place in society—they will refuse to be an underdog after the war." And from North Carolina, "Eventually the Negroes will revolt against their present status—demanding equality with the whites." One more specific was that "It is believed that all Negroes with college degrees try to marry into the white race." And, "There will be an upheaval of the Negroes after the war on the basis that Negro college graduates are denied employment utilizing their education."

The changing behavior of the Negro was reflected both in the actual demands which were made, first by northern Negroes, then more generally others, and also by the flood of rumors reflecting the fear of the southern whites that complete equality would be sought. Again, there was pathos in the chasm between what the Negro wanted and what the white South wanted him to have.

Here was treason to the southern credo. "Negroes went in white eating establishments demanding to be served." Again, "A group of Negro men went into a drug store and sat down at a table, demanding service. The employees of the store called the police and had the men arrested." Those were from North Carolina. From Virginia, "Negroes have actually tried to force their way into cafes and other places of business which are strictly for the whites." Again, "Negro women stormed a chain drug store and demanded lunch at the counter." And, "Negroes entered a white restaurant and ordered food—they were taken out by the police."

Cruelty and tragedy characterized many episodes. "When a Negro was served in a drug store, usually frequented by only white people, he was charged ten cents extra for his soda. After he finished and wanted to know why he was charged extra, the waiter very dramatically held up the

Negro's glass and dropped it to the floor." Again, "Negroes were then told that while the waiters would take their orders they must realize there was no limit to the prices. Food was quoted to them at $100 for a steak, $50 for coffee." In many places "They will not serve any colored person from a drug store counter, even in a paper cup."

It was of the essence of this story of rumors that chief emphasis was placed upon the negative aspects. There were, however, thousands of southerners who sensed the justice of the Negro's requests and who knew the South was wrong. Thus, one man commented on a story of wrong. "One man in a grocery store wouldn't sell a Negro woman any coffee—he told her he didn't have any; yet when a white woman came in, he sold her some. Seeing this the colored woman went back in and told the man that her money was as good as anybody's. The grocer slapped the colored lady and she was placed in jail. After such happenings we should expect some trouble with the Negro."

One of the chief places where the young Negro experiments is the fountain at the drug store. He may not drink at the fountain, although he can carry his drink out. On one occasion when a Negro bought a coca cola, the fountain attendant walked all the way around the fountain to avoid passing the drink to the Negro over the fountain. "A colored delivery boy of a drug store bought a coca cola. He stopped to drink it in the front of the store and the soda jerker told him to go to the rear." At another place, "A Negro stepped up to the fountain and ordered a drink. Asked to go to the rear to drink it, the Negro handed the drink back and said unless he could drink it there at the fountain he'd leave, which he did."

Other discriminations illustrated the basis upon which the Negroes were more and more demanding better treatment. "When Negroes come into stores to buy clothes, and they are asked to try them on in a Negro dressing room, they say they pay as much as the whites and think they should be allowed to fit them in the same place." Again, "Recently two Negro women came in and wanted to try on some dresses. When they found they were expected to use a separate dressing room from the white customers (exactly the same type, the employee says), they declined saying they would go elsewhere where they would not be discriminated against." And, "I have also noticed when Negroes come into a store or building they seem to think they are on the level with white people. They want to be waited on just as fast."

As a matter of fact, the best stores in many southern cities treated the Negroes exactly in this respect as they did the whites. Especially in cities where there were Negro colleges and the Negroes had earned the respect as well as the financial esteem of the stores, there was little discrimination. And throughout the South the tendency grew always to serve the Negro in his regular turn. Other examples of the successful elimination of segregation were found in the banks and in post offices everywhere. Crowded people in lines at cashiers' windows in the banks reflected behavior and conduct on the part of both races that "stands to reason," and no one complains about social equality there or at the post office.

Eloquent as symbol of segregation and of attitude was the young college white student's report on his own attitude and reaction. "Yesterday when I went to use a public telephone, whom should I see sitting using the 'phone but a big black Negro. I asked if he didn't know that only whites were supposed to use that telephone. He replied that it was a public telephone and that America was a free country. Much to my amazement, I knew that he was right, but I didn't want to admit it."

XII

The Ice Pick and Race Riot Rumors

One of the chief objectives of a new portraiture of rumor and story was to sense the sweep and power of emotional attitudes, rationalized through quick-spreading talk. This was nothing new and, of course, was not limited to stories and rumors about Negroes or to the South. Yet, if thousands of people who actually believed and passed on fantastic rumors just as they would actual happenings could sense the almost treasonable implications, it might go a long way toward checking the epidemic of so many emotional reactions. How true this seemed to be was illustrated in rumors that set off such riots as those in Detroit or Beaumont. How utterly unreasonable and how dangerous such rumors could be was well illustrated in the epidemic of stories that the Negroes were preparing to attack the whites with various types of weapons.

Perhaps the most fantastic of all the rumors, in this respect, was "the ice pick rumor," strangely alike in Mississippi, in Georgia, in Virginia, and symbolic of the wild, illogical sweep of the unreasonable story. While this was one of the common rumors that had the Axis earmark, its genesis and spread might very well have flourished in the soil of fear and excitement so prevalent in the early years of the war. Negroes perhaps did buy more ice picks because they owned fewer frigidaires, while the knife and the gun are companion pieces to a folk behavior of long standing. A few instances where such articles had been sold out and a few comments on who bought them might easily start another of those already unbelievable stories.

The ice pick rumor was also the precursor of those other rumors of uprisings, revolt, and riot, themselves numerous enough to constitute a special study. While the pattern in general was the same, namely, that the Negroes were buying up all the ice picks and waiting for the first blackout to start an attack upon the whites, there were some variations. Sometimes they were to attack on a holiday or a Saturday night. The humorous picture of a black army limited to ice picks in the dark ought to have struck the South's "funny bone," but it didn't for a long time.

Although the first, now famous, rumor seemed to have come from Virginia, others also came from many other places. Thus, from Georgia, "They say that Negroes are buying up ice picks to attack the whites." And another from Virginia, "Rumors during the past summer of impending race trouble, especially the buying of ice picks and other forms of favorite 'Negro' weapons. There was also a rumor that the Negroes were going to take over the entire area during a blackout early in September." It was also reported from South Carolina that Negroes had been buying ice picks, not for ice but for protection. And "I heard that on Labor Day at the Navy Yard the Negro workers were going to attack the white workers. I also heard that some stores had sold out of ice picks. I heard that many workers went to work on Labor Day with these weapons." And from North Carolina the story had it that "on the night of a blackout all ice picks were sold to Negroes. The whites expected a riot and had called out five hundred National Guardsmen during the blackout." In South Carolina, it was heard that the Negroes "had bought all the ice picks which they could find on the day before Labor Day, and that at the Navy Yard the

Negro workers were buying ice picks and slipping them inside the gates to use to attack the white workers."

One Georgia version said that "the Negroes were buying up all the ice picks in town to use in a wholesale massacre during the blackout scheduled that night. When the rumor was traced down it was found that only two ice picks were sold that day in the entire town and these two were sold to two maiden ladies." Another Georgia rumor was that "in a certain town the Negroes bought up all the ammunition, ice picks, and harmful weapons they could buy and were going to start a riot on Saturday night. The police found it out and would not let the Negroes out on the streets after 6:00 P.M."

From Mississippi the story came from the scene of two recent lynchings that "the owner of the hardware store had told personally that a truckload of Negroes came into the store not long after the lynchings and bought up every knife, ice pick, etc., in the store. It was rumored that the Negroes were going to start a lot of trouble around there." And finally from South Carolina a store salesman told "that there was not an ice pick in town because the Negroes had bought all of them. The Negroes had warned any white person who might come down in their Negro settlement that he would never come back alive."

Preview to the stories and rumors of riots and uprisings and similar to the stories of Negroes buying up all the ice picks were the rumors that they were buying all manner of arms and especially knives to be used against the whites at certain times. Instead of manifesting a sense of humor or checking up through common sense, the people had allowed such rumors to upset entire communities, including such cities as Atlanta, New Orleans, and Washington, where rumored uprisings might easily have led to actual race riots.

Here again there were many variations of the common theme.

In South Carolina, it was rumored all around that Labor Day week end was the big week end for the long suspected race riot. It was reported that all the Negroes had bought all available ice picks, guns, knives, etc., and were armed, waiting for a signal. "We were all made to stay at home from Saturday afternoon until Tuesday morning—hoping for the best and expecting the worst. We live in the suburbs and had to be extra careful for we didn't have the protection of the city police. Several of our friends came at night to stay with us just in case anything happened. Saturday night we heard that 18 white men had been killed and three military police wounded. Sunday night, it went around that a bus had been wrecked by a group of Negroes on a lonely highway and all the people had been slashed to bits. All this and more reached our terrified ears. Our loss of sleep was beyond possible imagination. But when Tuesday's dawn appeared and we were all still existing, we sighed deeply and, after investigating the rumors of the previous days, we discovered none of them was true."

From Florida, it was said to be "common knowledge and could be verified at the Police Department that Negroes had bought up the available supply of knives and other weapons." And from Georgia that "all the Negroes who had been turned down by the United States draft were buying up guns and rifles and ammunition; and that the white people were afraid to go unarmed."

Here were other samples. From North Carolina, "The Negroes are secretly arming themselves and will strike at the white population at an appointed time." From Louisiana, "The Negroes are purchasing firearms for protection against whites." And also "It was reported to me that $75.00 worth of knives were bought in one day by Negroes in one hardware store." From South Carolina, "At the stores the managers have complained about Negro men coming in and buying cases of shells and long-bladed, sharp knives. This is said to have been happening in all the stores to such a great extent that the merchants have refused to sell Negroes any type of knives or shells." And from Virginia, "Authorities are afraid to have blackouts inside Virginia for fear of race riots."

And so on and on with varying details. It was reported that "the police recently raided a Negro church in which was found an arsenal of firearms and ammunition to be used against the whites." Another story had it that "Negroes had bought all the guns and that girls from school had received letters from parents telling them not to come home." In another community it was reported that "when Negroes were paid off one Saturday night, their entire wages were spent buying shot, knives, etc. so that after dark they barricaded the highway leading through and started a riot. It was said again that hardware stores had noticed that a large proportion of their sales of guns and shells had been to Negroes. The implication was that the Negroes were preparing for an armed uprising of one kind or another. Also there was a rumor to the effect that no shot or shells could be bought, because the Negroes had already purchased them all and were saving them to use against the whites at a later date. They also said that the Negroes were ordering from Sears and Roebuck Co. guns, pistols, shot, and the like." The last cluster of rumors came from North Carolina, South Carolina, and Georgia.

Another series from Georgia showed little variation. "I have heard rumors that the Negroes in several small South Georgia towns are buying all the ammunition, having secret meetings, and planning to revolt against the white people. They say the Negroes are going to demand equal rights with white people." It was also "rumored that the Negroes who have had their incomes increased to $50.00 and $70.00 a week were buying guns, rifles, and other weapons to start a riot on Labor Day. All white women and children were asked to stay inside the house all day."

Two of the " 'rumorist' rumors I ever heard came from Mississippi and South Carolina. One was that a Negro undertaking establishment began to buy a great many coffins. The shipments were so large and so numerous that the suspicions of the stationmaster were aroused and he reported the matter to the sheriff. The sheriff went to the station to see the next shipment, but he made it seem as if he were visiting the stationmaster. He 'accidently' turned one of the coffins over and found it to be full of guns. The Negroes who were unloading the coffins ran away. Upon investigation the undertaking establishment was found to be a cache of guns which were to have been used in a Negro rebellion." The other was reported by a laborer who had been informed that the Negroes were organizing "shock troop units all over the country and were secretly storing weapons and ammunition in their neighborhood churches and basements. When the manpower of America reached its lowest ebb, which would be sometime soon, the Negro would strike and would defeat the white man. Then he was going to beat the hell out of Hitler and the Jews."

The remarkable catalogue of rumors with reference to arms, ice picks, and knives all appeared to be fabricated upon the assumption of race riots and uprisings. This was nothing new, of course. Especially was that sort of thing prevalent just after the other World War. In the first World War rumors, there were apparently more stories of the Negroes drilling and practicing, which proved to be based often upon the formal ritual of lodge meetings. In the present flood of rumors, the psychologist might find the chief characteristic to be the folkways of self-defense. That is, the whites were justified in violence if they "knew" the Negro was planning violence. It was not possible, of course, to explain fully such rumors in this way. Why, for instance, would hundreds of white women spread rumors of terrible things that were going to happen in Atlanta, when nothing happened, no Negroes even heard the rumor, and apparently there was no basis whatever for it?

Again there was pathos in the tales that went the rounds. Did not these rumors justify a distinguished writer's characterization of the South as "This tragic land"? A few samples would suffice. "During the blackouts down there armed trucks with police and soldiers drove through the colored section in case any white people had been stopped by colored air raid wardens and were trapped alone in colored homes." That was from Virginia. From South Carolina, "The Negroes tried to take over the armory which resulted in the State Militia being called out." And from Louisiana, "A rumor was started that on a certain Friday all the Negro maids were going to put poison in their employers' food because they felt that they were being too sharply discriminated against." And also, "A white man discovered through one of his Negro employees that there was going to be some kind of trouble on the following Saturday night. The man reported this to the mayor and he called the sheriff and a group of men to go to the Negro district that night and watch for anything that might happen. The sheriff found about ten Negroes with weapons of some kind on them and promptly arrested these as the leaders." So, too, "Many people believe that we are going to end up with a race riot, but that the police will merely shoot a few Negroes and that will be the end of it."

Then there were other rumors of what would happen after the war, slightly different from the earlier ones, in which the Negroes predicted the "turning of the tables" on the whites. A few samples: "After Christmas all the Negroes would rise up and control first city and then state legislatures, most probably using forcible means." This was from North Carolina, while from South Carolina, "There are going to be a great many Negro uprisings in southern cities. The Negroes are going to go against the white people." And from Louisiana, "The Negroes will take over government after the war through an organized Negro revolution." And again, "There are rumors that the liberation of the Negro race will be gotten in this time of crisis and that the Negroes are prepared with different types of armaments to get it by force in case they don't get it by peaceful ways." North Carolina again, "A great southern revolution will occur, the whites on the defensive with the aggressive Negroes, headed by a powerful Negro leader, on the offensive. This is liable to end in the domination of the whole southern system by the Negro." And again, "I have heard that Negroes are organizing to overrule the South, not only to gain social position but really rule the white people."

Stories and rumors of violence against Negroes were intermingled with most of the other stories and were also mixed up with actual happenings. Samplings of what was heard and told and talked about with reference to the violent treatment of Negroes reflected the tragedy and pathos of a behavior that often falls little short of barbaric. Fear of the Negro was ascribed as the justification of the folkways of self-protection which resulted in a long list of indefensible acts. From South Carolina, "It had been rumored that there were 26 Negroes killed and thrown in a lake. There had been quite a bit of upset between the Negroes and whites. They claimed that the lake was dragged and they found 26 bodies. The Negroes were trying to take advantage of the whites since so many of the young men were going to the

Army. Some of the Negroes had made remarks about the white women, which the southern whites would not take." And from Alabama, "Yes, a rumor went through the night, the rumor grew, and mill hands dragged a young Negro out of his house. They tied his feet to the back of a model A car, dragged him at seventy miles an hour through the thickly populated Negro district, and then burned his mutilated body with gas. The Negro undertakers were afraid to take his body. No more news came about the incident, it was hushed up, the state made it quiet." From Georgia, it was reported that "the police force had treated the Negroes cruelly—beating them for no reason at all, and that a middle-aged Negro man, for stealing a loaf of bread, was tied to an automobile, dragged a distance, then bumped against a tree with the car until dead or left for dead."

There was often protest by those who reported the rumors. Thus, "A police force in a small town ran all Negroes out of town one Saturday night, for no specific reason, except that they were afraid of the crowds of Negroes that flocked to town on Saturday nights." And also, "A policeman beat a Negro boy unmercifully for stealing. It seems that the police force is responsible for much of this cruelty." Another, "I heard that a Negro was shot down by a white man because he came with his car inside a white man's garage."

Tragedy in this one: "One Saturday night when the streets were crowded several white women were attacked by Negro boys. This attack resulted in several Negroes being 'beat up' by respectable white men, some being cops. At last, when the boys who caused the trouble were found, it was revealed that they were white boys who had painted their faces black and gone out just to have some fun and excitement." And finally, "I saw a white policeman strike down a small Negro girl who timidly started across the street after he had blown the whistle for pedestrians to stop."

XIII

The Negro in the War Services

The stories about Negroes in the armed forces reflected one of the most tragic of all the tragic situations. Here the conflicts and injustices already reported were repeated over again in an unending line of unbelievable complex situations. For to the practical and theoretical discriminations that were prevalent and logical in a biracial culture were added the technical violations of the rights and courtesies due members of the armed services. Here again, the war had accentuated the situation, both in the sense that the opportunity for discrimination and injustice and the occasion for conflict had been multiplied many times; and the appearance of Negro soldiers from other parts of the Nation and of white soldiers from all parts of the Nation had been the occasion for criticism and denunciation of the southern behavior.

The southerners again faced their dilemma of complex and paradoxical situations. They complained that not enough Negroes were sent to the services, and they maintained that the Negro was incapable of making a good soldier. Here was the dilemma of having too many Negroes at home and too many in the Army and too many returned soldiers for the post-war world. If the Negro remained at home there was fear of his presence there. If he went to the Army, there was fear of what he would do when he came back.

In this portraiture it seemed best not to present any catalogue of what actually happened to Negro soldiers in the

South or what Negro soldiers did. This was a technical field for official reports and a field in which detailed reporting would not be in order. It was, however, of great importance to catalogue rumors and stories that were heard here, just as in other areas. First, perhaps, were the rumors about the kind of soldier the Negro was. The common version was that "the Negroes in the last war were cowards. They simply would not fight, but turned and ran when faced with gunfire. This was perfectly well known. All of the officers reported it when they came back. No use was, therefore, made of the Negroes except to do manual labor behind the lines. Again, the common talk was that all the officers in this war were finding that Negroes were not capable of fighting. That it was dangerous to be in command of Negroes because they would turn on you and kill you if you ordered them into battle. That this was actually happening. That Negroes were such children that they could not be trained adequately in the use of the mechanized instruments of modern warfare."

There was another damaging rumor to the effect that in the camps where Negroes were in this country there was a great difference in the way Negroes were treated and the way whites were treated. That the Negroes were allowed to get away with anything because the officers were afraid of what they would do if an order was given which they did not like. That white soldiers could be depended upon to understand that an order was an order, but that the Negroes would resent it and "answer back," and the officer giving the order could do nothing about it.

One example was given. "On a Saturday night an order was given to clean the guns before going on Saturday night leave—an unreasonable order because the guns could have been cleaned on Sunday morning just as well. But the whites quietly went about cleaning the guns, knowing that an order was an order, but one Negro said to the officer in a belligerent tone of voice that he did not intend to forego his Saturday night for any such unreasonable order and so refused to obey. That the officer knew that he could not do anything about this because if he did the rest of the Negroes would rise up and do something or other. He reported it to his superior officer and the latter said it could not be helped and that the Negroes had to be handled with gloves on."

The facts of the actual participation of Negroes in the armed forces were being studied and catalogued. Many of their exploits were being given fine publicity, and that story will be told in due time. In the meantime, there was the problem of caste and status again. Would the white privates salute Negro officers? It ought to have been a simple question, but it was not. For example: From Louisiana, "A Negro officer was walking down the street. No white men in uniform would salute him even if he was below him in rank." And again, "A Negro second lieutenant was walking down Third Street, and he saluted a white first lieutenant. The first lieutenant refused to return the salute." On the other hand, "A private said that he saw a Negro officer on the street. He had known the Negro before either had been inducted into the Army. The Negro crossed the street in the middle of the block and did not look in his direction, although he felt sure he had seen him. He turned and walked to the end of the block and crossed the street so he would have to face the Negro. He saluted and the Negro corporal returned the salute and said, "Thank you, Mr.——. Most white soldiers do not salute me in Virginia.'" And again there was a similar one from Georgia. "A citizen picked up two privates who were white boys from small country towns. As they turned into a filling station, the citizen saw some Negro officers and so he turned out and went into the next

station, saying to the two boys that he had saved them
from the embarrassment of saluting superior officers who
were Negroes. The boys flared up and expressed respect for
the Negroes and willingness to salute them just as they
would salute white officers." And still again, "A student saw
a group of white officers chatting together when a group
of Negro officers came along. Seemingly the groups were on
a footing of complete equality, as the Negroes stopped and
chatted on a basis of intimacy with the white officers. The
student was indignant."

The pathos of much of the sort of discrimination that
was depicted in the failure of the White South to respect
the Negro soldier was reflected in the fact that many did
respect and salute the Negro soldier, and that nothing but
good came of it. Also, the fact that trouble arising because
of Negro troops had arisen in nearly all camps in the
Nation outside the South only emphasized the tragedy of
the situation. What could the Negro do? What could the
Army do? What could anybody do? Hence, conflict, rumors
of violence, actual violence. One southern college president,
when criticized for feeding a Negro soldier along with
the whites, replied that he was feeding the United States
uniform.

However, there were adequate samplings of the other
side. "A Negro soldier was killed in a cafe for demanding
service. A white patron hit the Negro over the head with a
chair in his anger and accidentally killed him." That was
from Georgia. From Louisiana, "About twenty Negroes were
supposed to sleep in the same barracks with the white soldiers. The whites of course were furious and sent a petition
to the officials saying if the Negroes weren't segregated there
would be some dead niggers." In Georgia, "Some Negro soldiers went into a white drug store and sat down to order.
The owner explained that they could not stay there but said

he would be glad to show them the Negro drug store. They refused to leave and an actual fight occurred." And again, "A group of Negro soldiers went into a drug store, sat down at a table, and ordered soft drinks. The proprietor asked them in the nicest way to leave and explained that down South whites and Negroes patronize separate soda parlors. The Negroes refused to leave and finally the military police had to be called to break it up." So, too, "Some Negro soldiers had specific written orders to eat at a certain cafe. Since the cafe was a white cafe the manager refused to fill their order. The situation was both unpleasant and awkward."

The extremes of embarrassment and unfairness were illustrated often. "In Georgia, a high-ranking Negro officer went into a white restaurant to eat. When he declined to leave at the manager's request the M.P. was called and finally the civilian police had to be asked to help with the case." In Tennessee, it was reported that Negro soldiers have been "jerked" off busses and beaten by police. In Georgia, "A Negro soldier was alleged to have walked up to a white girl who was working at the base and told her that he had dreamed about her the night before. Before he finished speaking a white soldier jumped up and cut the Negro's throat."

Serious conflicts were reported in which the pathos and tragedy of American soldiers fighting each other presented a sad spectacle. "In Tennessee a Negro soldier was arrested by a white M.P. A Negro M.P. attempted to take the prisoner from the white M.P. In this he was assisted by a group of Negro soldiers who tried to overturn the car occupied by the white military police. City police arrived and dispersed the Negroes with tear gas." In Alabama, a tragedy: "A Negro soldier evidently from the North boarded the municipal bus and sat in the white section next to a young white girl. When the driver noticed this, he immediately instructed the Negro soldier to move to the back colored section. At this request, the Negro grew very resentful and instead started getting "fresh" with the white girl seated beside him. The bus driver, instead of calling the police, drove on to the end of the line and then shot him." From South Carolina, it was reported that a white man was killed in a fight and a Negro was believed to have been the killer. "The white soldiers then brought out machine guns and killed almost a hundred Negroes. The entire Negro division fled from the area." And from Florida, the story had it that "a white soldier happened to find a Negro soldier in front of him as they marched into mess hall. The white soldier became so 'mad' that he knocked the Negro all the way across the table. The officer being from the same part of the country as the white boy did nothing about it." A Virginia story told about "a Negro soldier in a small town, when talking to a white civilian, said, 'After this war, I'll have the same rights as you. We aren't fighting this war for the whites.' The white man knocked him down, then reported the incident to a policeman. The policeman said, 'That's all right, sorry that I wasn't there to give him a punch myself.'" Finally, from Alabama it was reported that, during the summer, there was quite a bit of alarm over the Negro soldiers in one of our southern airports. Said the reporter, "And I know for certain that two Negro soldiers were killed one day by some white officers, for some disagreement between them. Little was said about it and it was kept out of the papers."

The prevailing story that fewer Negroes than whites were being drafted was the basis of many of the conflict rumors. The rumors were of several sorts. One was that the community did not want so many Negroes in the armed forces because people would be afraid of them when they returned.

One was that the community was afraid of so many Negroes, not being drafted, who are left behind. Another common story was that so many Negroes were rejected for venereal diseases that the communities were in still another danger. Still another was that Negroes tried to contract these diseases in order to be rejected.

From South Carolina, it was reported that draft boards were not drafting men proportionately because they didn't want to put weapons in their hands. And from Virginia, that colored men weren't being drafted as rapidly as the white men because they were afraid to let them get their hands on guns. From Alabama, "I don't know what the draft boards are thinking of by drafting so many whites in proportion to the Negroes. This town is going to have a serious problem on its hands. From numerous sources has that complaint about the disproportionate number of white and Negro draftees been heard." And from Virginia, "It seems that some of the Negroes there wish to enlist but are not allowed to do so, because only a certain percentage of the Negroes are taken. The Negroes feel that this is unfair and that all Negroes should be allowed to enlist." And from Louisiana, "There is a rumor that the Negroes are deliberately contracting venereal disease in order to avoid being drafted." And from North Carolina, "Army prospects undertake to get disease so they will fail examination and keep out of the Army."

Complaints poured in criticizing the draft boards both ways. Some said that the boards sent off too many Negroes with families; some said that too few Negroes were accepted. There were many versions of the folk-feeling. From North Carolina, it was said that "since so many Negro men have venereal diseases they are not fit for military duty, and therefore will be left at home. There had been a good number of cases of rape in this section also, but as a remedy, it is rumored that all Negro men are to be drafted and sent to medical centers where treatment for these diseases will be enforced." From Florida, "Negroes play ignorant and crazy when they appear before the examining board. Great numbers are turned down for this and other causes." And from Georgia, Alabama, Virginia, and South Carolina they were saying, "The Negroes are talking among themselves that they shouldn't fight, that there is no democracy for them." And "Some Negroes avoid the draft because they have been told it is not their war." And another funny one, "As to the war situation I have heard the comment that Negro soldiers are not accepted in the Army because the whites want to win the war and the world for themselves." A variation, "I have heard of a good many cases here and other places where they have refused to register and refused to report when inducted and had to be run down. They say they are not going to fight when they have no place in the government."

XIV

The Negro and Travel

For another cross section of the whole drama of attitudes, behavior, and the resulting episodes, the rumors and stories that centered around bus travel perhaps afforded the best possible exhibit. For here was an experience which perhaps more than any other hurt the Negro's pride, gave him handicaps that he could not overcome, and reflected the worst aspects of segregation. For the bus, the streetcar, and the train were public services. He had to use them. Perhaps the bus travel was worst, a situation in which the South's millions moved from place to place in crowded busses and under all the trying circumstances that abounded. Here were experiences which portrayed again the South's reflection that the Negro was just a Negro. And yet there was the contradictory implication that sitting together or riding together constituted social equality.

Said one white soldier to his charming woman companion as they observed some Negroes boarding a bus well up in line instead of at the rear, "We don't do it that way down our way." "Well, why not?" they were asked. "Isn't it true that the Negroes must move to the rear? Why shouldn't they go first?" The young man was gracious enough to grin apologetically as he said, "Well, they can do that after all of us get on and sit down." As a matter of fact they often could not. In this case the bus was crowded to standing room. The bus was delayed, the Negroes embarrassed and many whites inconvenienced while Negroes slowly crowded back with their baggage to the rear. Logically it just didn't make sense.

It should be repeated that there were thousands of incidents that reflected great courtesy and patience on the part of both whites and Negroes. Yet, since travel on bus lines reflected so great a proportion of conflict and unfairness, the catalogue of rumors and stories has been presented primarily to interpret further the tragedy of the situation as most commonly observed.

A young college white woman, in the depth of discouragement and wondering whether she could live in the South of the future, was brought to her low state of morale by two incidents on the same day. First, a bus driver stopped at a midcountry crossroads, making a Negro man get off the bus and wait an hour or two for the next bus in order to let a young white girl get on. Second, when a young Negro college girl politely asked a taxicab driver if she might sit in the front seat and, after other passengers were delivered, be taken to her destination in an emergency, the driver slammed the door in her face and said he'd die before he would ride with her. Then, he said, "I wish everybody loved 'em as I do." Another said, "These Negroes think they can do like white folks, but we'll show 'em and no law can stop us." In the meantime how were these Americans to get to their destinations? And was it their fault?

It was difficult to find a place in American life where the sense of unfairness seemed more pathetic. Waiting in line for tickets, waiting in line for busses, the Negro never had an equal chance. Again a few samplings from thousands. "In a bus station a Negro was buying a ticket and apparently gave the clerk a little less than the actual fare. Instead of the clerk asking him for the rest of it or explaining that fares were higher, the clerk called a cop who forcibly took the Negro out of the station." In Tennessee, "white people crowd

on busses first, making Negroes take any seats left if there
are any." In Louisiana, "a bus conductor struck and threw a
Negro off because he sat next to a white person, although
the white person sat in the back of the bus."

It was pointed out often that the picture was a mixed one
even as was the living reality which it portrayed. Here was
the viewpoint of many southern whites. "When a crowd was
waiting for a bus, Negroes no longer stood back and let
white people enter first. Negroes pushed white people aside
and, if possible, got into the bus first, and secured as many
seats as possible, beginning in the rear." Observers from
South Carolina reported that Negroes had refused to sit in
the Negro section of the cars and busses. So, too, many
Negroes from the North wanted front seats on the busses
in the South and the drivers had to call policemen to take
them to court for violating the laws and not moving when
the driver asked them to.

There were literally so many stories being told about experiences in bus transportation that it would have been impossible to list all, even if it were necessary. Not a day, nor
a traveler but could add and add to the unbelievable total.
Yet, it was repeated again and again that hundreds of examples of courtesy and patience, as well as just ordinary human
relationships were mixed up with the greater number of unfortunate and unfair practices. The special point in presenting the negative side, it was urged, was to explain levels and
causes of tensions and to portray occasions when conflict
arose and rumors multiplied.

From all the States came the same general story. From
North Carolina: "If a Negro woman refused to move her
seat for a white man, the bus driver stopped the vehicle and
threatened to put her off." Also "when busses were over-
crowded, there was room for the white soldiers but not for
the Negro soldiers." And "they had to have separate busses

for Negroes and whites as there were so many fights when both rode on the same bus."

From Georgia, it was rumored that the Negroes were going to stop riding busses because of the treatment they received. A story full of pathos: "A bus was filled with the exception of three or four vacant seats. One of the empties was second from the rear. Across the aisle from this empty was a white woman. The bus stopped to take on a Negro man and woman. They went back to the rear but remained standing in the aisle by the side of the empty seat. The white woman seemed to sense the situation and was apparently in a quandary wanting to move up toward the front, but didn't. The Negro woman began crying as she swayed straphanging by the empty seat. It was night and no lights were on in the bus. At a stop, later, the bus driver went down the aisle toward the back, as if to see whether everything was O.K. Simultaneously two white men in the bus said, 'Captain, if you need any help let us know.'"

From Georgia also was reported the other type of behavior. "One of the city bus drivers was so officious with his Negro passengers, shoving them around and making them wait unduly for their transfers, they finally complained to their employers. One or two of the employers observed the situation for themselves and then took up the complaint with the bus company. The driver lost his job." So also, "On a bus not long ago a lieutenant in the Army asked an old Negro man who was being forced to stand to share his seat." Likewise, in North Carolina when an older white man, seated temporarily toward the back before Negro passengers got on, got up to give Negroes his seat, three southern soldiers offered him their seats in appreciation.

In Virginia, "A young southern man was on a bus which was crowded, with only one seat remaining by him. A Negro got on the bus and sat down next to him. The white man advised him to go to the rear of the bus, but the Negro refused and began to set up his arguments of all men being created equal. The white man became furious and warned the·Negro, but the Negro still refused to move. When they got off the bus, the white man immediately grabbed the colored man and hit him on the jaw. The colored man fell to the street where the white man kicked him into the gutter." From Alabama came the story that on one occasion an old Negro woman attempted to enter a bus and was told first she would have to wait for the white folks to get on. As she stepped back, some white women laughed. The Negro turned to another and said, "What dat woman laughin' 'bout? Ain't nothin' funny as I kin see." A different type from South Carolina told about "a Negro woman asking a white woman to move up a seat. The Negro woman was seated behind the white woman. The white woman did not pay any attention to what the Negro had said. The Negro woman slapped the white woman. A warrant was sworn out for the Negro."

So many complex and varied situations arose that it was relatively easy to understand how tense nerves and crowded busses led to all sorts of unreasonable behavior. As strange as many happenings appeared, further inquiry indicated that always there were more and stranger episodes waiting to be found. Again samplings from what appeared limitless numbers: "A Negro girl tried to sit by a white girl on a bus. As she refused to move, the conductor took her by the collar and pushed her off the bus." That was from Georgia, and from North Carolina another weird one: "A Negro soldier got on a bus and sat down by a white girl. He insulted her and tried to hold her hand. The bus driver dragged the Negro from the bus, beat him up, and then called the bus company and resigned his job. He then walked off and left his bus load of people." And from Tennessee, "A Negro secretary of the Fellowship of Reconciliation, while riding a bus early last summer, refused to move to a back seat. After some abuse, he was taken by the police and was released when a southern white man interceded for him." Florida complained that "during early morning or late afternoon hours, when most of the bus passengers are Negroes, they are sitting within two or three seats of the front. No matter how many white men or women get on later, the Negroes will not get up and move to give white ladies their seats, although white people have to stand in the aisle with Negroes on all sides." Again, "A white man, seeing Negroes sitting almost all the way to the front and white women standing, asked this same bus driver if he could not ask them to move back and let the white ladies sit down. The driver said that the man could ask them if he wanted to, but that he (the driver) would not dare to ask them." "A Negro sat down beside a white man on a bus. The bus driver asked him to move, but was forced to throw him off. Bus drivers have been given police authority in this city."

Many instances were reported in which Negroes were made to wait for later busses or to give way for white passengers. Thus, it was reported in North Carolina that a "Negro woman was rudely deprived of a bus ride at seven P.M. by the driver who curtly explained, 'No seats for colored people.' The woman protested, saying that she had a sick son to whom she had been trying to get since nine that morning, having not been permitted to ride on any of the busses since that time. The driver only said, 'Sorry' to the soldier who offered the woman his place on the bus." Another from the State which usually accords the Negro a fairer chance than others. "After all the white people got on, the three Negroes who were already on the bus were told to get off and wait for the next bus. On another occasion a bus driver passed up three Negroes standing waiting for the bus and stopped a little further up to let three white people on."

One of the tragic patterns of behavior frequently reported was that of homicides growing out of bus friction. There were enough authenticated happenings to indicate the seriousness of the stories and rumors. From Virginia it was reported that "on one occasion a drunk Negro insisted on sitting next to white people, or rather, in the white section, and was ordered back to his place, whereupon he drew a knife. The bus driver took him outside the bus; they had a few words and the driver shot and killed him. The Negroes were infuriated, and for many days thereafter shot at that bus." Another similar story from the State told of "a Negro who was abusive, being reprimanded by the bus driver. When the Negro started toward the front to attack the driver he was shot." In Alabama, it was told that "a Negro sailor got in the bus and insisted upon sitting in the white section. When asked to move back, he refused and the driver became infuriated and struck the Negro with the end of his gun. In defense of the sailor another Negro man attacked the bus driver and stabbed him. It finally resulted in a riot in which several people were injured."

Even the longest possible list of samplings of rumors and stories concerning Negroes and bus transportation would be inadequate. Yet the examples given were adequate to typify what the Negro-white folkways were with reference to this aspect of life. As a matter of fact, both rumors and stories often understated what sometimes appeared to be the facts. The bus drivers utilized a varied strategy. It was necessary to recall that the law in the South required Negroes to sit in the rear part of the bus, and that the bus driver was often instructed to take positive action. Yet there were many variations. One driver would revert to force, while another would remain more poised. All were positive. Thus, some-

times bus drivers deliberately misinformed Negroes that another car would come along, or that this particular bus did
not go where they wished.

One driver, being unsuccessful in getting a Negro soldier
to move back, simply shut off his engine and announced
that his bus would not start until the soldier moved. Negroes
persuaded the soldier to move back so that they could get
to their destinations. Here again it must be repeated that
in many cases the Negroes were defended by southern
whites and that for the most part the Negroes themselves
were extremely orderly. Always there was the folk-drama of
everyday life, in which there was good and bad mixed together in a southern human ratio.

Many of the stories blamed the Negroes for the way they
behaved. Thus, "Negroes occupied most of the seats and
the white people stood. At times they were as near the front
of the bus as the first seat. They were loud and boisterous.
Only one bus driver when I was on the bus ever made them
quiet down or move back as the back seats were emptied."
And again, "The Negroes are beginning to crowd on busses
ahead of white people, and, surprisingly enough, the whites
let them do it. The rabid southerners around here, who a
short time ago seemed to think that the Civil War was still
being fought, are giving in to the Negroes as they have
never done before." The two instances cited were from
North Carolina. From Louisiana, "Several times when I have
tried to get on a bus going from one town to another
Negroes have pushed and nearly knocked white passengers
down in their persistence to get a seat before they are all
taken. Naturally this shoving and knocking about is resented
by the whites, and some sort of conflict, whether in mere
words or actual blows, inevitably results."

Then back again to the "blame" of the white drivers. "It
was a bitterly cold day and even the inside of the bus was

none too warm. The bus driver came on the bus and told the only Negro passengers (a Negro woman and her two-year-old child), that they would have to get off the bus and give their places to white people. He said that an extra bus was to be 'put on' for the Negroes; however, he did not direct her to another bus and she stood against the wall of the bus station for half an hour or more. The wind was blowing and she and her child were not clothed very warmly. The driver did not even show her common courtesy." That was from South Carolina. A story from Louisiana reported: "A crowded bus stopped on the hail of a Negro woman. The driver brusquely told her that she would have to stand if she got on and when she seemed undecided as to whether to ride or not he curtly ordered her to make up her mind. Almost every white passenger within my hearing range made some remark about how discourteous the bus driver was. I was seated near the Negroes in the bus and did not hear a single remark about the bus driver's conduct." And from Alabama, "Bus drivers seem to have no respect for Negroes' feelings. I have heard many of the drivers 'holler' and talk very unkindly to colored people when there was no reason for them to be so angry."

Finally, the pattern of disrespect for the Negro's personality was so prevalent that its portraiture reflected upon the intelligence and chivalry of the southern people. Especially was this true in cases when white men "slapped" Negro women. There was an Alabama story, in which resentment was noted among white students who observed such unfair practices. "On the day when the university students were returning after the holidays and the crowded travel was made even worse, no Negroes were allowed to get on the busses until all of the white people had gotten provided for. Consequently, they had to wait a whole day trying to get on a bus. When I got on a bus as late as 10:00 P.M., Negroes were still *not* allowed to get on." And again, "There was one colored woman in the very back seat on the bus. This seat extends across the back of the bus, so of course no white people would sit with her. Upon arriving in a fairly large town some white farmers wanted to get on the bus and the driver insisted that the colored woman get off the bus and wait for a second bus that would arrive in half an hour. The Negro woman refused to do so and one farmer became very angry about the whole matter. He, himself, was not willing to wait for the other bus either, so he said everything to the Negro woman and told her that just as soon as he got the other bus and could get to the next bus stop, he was going to give her a most severe beating." And from South Carolina, "I was riding on a crowded bus. A young Negro was sitting alone in one of the seats, and quite a few white and colored people were standing; a white woman got on, marched up to the Negro and said angrily, 'Get up out of that seat you "nigger" and let a white person sit down. Who do you think you are?' Looking very frightened, the Negro got up. When the woman sat down, however, she took up all the seat instead of letting someone else sit beside her. The rest of the time I was on the bus, she muttered about how impudent the Negroes were getting, thinking they were as good as white people. I've never seen a white woman make herself more disgusting." And from North Carolina, "I heard a Negro woman with a small baby in her arms ask a white woman, who was sitting in one of the two very back seats for whites on the bus, if she minded if she sat down in the empty seat beside her. The white woman said that she would prefer for her not to do so. There were no white people standing on the bus. There were two or three Negroes standing. There was one empty seat by a white woman and yet the seat remained empty."

Why continue more and more when the portraiture has

been so vividly presented? Even though the samplings here were but a small part of what was told, they appeared more and more monotonous and repetitious. Yet, a part of the picture was its extraordinary sweep and intensity. Could the public by repetition and vividness be made to look at the picture? Not even most southerners had any idea of what was happening. Over and over again there was the tug of conflict; the whites feeling the Negroes were to blame, the Negroes knowing the whites were wrong. There was no inclination to deny the facts about the behavior of both white and Negro. The facts were true!

Now again there was the alleged behavior of the Negroes. "There is increasing lack of consideration on the part of the Negro in busses. Considering how most of us are today riding the busses and using public facilities, this is becoming a very alarming problem. I have, personally, had Negroes almost knock me down to get on a bus. They shove and push people aside." So, too, "It just so happens that I ride the same bus that many Negroes ride back and forth to work. At all times I have quite a struggle to get on the bus, because the Negroes push everyone out of the way and scramble on. The drivers, for the most part, are polite in their remarks to them, but the Negroes are free with their retorts. I am in favor of equality of race, but I don't like being pushed around by a Negro or anyone else."

Now back again to the behavior of the whites and the bus drivers, primitive and brutal. "After a heated argument with the bus driver, a soldier entered the bus that was waiting to be loaded and bodily dragged a Negro soldier off —pushing him with such force that the colored boy sprawled on the sidewalk, with these accompanying words, 'When a white man can't ride before a damn nigger—there is something wrong.'" That was from North Carolina. Another from South Carolina, "The bus was loaded and presently it stopped to take on a Negro. There happened to be a drunk marine at the front of the bus who had caused considerable disturbance all of the way. As the Negro went to pass him he hit the marine accidently, which immediately got the marine hot. The marine told the Negro to apologize in the name of the United States. The Negro said, 'Hell, I have not done anything wrong.' The marine asked him once more and not getting any response hauled off and hit the Negro with such force that it piled eight people in the back seat of the bus. Then the bus driver and the marine calmly took the unconscious Negro and put him behind his baggage by the side of the road and said the next bus would pick him up." Another, "Just as we were getting on the bus a Negro man walked up as if he wanted to get on the bus. There were about ten students sitting in the back of the bus in the colored section. (There were no Negroes on the bus.) One of the boys yelled to the bus driver, 'Hey, Skipper, don't let that Negro on here.' The bus driver told the Negro there wasn't any room for him. We drove on another block and at the next bus stop the boys got off the bus, leaving the colored section completely vacant."

That long catalogue of bus travel rumors and stories was revealing both to the South itself and to its critics. Out of the picture came a powerful sense of pathos and a sort of pity for both the white South and the Negro South. It was clear that the never-ending stream of difficulties was made more so by the war, by limited facilities, by nerves and tempers reacting to new situations and to manifest injustices. Their portraiture was the picture of crisis and conflict, because that was the thing to study. Yet many Negroes and many whites reacted with that wisdom and kindness which might have come to all if only they had said: "Yes, we understand. We know these irritating circumstances are going to be repeated over and over again. So what? What, then, is the best way to help the days and the people along to a happy ending?"

Close study of most of the rumors and stories reflected a continuous and never-softening level of tension. Most of the college students who told of the injustices in bus travel showed their impatience, and thus reflected on the white side a reasonably large reserve force for improvement. Also, many Negroes recognized the difficulties that were inherent in detail and incidents that are "natural." Many a bus driver showed fine patience, alongside many a one that did not. They had their problems, too.

There had been numerous examples of southern whites taking the part of Negroes and denouncing the treatment accorded them. Many leaders had appealed to bus drivers and bus companies for fairer treatment. There had been occasions where, for instance, a southern white youth would "knock out" another southern white youth for his treatment of Negroes. There was the case of a white soldier knocking another white soldier "cold" because he had beaten a Negro unjustly in a bus. And the greater part of the stories reflected a promising tone on the part of many white youth, alongside the contrariwise, combative attitude of many others.

The final catalogue of stories reflected this aspect of the situation, while outside, on the roads, day and night, the drama went on. "I've seen white people get up from seats on the busses where the Negroes were supposed to sit so that the Negroes could sit down while the white people stood up." And again, "Our school principal went with a group of basketball students to a near-by school on the bus. The bus was crowded and when a Negro woman got on, one of the school boys got up and gave her his seat by a white girl. The girl sat still and there was not a single remark made." From over in Tennessee, "A Negro woman with a baby entered a crowded city bus. None of the Negro men who were seated offered her a place. As she stood in the aisle the bus lurched to one side and caused her to hit the baby's head on an upright support. The baby screamed in pain. A white man arose from his seat and said to those around him, 'I can't see a woman with a baby treated like this.' He then offered his seat to the Negro woman. When she sat down, a second white man who was occupying the other part of this seat protested that he was not going to sit beside any 'nigger.' The first white man replied, 'Then I think you had better stand up.'" From Georgia, "I have also seen bus drivers be very polite to a Negro passenger, making white passengers move out of the section set aside for colored passengers and to the front of the bus." And again, "I have recently traveled 2800 miles through the States of Louisiana, Georgia, Alabama, Mississippi, Tennessee, and Arkansas. I have noticed bus drivers being unusually kind to Negro women and children." From North Carolina, "Coming up on the bus last week-end, we had to change busses and by the time the bus arrived there was an enormous crowd waiting. All the white people swarmed on the bus, until they were standing in the aisles. One colored woman was left on the platform, and the bus driver said he was not going to let the Negro miss her ride, and he made all the white people stand to one side so that the Negro woman could pass to the back of the bus." And once again, "I have seen white people help Negro mothers with their children get on and off the bus. I have seen white men give up their seats to Negro women with children at their knees."

XV

On Streetcar and Train and in Other Segregated Areas

The picture of travel on streetcar and train needed less emphasis in the portraiture of conflict and tension in the early war years for several reasons. It was not that the same irritating forces and experiences were not observable. They were. On the other hand, the picture of the streetcar tensions was largely the same picture as for bus travel for two reasons. In most of the cities busses had supplanted many of the streetcars, and, in the second place, the rules of the game were similar to those in the busses, namely, the law required the separation of the races, front and rear. In general, therefore, the stories and rumors repeated and reproduced the picture of the bus situation with one or two exceptions. One was that there was often conflict of a body of whites with a group of Negroes as when laborers, working at the end of a line or boarding the streetcar in a body, would either fill up the car and leave no space for the Negroes, or the two groups would compete for seats. This made a sorry picture and was reflected in cities outside the South as well as within it.

The second main way in which there were differences in the streetcar situation had to do with the congestion of traffic in Negro centers of large cities and with the passing of cars heavily crowded with Negroes through white sections or crowded with whites through Negro sections. A source of conflict was found where the streetcar, starting in the Negro neighborhood, would be crowded before it reached the white part of the city.

Here were the same stories and rumors all over again.

The Negroes crowded the whites off.

The whites crowded the Negroes off.

A white man abused a Negro.

A Negro was impertinent to a white woman.

A Negro was shot for not conforming to the rules and for quarreling about them.

There was trouble between Negro soldiers and white soldiers.

A Negro soldier refused to go in the back part of the car. He was attacked by whites.

The conductor refused to stop for Negroes to get on, but let additional whites on.

The conductor advised white women not to ride on that car.

Special cars for Negroes were used without designating them as such. Some cars stopped for whites; some cars stopped for Negroes.

And so, on and on, the old story.

The situation with reference to trains constituted a special story. It was different, too, in several ways. In the first place, there were no such opportunities and occasion for conflict as there were on streetcars and busses, since the Negroes rode separately from the whites. The trains, therefore, were not the occasion for either the cumulative conflict or war-incited conflict which was reflected in so many other aspects of race relations. For this reason some Negroes among the common folks advocated separate busses for Negroes.

The whites for the most part did not even know about the discriminations, and the Negroes' complaints were not the basis for daily physical conflict. There were relatively few stories and rumors about train travel from the same sources from which the others came, for the simple reason that few observers were there to tell the tale, few actual conflicts occurred, and quantitatively the issue was different. Likewise, the stories here were stories told by Negroes and constituted a special complaint of injustices and unfairness, rather than observations on conflict. There were, however, adequate samplings to indicate the nature of the problem.

In contrast to many of the other aspects of conflict the story of passenger travel on trains was one which reflected considerable progress, especially in provisions for Negro passengers in Pullman cars and in dining cars. Hardly a through-train but carried Negro and white passengers alike in Pullman cars with hardly ever a complaint or an insult by whites as would have been the case in the earlier part of the century. Yet the catalogue of injustices was long and added to the points of tension between white and Negro in the Nation in so far as it represented one of the most embarrassing and humiliating of all the levels of segregation for the Negro in the upper brackets of his life and culture.

Also, one of the chief points of tension and unequal treatment was found in the ticket office, where with crowded schedules and limited services, the Negro had to wait and wait his turn. It was almost an impossible situation, one in which again thousands of ticket attendants showed fine courtesy and service to Negro passengers. Yet the main story was the same, reflecting an unspeakable embarrassment to the thousands of Negro travelers moving more than ever about the land. This waste and injustice, discomfort and unhappiness would not appear intelligible in any situation except the South.

While the complaints about railroad stations and travel constituted a special technical problem and a separate story, there were, however, samplings of discrimination and tension which, added to the other totals, helped to interpret the whole picture and point the way to next steps.

The Negroes always had unequal accommodations in the railway stations.

They had difficulties in the use of taxi services, suffering the same indignities as in other special services.

They had difficulties in buying their tickets and arranging for baggage. They nearly always had to wait. If they had to catch a train without a ticket they were abused.

They rarely ever had the best equipped passenger coaches on the trains and rarely ever enough in the crowded, war days.

They were more crowded than the whites; especially Negro soldiers in such periods.

Negro soldiers on furlough and in civil travel had great difficulties, in travel and dining facilities.

Northern Negroes, both in army and civil life, suffered more especially under the southern segregation rules.

There were many incidents of conflict below the "Line." Negroes often refused to go back to the colored car. They abused the conductors. The conductors abused them. Negro soldiers were often treated with unbelievable discourtesy and cruelty when passing from North to South. They were often required to wait for special trains or to find special facilities for eating.

There were other areas of segregation and discrimination that reflected the difficulties involved. A part of the story of treatment in restaurants, drug stores, and merchandise stores was told in the catalogue of stories about their search for equality. The Roland Hayes episode of disgraceful treatment at Rome, Georgia, and the defense of this by southerners constituted what appeared to be the most disgraceful incident outside of the lynchings and brutalities that had been pictured. Although in hundreds of the best stores in the South, in the banks, and in the post offices, there was no segregation, there were nevertheless still thousands of cases where unnecessary discrimination led to increasing tension and trouble.

XVI

When Hitler Takes Over

It was not a part of this story to trace out the influence of propaganda upon the Negroes. That was a special job being done by authorities in the field. While many of the mass rumors such as those which excited the city of Washington or New Orleans or Detroit bore the earmarks of having been planted, the effect was the same in any case, whatever the source. Here, as was the case of actual happenings in the armed forces, where Negro and white soldiers were quartered, the story was necessarily left to the governmental authorities to tell. Yet there were demonstrably certain points of tension in which the Negro was represented as preferring Hitler or the Japanese to an America in which he was not free. Some of these were worth cataloguing as were many of the idle boasts of Negroes.

One aspect of the Hitler story was reflected in the mass of rumors in which the Negro predicted that "his day" would come. Well, since the country was fighting Germany and Japan, and since the Negro was "mad" with the whites, the natural reference would be to the enemy. "Some Negro girls stayed in the white section of the train after it had passed the Mason-Dixon line, and they made some remarks about how 'the Japs and Germans would show up a thing or two.'" Again, "in the back of a bus, the Negroes began to say in a low tone that when Hitler got over here he would fix the white people." From South Carolina, "A Negro woman got on a bus in a small town in the upper part of the State. She sat down in the front of the bus. The bus driver naturally told her to move to the back. She said, 'When Mr. Hitler gets over here we will sit in the front of the bus.' This angered the driver and he slapped her and put her off the bus. Three Negro men then attacked the driver. They were unsuccessful as another white man who was riding the bus promptly got up and shot all three of them. Another Negro girl began talking to a Negro girl, but loud enough for those around to hear her. She said, 'I'll be glad when Hitler comes. We couldn't be any worse off.' "

Other short versions were, "When Hitler wins the war and comes to America, the Negroes will be given the best jobs and positions and the white people will have to work for the Negroes." And "Hitler will make white people slaves and the Negroes the leaders." And again, "A woman had had the same cook for a number of years. One day she said, 'Ise cookin' fer ya now but when Mr. Hitler comes over here you'se gonna be cookin' fer me.' " So, too, "A Negro cook when told by her mistress to go scrub the floor of the bath-room said, 'Well I'll go scrub it, but when Hitler comes you'll be scrubbing mine.' "

Even if the retorts of Negroes against the whites had little specifically to do with Axis sympathy, it was a vivid way of "getting even" with the whites in the same old segregation patterns. "A Negro maid told the lady for whom she was working that she wouldn't work one certain day, that from now on she could do as she pleased because when Hitler takes over, we won't have to work—the white folks will have to work for us." Another housewife had her Negro cook confront her with this statement: "You just wait until Mr. Hitler gets over here; then you'll be working for me." And still another report had it that when a lady and her cook had argued, the cook said, "After Hitler wins this war you will be cooking for me." And the same pattern of retort, "A Negro washwoman returned the washing of a white woman. The washing was not as well done as it usually was. When the lady asked the Negress to do better the next time, she replied, 'When Hitler gets over here, you'll be doing my washing.'" And finally, "A lady in town went to see why her washwoman had refused to come after her clothes the previous week. When she asked her why she did not come after the clothes she replied, 'I'm waiting on Mr. Hitler. When he gets here I won't have to wash for you but you will have to wash for me.'"

Some stories went the rounds that the Japanese were the Negroes' friends, kinsfolk as a colored race, and all that. And it was well known that the Japs provided a bill of particulars showing discrimination against the Negro. One way in which Japanese propaganda was promoted was for the Negroes to repeat what the Japs had said but to protest and ask the whites to prove that it was not true. This also gave the Negroes a fine opportunity for their own protests.

Samplings of the common rumor about the Japanese were about the same as for the Germans, with the exception of the element of race kinship. "Organizations are believed to exist among the Negroes. They talk of the Japanese in a friendly manner. They sympathize with any colored races and believe that the Nipponese are their kindred. They speak of how they will govern and rule when the Japs attack California."

There were also stories of organized alignment with Japan. "I have heard some talk about the Black Dragon Society which was organized in 1931 by a Japanese agent." And again, "They say the Negroes are banding together and call themselves the 'yellow shirts.' That is one society. It is a secret organization. Another is called 'Black Dragon.'" Another report, "The most startling news I have heard of the Negroes is the fact that one Negro informed his employer that they were told in church by their preacher that the Japs

were coming to free them and make them above the whites."
And finally, "I heard that an organization which had been
formed by an 'outside' Negro had been discovered. They
stood for the superiority of the black race, with the Japs second, and the whites third in order."

There were, however, some stories and rumors about Axis
propaganda and funds available for the Negroes. "I have
heard a Swastika Club had been formed all over the country." "Hitler has told the Negroes he will give them the
South for their help." "The Nazi party is going to give some
propaganda to the Negroes and lead them to sabotaging the
whites. They will have good opportunities in their jobs as
maids, butlers, chefs, chauffeurs, etc." "Because of Nazi influence, many Negroes have quit their jobs and are slowing
up the war effort." "There have been several rumors circulating. One of them is that the Negroes have stores of arms and
ammunition and that when Hitler gives the word they will
start killing the white people." "Negroes are being influenced
by Nazis and are planning to revolt against whites in this
emergency." "The Negroes are all organized through the
churches. They have received and are still receiving Nazi
propaganda. They can arise and attack the whites whenever
they want." "The Negroes have organized a 'Victory Over
There, Victory Over Here' Club. The Germans, the rumor
goes, have promised the Negroes supreme rule over the
white people in the United States if they win the war over
there." Then there was another report that Negro children
were singing to the tune of *America:*

> My country's tired of me,
> I'm going to Germany
> Where I belong.

XVII

Rumors and Stories Among the Negroes

There was yet one other level of story and rumor that had its dynamic influence upon the situation and contributed to tensions and conflict. This was the sweep of rumors that spread through the Negro population and the stories of what happened to Negroes and what Negroes themselves said and did.

There are two reasons why this level of story and rumor was of minor importance in the present story. One was that the record of the Negroes in the South was an extraordinarily fine one in this respect. There were surprisingly few rumors to be heard and the Negroes themselves showed admirable restraint. However, no special study of this phase of the subject was made, and it is likely that the story of rumors as they were current among the Negroes would also prove to be an interesting one.

The second reason, therefore, why only a short chapter is devoted to this phase is that the main current of stories and rumors studied was that which swept through and influenced the white community and the resulting behavior towards Negroes. Nevertheless, especially in the latter part of the period there were many similar rumors among Negroes who were becoming increasingly articulate and vocal in what they said both about the whites and to them. While this was a special story on its own account and not fundamental in the structure of the present work, it was important to record something of the role of Negro stories and rumors in the total picture.

To the extent that rumors among the Negroes, as was the case in such riots as Detroit and Harlem, were likely to lead to unfortunate results, the cataloguing of such rumors, exactly as was the case among the whites, might be of value in the interpretation of the whole phenomenon of rumors and their effects upon behavior. Thus, if it were shown clearly that rumors which set fire to riots in various places were unfounded and the resulting tragedies were shown to be the result of unreasonable stories, the same prophylactic effect might be anticipated as was hoped for in the case of rumors among the whites.

A study of this level of rumors also would be profitable alongside the studies of similar rumors in the Far West with reference to the Japanese in the total interpretation of certain fundamental psychological aspects of rumors and their influence upon the public. From the Gallup Poll as a sampler there were examples of fantastic rumors with reference to the Japanese, the work they did, the plots they threatened, the food and special privileges which they received, and a great many other types. Similar studies in Philadelphia and New York and in Boston resulted in certain basic materials, the presentation and interpretation of which would be of importance in comparison with the rumors in the South.

These, however, were special studies that might or might not be made. In the meantime, it was important to look at a few of the rumors and stories that were a part of the total picture presented in this work. First of all, there were such rumors as precipitated the riots in Detroit and Harlem, as vivid examples of what in a minor way was going on in some southern communities. Thus, at Detroit the story was circulated among the Negroes that a white man had thrown a Negro woman and her baby into the river. There were variations of this, some being that a white man had killed a Negro mother and her baby. Very similar was the story that swept Harlem to the effect that a Negro policeman had killed a Negro soldier in the sight of his mother. In some southern communities there appeared on the horizon from time to time stories of the number of Negroes that had been killed by the whites or the number of soldiers that had been shot by white M.P.'s. Most of these rumors failed to reach the stage of conflagration, but they illustrated the growing hazards of an increasing number of rumors among the Negroes which might approximate the proportions that existed among the whites.

There were other rumors easy to start and to grow. There were stories to the effect that white soldiers in the South were mistreating Negro women. There was specifically, for instance, a rumor that a white M.P. had beaten the wife of a Negro soldier in a Georgia camp. In Mississippi, there was the story of the beating of a Negro soldier and the alleged molesting of the wives and women companions of Negro soldiers by civilian police. There were stories about Negro women being arrested and beaten for protesting to policemen of mistreatment in the busses. There were other stories to the effect that white soldiers in and near camp cities were planning to prevent Negro soldiers from riding on the busses. There were threats of armed groups of Negro soldiers made against the whites and there were rumors of conflict when no conflict occurred.

Another type of influence was found in the alleged common talk of Negroes in and out of the Army. Such talk was reported by newspapers and was reflected in what white officers were alleged to have heard and feared in the various camps. Just as the white soldiers are alleged to have said, "The next war is going to be in Mississippi," so the same words were reported by Negro newspapers and others to be common talk among Negro soldiers. In the chapter dealing with rumors and tensions among armed men it was

reported that there were rumors among the whites to the
effect that they were afraid to send Negro soldiers abroad
for fear they would shoot their white officers. This same
rumor had been reported as coming from a Negro newspaper
man.

There were also many recorded conversations of the
Negroes who protested against discrimination. Sometimes
they constituted threats of violence. In the long catalogue of
rumors and stories among the whites with reference to bus
travel particularly, there were recordings of the resistance of
Negroes to segregation. Among the Negroes there were uncounted examples of such protests. The protests were facts,
not rumors. It was the cumulative talk about them that increased tensions. An example: In reporting the causes of the
Harlem riot, one of the national weeklies quoted a young
Negro soldier as saying: " 'I made up my mind right then
that I had taken the last insult from crackers I was going
to take,' the Negro officer told me grimly. 'If I had to die for
democracy, I decided that there was no better time or place
than right then. I told the driver I was not going to sit in
any jim-crow section and that if he was man enough to
make me do so, he would have to do it. I sat down in the
"white" section and rode into Washington.' "

The continued narration of stories of actual violence and
the recounting of the murder of Negro soldiers in the South
inflamed both the Negro soldiers who were nearby and
those who heard of the acts in the distance, and under-
mined the total morale of the Negro civil population
throughout the Nation. Resentment and talk about neglect
and about the treatment of Negro soldiers in camp and about
the failure to give them protection, often resulted in groups
of Negro soldiers threatening violence. The common talk
that much of the violence against Negroes did not get into
the newspapers accentuated the opportunity for rumors to

exaggerate the cases even worse than they were. There was an apparent acceleration of both actual violence and of the rumors and stories that resulted.

Back again to the simple rumors that were sometimes heard among the Negroes, there were some that were fantastic in some such way as were many of those among the whites. Thus, the rumor was widespread in some communities among the Negroes that Negro girls should not join up with the WAC's, because they would only be permitted to clean up camps and do menial service. A common story also was told that Negro soldiers were occupied in cleaning the sanitary parts of the camp and were not given regular training or equal treatment. And there was one fantastic rumor that before going into battle every white soldier was to have a Negro soldier in front of him.

Again, as in the case of many of the rumors among the whites, there was pathos aplenty in some of the stories and action. It was told in many communities that the Negro soldiers would come to town and take all the women away from the civilians. From this grew tensions and riots and trouble with Negro M.P.'s and white M.P.'s and civilian policemen, from which again would arise other rumors and stories, complicating the situation. And there was resentment against the Negro M.P.'s because they would sometimes turn over a Negro offender to a white M.P. and would not stand up and fight for their own people. And there was the case in which a Negro M.P., undertaking to protect a Negro soldier from whites, was in turn attacked by the Negro soldier and shot him in self-defense.

Finally, there were, as yet to an unknown degree, many stories and much talk among the Negroes about whether they should fight for the Axis or at least whether they should fight for an American democracy which ignored their claims. There were bitter letters from Negro mothers and other civilians frankly stating that there could be no sound reasons why, with their sons treated as they were, they should fight in this war. This type of sentiment and the increasing mass of rumors and stories about mistreatment of Negro soldiers was increasingly a powerful hazard in the total problem of race conflict and tensions. It was utilized, in particular, by a great many of the agitators outside the South, and thus was contributing largely to the substance of protest. Something more of this will be seen in the story of the role of outside influence.

XVIII

The Role of Outside Agitation

In the attempt to explain the intensity and sweep of the new crisis of race tensions, a substantial part of the evidence was clearly the psychological reactions to what the South, the white South, considered outside interference. "They are trying to make us abandon our fundamental policy of race segregation," they would say. "If they would just let us alone, we would work out our problem," was a constant refrain that was not always couched in such mild language. And again, "We won't have any trouble with the Negroes down here if you will just hush up and let us alone." While it was pointed out that a great deal of the tension and conflict would logically have occurred in the normal evolution of a quick-changing world, even without the incidence of war and outside pressures, it was clear nevertheless that the chief immediate incidence of tension and conflict came from these two sources.

These have been reflected in most of the rumors and stories which have been catalogued as a chief portraiture of the total situation. Now it was important also, however, to catalogue certain evidences to substantiate the main assumptions. One way was to associate the range and nature of the rumors, stories, and incidents with the war incidence and with the real or imagined causes which rested in outside influences. This was done in the case of the rumors and stories.

It was, however, important to catalogue many of the evidences to indicate the extent to which individuals, agencies, and the press had been articulate in demanding radical changes in the southern way of life. Were there individuals, agencies, editorial policies, New Deal representatives, and others who did actually advocate what the South affirmed they did and what much of the South actually believed they did? If, for instance, there was great pressure, both intense and widespread, to urge the complete abandonment of racial segregation, and this was known to the South, then that was, in many places and with millions of southerners, tantamount to a declaration of violence, because the South was on record as being willing under no terms to do what was wanted. It was clear, therefore, why there was such sudden flare-up and inflaming of emotions as would set the stage for race conflict. And always it was the Negro, South and North, who bore the greatest burden of tragedy.

The answer to the question as to whether "outside" influences were trying to make the South change was plainly from multiple sources of evidence. "Of course, it was true. Who ever said it was not true?" It would have made a magnificent chapter in American history if the South could have replied: "Sure we know you urge these things; we understand from your viewpoint why it is natural that you should. We will try to understand you and will try to show you why this is an impossibility. So what and what of it?" This, however, was not the way of the South or of the North or of any other part of the world of warring conflicts. The result was continued growing animosities, conflicts, and approaching hate, and a well-nigh universal inflaming of Negroes against the whites and of whites against Negroes.

But what was the manner of published evidence of this outside agitation which inflamed the South? Was it in the programs advocated by the liberal leaders of educational institutions and the press? Was it in the Negro leadership of the Nation? of the South? Was it in the great Negro newspapers? And where else? The answer again was that it was in all of these. Here, again, the issue involved in this story was not whether segregation was right or wrong, but whether its complete elimination was recommended and the consequent effect of this impact upon the South and upon the Negro.

As was the case of rumors and stories, samplings that were representative would have to suffice in the place of volumes which would have been necessary to record the total. One type of sample was that of a popular national university round table which, summarizing their findings, emphasized the fact that a chief conclusion was that race segregation was wrong and that a chief objective was to be its abandonment; and, furthermore, that a strong federal action program was a necessary next step. This conclusion was reached after a review of the facts and after mention of the much-quoted statement that there were not enough armed forces in the world to enforce such a policy. This statement, the round table concluded, was evidence that there should be all the more effort put forth toward the desired ends. To the South, then, this was a declaration of war.

Here again the question was not what was right or wrong, nor even whether the public advocacy of such a policy was advisable or courageous or whether it might add still other troubles to the Negroes, but what was its effect upon race tensions and conflicts in the South? The same was true of samplings from the press: Did they advocate the doing away with segregation and what effect did they have upon race tensions?

One of the chief complaints of the South was that the people of the rest of the Nation were irresponsible in their agitation to make the South over. They were not acquainted with the facts. Another complaint was that the Nation itself did not treat the Negro fairly and that it should begin at home before it tried to reform the South. While this had little to do

with the merits of the demand that the South give the Negro
better opportunity, it did have a great deal of effect on the
South's reaction. The South felt that there should be an
equally realistic picture of the total national attitude and an
understanding of what ratio of the people at large constituted the basic power of the drive against the South.

It seemed important, therefore, before cataloguing samplings of extreme attacks by the Nation upon the South—
those which inflamed the majority of the southern people—to
look at a sort of composite estimate of the division of people
of the Nation as they looked at the Negro, as estimated by
those who were both national and southern—that is, native
to other regions, but seeing through southern eyes and from
southern experience. This was an extension of the "northern"
credo.

First, the outstanding feature of the attitudes among all
sorts and conditions of men appeared to be their lack of pattern in the mind of the individual. Each man seemed to have
as many packets of attitudes toward Negroes as he had in-
groups to which he belonged. There was a second general
observation, namely, that except for the class of whites who
entered into direct job-competition with Negroes, "The
Negro" as an abstraction in the ideal culture pattern bore *no*
kinship to Negroes who lived and moved and had their being
in the community.

At least four groups of people whose attitudes made any
difference (excluding recent immigrants) could be set apart.
One group, perhaps the immature intelligentsia, saw everything as entirely black or entirely white. They recognized—
sometimes because of ignorance, sometimes because of tem-
perament, sometimes because of ulterior motives—no distinction between things as they could be tomorrow and things as
they might well be millennium after next. Negroes were citizens. Citizens were all alike in their rights and privileges.

Ergo: Negroes must get now everything everybody else gets (except me). They were the cutters of Gordian knots. They espoused legislation of a frequently hysterical and abolitionistic tenor. Perhaps they comprised one or two percent of the population, but fifty percent of the articulate journalism.

There was another one to two percent of the population, and the other fifty percent of the articulate journalism, that were more mature and stable. They were searching—especially through education in industry and the schools—for ways to break up job stratification and social immobility in the Nation as rapidly as could be done without social explosion or psychological dismay. They saw discrimination in industry and insult in social relations as increasingly a threat to the welfare of America as a whole. Most of them pointed with alarm to discrimination and insult directly; a very few worked on the assumption that making a better world for all men to live in would make a much better world for Negroes to live in. The attitude of this group toward the state of affairs in the South was one of eagerness to lend aid and comfort to sound southern leadership when asked to do so.

Perhaps a third of the population, representing the great mass of privileged folk, found the prime characteristic of their attitude as one of ignorant detachment, with an admixture of benevolence increasing as one moved up the ladder. As a whole group they saw the Negro as a cultural incompetent and a natural-born servant who was at the moment in danger of getting too big for his shoes. He was not to be denied educational opportunity, but he was not to attend the schools or colleges attended by one's own children. He was to be quietly but firmly bound by housing covenants but he was not to be denied equal opportunity for good housing. He was to have equal job opportunity. (But if I hired him my men would walk out, and I have enough headaches as it is.) There was a Negro named Carver, written up in the *Readers*

Digest, who was so atypical as to represent no threat to mores or business. (I admire Marian Anderson, too, though I have never heard her. Frankly, the New Deal coddles the Negro, but they treat him like a dog in the South.)

And finally the estimate, paraphrased to represent the common man, characterized a ratio of perhaps sixty percent who might be termed the masses. "Me? I get along with everybody. If a man minds his own business it don't make no difference to me what he is. Hell, I seen colored men doing a day's work, you couldn't say they was lazy. I eat right along side them. Why, I got a friend is colored. We don't have no trouble. My God, no. If he was to move in my neighborhood property wouldn't be worth a dime in two years. No, we can't let them black bastards in our union; they'd ruin it. You think I want to take orders from a nigger? Well, I wouldn't work in the South if I could help it. I seen some of the crackers and hillbillies here in the plant. To hear them you'd think colored people wasn't really human. Oh, it don't make no difference at school; they got a right, but outside, that's different. Would you want your daughter to marry a black man?"

To these then were added the other small percentage of immigrants and ethnic groups whose prejudices and attitudes stemmed from a heritage of folk-conflicts and from specific situations and tensions in labor and community relationships. Much of their attitude also stemmed from their pattern of inferiority feeling regarding other peoples and, especially historically, regarding the Negro. In race riots outside the South these factors and attitudes were of great importance and the South resented being held responsible for race riots in other parts of the country, although it was clear that southern influence North was always a dynamic factor in race relations, and southerners didn't change much.

In the samplings from so great a catalogue of bitter denunciation of the South it was scarcely possible to estimate how many of the total people or how much of public opinion was represented. As was the case with rumors and irresponsible stories that swept the South, the effect was about the same, whether representing a few or many. The patterns of spread and of inflammation were similar—often the least representative but the most extreme fanned flames most. In general, there were four or five main sources and currents, namely, the New Deal, the First Lady, the earlier radical and Communist agitators, the main body of "liberal" writers, editors, and reform groups, and the Negro press.

The catalogue of stories and rumors reflected very well the South's reaction to the New Deal and to the general theme of outside interference. There were immature and emotional extremes on the part of southern representatives in the Congress which reflected much of public sentiment that hadn't thought the situation through. Thus a senator from Texas was reported as saying that "Thaddeus Stevens, in the days of Reconstruction—in the deepest wells of his hatred . . . never proposed an outrage such as this which is now tendered us by our own party and by our own leaders, who prefer a few little votes somewhere to the support of the respectable Southern Democrats."

There were hundreds of editorials and columnists' verdicts adequate to confirm what the rumors and stories had told. And there were new fears on the part of the upper brackets of southern leadership that they were being maneuvered into situations in which either they would have to desert the South or else be labelled backsliding liberals. And there was growing resentment along with fears.

There was also growing up a well-nigh unanimous feeling of discouragement in so far as it became clearer and clearer that no white southerner was to be approved on any general basis, and that no matter what was done it was too little, and it was wrong. And there were both fear and resentment growing out of the tendency to force southerners and northerners to "take sides," which meant automatically "opposite" sides in a crisis where unity and fellowship were needed. Whether "right or wrong," there was practically unanimity in the South as to the unreasonableness of the situation.

There were, to illustrate, general resentment that the South was regularly accused of holding the same principles and using the same tactics as Hitler, and impatience that intellectuals were saying that, at Detroit, "the planting of bitter, unreasoning race hatred was entirely on a par with the worst actions of Nazi Germany." This appeared to the southerners as a treasonable accusation of motives, principles, and national ideals where local conflict abounded. There was no doubt that southern leaders were troubled as that generation had never been troubled, and it was but natural that to the charge of Hitlerism they began to raise questions of wartime treason, when one part of the Nation was set against another, and always on pretexts out of perspective, either to the fundamentals or to the majority of the American people.

Yet, it would have been profitable if the South could have stood off in time and perspective and asked itself: To what extent is the southern credo, ruthless in its enactment, based upon the same kind of laws of biological, animal life, as were Hitler's powerful drives?

Here, for instance, was a sample of what, in the newspapers, corresponded to the worst rumors among the folk, in so far as it inflamed the people, North, South, white, black: "Since the South has all the ideas of Hitler in its head, from labor-baiting to Negro hating, it had just as well go on and join up with the Nazis and stop fooling around pretending to be democratic. Then we would all know where we stand, and we could take armies and go down there and fight it, just like we are taking armies to Europe now to rescue the French and the Greeks from Hitler who treats them like Mobile treats Negroes. I think we ought to rescue democracy in the South."

And again, "The Southern bloc, like Hitler, has felt these appeasements [of President Roosevelt] were their 'go-ahead' signal . . . like Hitler, too, the Southern bloc has launched out on a program of white supremacy, to be accomplished despite hell and highwater, and even at the expense of losing the war."

And still again, "What sticks in their throats [the Negroes] like a great, bitter lump is the feeling that reactionary white forces, especially the dominant Southern group in Washington, would prefer to stalemate this war in defense of democracy, rather than win a clear-cut victory, if victory required total cooperation by the Negro and therefore fundamental revision of the white-supremacy pattern of Southern life, and of its less obvious counterpart in the North."

Even a liberal sampling of the extremes to which race tension had brought attack upon the South and its consequent reactions would make a big book. Yet, like the rumors and stories, in general they were about the same. Repetition was important for vividness and minor variations. In the midst of all the South's vivid reaction there were some who urged a complete moratorium of all emotional reactions to any sort of criticism. What the South needed was to examine itself and to ask again and again if some of the accusations were true. There were many clear-cut appraisals in the national weeklies and elsewhere which, although extremely critical of the South and advocating extreme Federal policies, were nevertheless cognizant of the difficulties of the situation. There was one, for instance, which, perhaps following James Truslow Adams' *America's Tragedy* felt that her greatest tragedy was a great southern people who were blind. "The race problem, centered as it has been in Southern states, has been a cyst in our national anatomy. We must break it up, absorb it. Like a wounded man who, in his pain, lashes out against those who would help, the Southern people turn on the proponents of any kind of change, and resent any discussion of the problem. This is the deepest tragedy in American history, a people of virtue and courage, who have been blinded . . ."

And again, "It is hard to convey in words how deep-seated and ineradicable such intellectual brutality can be in the South. But the migration of the Negro northward and westward must continue; and it must continue under the guidance of sound Federal policy so that congestion in a few Northern cities will not lead to friction and riots as it has in the past. But even with the riots of the past, even with ghettos like Harlem, the Negro people have been helped by the migration northward. The United States never needed more gravely than it does today a strong and intelligent Federal policy on the race issue. What shield can it be, what group of men, what one individual, what set of circumstances, which stand between the President and this fact? Whatever it is, may its place be accursed in history."

What the South feared and believed was happening was voiced by many southern leaders and some in other regions. In substance, the fear was expressed by one of the South's younger liberals, and it was a measure of the South's reaction and mood. It was, he was sure, a foregone conclusion that if an attempt was made forcibly to abolish segregation throughout the South, violence and bloodshed would result.

The chief blame was placed upon the small group of northern white intelligentsia and a small group of Negro agitators and not upon the great body of southern Negro leadership. One count against these extremists was that they did not count the cost and were willing to throw the Nation and the races into a war of brothers again just to satisfy their egoistic "courage," their new-found freedom, and their journalistic scooping. "A small group of Negro agitators and another small group of white rabble-rousers are pushing this country closer and closer to an interracial explosion which may make the race riots of the first World War and its aftermath seem mild by comparison. Unless saner counsels prevail, we may have the worst internal clashes since reconstruction, with hundreds, if not thousands, killed and amicable race relations set back for decades." And another observer was sure that, "as matters are developing, the attitude of some leaders and of most Negro newspapers intentionally or not is tending to produce a race war. If this attitude is intentional and if it is adopted by the Negro people, it will have to be justified by results. If it is not intentional and this war occurs as a sort of mass accident the tragedy will be absolute."

The Negro press itself constituted a special exhibit. Here again, the picture was a mixed one, with the emphasis placed upon the extreme agitators. Again, the fact that Negro editors and their friends justified their journalistic extremes on the grounds that they had to have readers and financial success and were only following the earlier patterns of white extremes, had little to do with the total effect upon the great mass of both Negro and white people. Nor did the fact that they had been influenced greatly by many irresponsible white agitators alter the case; nor again that the Negro newspaper was really an epic of achievement for the race and the times. The total effect was the same.

The case of the Negro newspapers was reported and interpreted often and by varied writers. Their contributions were made in the more "literary" *Saturday Review of Literature* and *The Atlantic Monthly* and in such standard liberal journals of public opinion and social interpretation as *The Nation, The New Republic, The Survey Graphic,* as well as in the specialized Negro mediums, such as *The Crisis, Opportunity,* and certain professional and learned journals of education and social science. The record was both representative and adequate to portray the picture of what was happening.

Here are samplings. "A highly disturbing thing about this group of colored papers is their unwillingness to grant sincerity of motive to the whites who disagree with their attitude, and who argue that this attitude will be much more harmful than beneficial to the Negroes in the end. The same papers are equally intolerant of Negro leaders who try to put on the brakes. Any colored person, especially in the South, who urges a more conservative policy upon the Negroes, on the ground that a continuation of demagoguery and abuse is bound to end in disaster, is promptly assailed as an apostate, an 'Uncle Tom,' or a 'handkerchief head.'"

And again when a distinguished white newspaper editor who had been "defending the civil, political, and economic rights of the Negro in a distinguished newspaper career extending back over more than two decades . . . declared as a member of the committee [Fair Employment Practice] that the South has no intention of giving up the legal segregation of the races . . . his reward was excoriation from the Negro press that could hardly have been more extreme if he had been caught heading a gang of lynchers. He was assailed . . . as though he had been a common pick-pocket."

Sometimes the South's reaction to the agitation of the bitter calling of names by white northern publications appeared even more violent. Like the extremes of the Negro press, many writers with extraordinary ignorance and provincialism assailed all southern leaders, white and Negro, as false liberals in whom there was no hope. The great group of Negro southern leaders, measured from any standard, one of the most statesmanlike in the Nation, were still dubbed as "Uncle Toms," "White man's Negroes," "hat-in-hand" college presidents. This, of course, was following the lead of the radical and "smart" writers.

A sample of their statements, pointing to the younger Negroes, predicted a new sort of Negro leadership, without offering a level of cultural and economic foundation upon which they could work. The "new forces in southern life," so they predicted, would be different. "The emerging groups of articulate Southern Negroes are not the 'handkerchief heads' and 'Uncle Toms' drawn from among the hat-in-hand ministers or college presidents. They are the younger intellectuals, the trade union leaders, the courageous organizers of the National Association for the Advancement of Colored People. They will not be downed by Southern fury, for already they have confronted it and stood firm. They will seek further ties with their fellow Negroes in the North and East and will secure further use of the Federal authority in their behalf."

So, too, there was the collegiate type of writers, not always young in years, who satirized the "southern liberals" and the decent southern white people, meaning that there were but few decent such in the South. "The 'decency' of 'decent' Southern white people about which too many 'decent' southern editors have written has been very shallow and narrow. Too often, what is merely indifference and mental laziness is interpreted as a genuine and sympathetic tolerance carrying a sense of social responsibility. But the moment that such 'decency' admits of a modification of white, and a fundamental improvement of Negro, status, then the 'decent' Southern white man sees the real implication of his beliefs. He is afraid, and is quick to recant."

It seemed clear that the net result of all this sort of thing was not only in its effect upon the South and its undermining of the best genius and wisdom of the Negro people, but in its alienating millions of white people in other regions of the Nation from their natural allegiance to the Negro's cause. This was tragedy of the highest order, tragedy of the Greek, as it were, because it was the innocent Negro who suffered. From a swing around the country, the verdict of the young white southern liberal, perhaps more nearly trusted by Negroes than any other, was: "I gather that if and when the people of other areas have to make a decision on race matters, they will do about the same thing as the southerners have done. As I see it, there is literally no part of the nation which stands in opposition to the southern racial policy. In most areas, tragically enough, there is an inclination to make the same decisions the South made without the same reasons for having made them."

And so the tide was rising. Even in the confidence in nature's great capacity to survive and renew and in the light of America's great capacity to weather crises, it was difficult in these early years of the war to see the way on. This, then, was the problem, to find the best way out of crisis and the best way on to the general integration of American culture and ideals.

XIX

Science, Technology, Education, the Press, and Radio

Perhaps the great majority of people in the South found themselves impatient with the whole situation and especially with the necessity of considering this rising tide of tension and conflict. "Why," they seemed to feel, "can't we be let alone?" "Why keep stirring things up?" "Why keep agitating for this, that, and the other?" For this, they thought, was the cause of much of the trouble. And why couldn't folks let well enough alone? And besides "Christian men and women of both races sitting down together and planning how best they can render service to a needy world will do more for mutual understanding than all these highly publicized race relations meetings." "And the professors and scholars, why do they have to study and discuss such problems? Why can't they teach their subjects?"

And many people in other parts of the Nation found themselves regretting that the problem of race had come to them. "Why," they seemed to feel, "couldn't the people let the race problem of the Negro stay where it was, namely in the South? And why must they always be agitating this and that? And why especially should they expect us to solve the problem? It's the southerners' problem, let them solve it." And also "it is the southerners in other parts of the Nation that cause the trouble. Of course, there is Harlem, but that is different. But why should the Negroes and some intellectuals keep saying that the great newspapers and city administrations are always carrying on a campaign of race hate or

156

discrimination. Why can't they let us alone?" These were natural questions based upon plausible assumptions. Yet, always there were then the other inevitable questions: "Now since we have this problem what can we do about it?" "Ought there to be some great study of the situation?" "By congressional committees?" "By university professors?" "By representatives of special agencies?"

And always there appeared to be a common twofold answer. First, because of the reach and power of communications, of science and technology and education and of modern world movements; because of books and periodicals; because of the press and the radio; and because of new personalities made articulate through these media; and because of the new Negro in the Nation at large—the situation could not be let alone. It simply wouldn't and couldn't stay put. Something had to be done about it.

And the second answer was clear, always needing repeating, namely, that the first thing to do was to understand the complexity of the situation and all the factors that went into the making of crisis and conflict. To know about, for instance, the importance of the factors of communication and propaganda; to know that there could no longer be isolation of a human problem; to know also that because of all these neither could there be quick solution by edict. From a clear understanding of all these would come the ways and means for determining what was best to be done.

There were many phases of the new world that changed the situation of race, including education, the chiefest of America's pride of national achievement. It had been pointed out that four general factors had conspired together to make the situation with reference to the Negro more dynamic and more subject to rapid change. The first was the general conclusion of the psychologists, sociologists, and anthropologists that evidence of inferior and superior races did not justify the world's previous appraisal and action in relation to races. This factor, communicated to all races, contributed to the dark races' as well as the white races' attitudes. A second factor had been the extension of learning and technology to all races and their consequent increasing use of common tools of economic and political development. A third factor was the increasing tendency toward racial and national consciousness. The fourth was the rapid rise and increasing articulation of the American Negro in contradistinction, on the one hand, to his earlier status, and, on the other, in relation to his proportionate part in southern life.

There was no longer the possibility that the South could ignore all these great trends in looking at the reality of its own problem as it was seen by other parts of the Nation and the world. Where once the South had been pointed to with pride as the finest example of two different races living harmoniously side by side, the finger of criticism had long since been pointed, on the ground that the races were not in harmony and that the earlier premises of the good biracial society were not in line with either the American credo or of world trends. There would, therefore, have to be important alterations in the plans and structure of the South in its rebuilding programs.

If the South could not ignore change and if the situation could not be "let alone," no more could it be changed at once by legislative edict or the use of power to enforce unexamined moral principles. There were always the elemental processes of cultural evolution and the dynamic processes of education as powerful twin forces at work. It was constantly being said that America held one weapon that would obliterate the Hitlers and the Axis type of civilization, namely, American education, key to "achieving our vision of a better post-war world." Education had long been the key to America's mastery of her own destiny. What, therefore, had been the rate of education in the cumulative race situation in the South and in the Nation?

Now the most common concept of education that had been accepted by America's foremost educators and philosophers was that it was a process by which cultural heritage was transmitted from one generation to another. Applied to the Nation and in particular to the South it was clear that education had fixed the racial folkways and mores firmly in the total fabric of American culture and in particular of southern biracial culture. It appeared fantastic, therefore, to ignore the role of America's chief force, namely, education, which was working steadily to transmit the old heritage; or to expect a new generation, in the twinkling of an eye, to ignore all that it had been taught. Rather, it was apparent that some new forces and levels of educational effort were undertaking to transmit certain different types of cultural heritage, which in turn must compete with the larger current of traditional heritage and take ample time to change the current.

In the realm of evolutionary reality there were many factors that had contributed to the stubbornness of the situation, in addition to the general cultural heritage of the South and its educational teachings. There were certain fundamental "errors" of mankind. One was the age-long tragedy of race prejudice and conflict. One was the assumption that race was a purely biological phenomenon, and different in this respect as superior or inferior groups. Another was the assumption that because race conflict always had been a major cultural phenomenon, it would therefore always be. Still another was the assumption that the Negro was an inferior race subject to the logical processes of exploitation and domination. The South was a fine example of transmitted culture, following in the wake of all these human heritages and intensifying them through its own concentrated folkways of racial purity.

There were other important factors in the evolutionary heritage. One was the American heritage of the will and fact of extermination and exploitation of the American Indian. This American pattern, first grounded in the religious intensity of the New England forefathers to convert or to kill was still reflected in the tragic Custer's last stand. There could be no doubt that this American heritage set the stage for much that later flowered into the tragedies of race conflict throughout the Nation. Here, again, the South was following in full force that heritage long promulgated through American history and education.

There were also economic factors involved alongside the total struggle for societal as well as biological survival. Under the premises of what had actually been the racial backgrounds and the historical development there were honest bases for questioning whether a completely changed culture-economy could survive under the pattern of frontier and American economic framework. Rather, the problem was one of logical and sure integration of all the people, equally alike in opportunity, into the total unified system. The admission of the chief accusations against the South, namely, that the Negro had not been trained, educated, given experience in the normal processes of societal control, automatically reflected a picture of a people unprepared to measure up to what could be done in the absence of these limitations. The problem, therefore, again, was first to insure facility and capacity to succeed and then to follow with the consummation of laudable and attainable ideals.

Now, over against these organic factors and in sudden impact upon all that powerful cumulative heritage, came the sweep and power of new demands made possible by the reach of technology through communications and propaganda. The result was bound to be what it was. Here would be an individual who, because of some incident of world experience, would come to the public over radio or through thousands of pages of periodical and newspaper publicity. Perhaps one would fly around the world. Another would write a beautiful book and appear dramatically before the public. Another might be in on the sinking of a great battleship. One might go around the world. One might be a race-hater and set up a radio station to inflame the people and multiply their folkways. One might own a chain of newspapers. Another might function through powerful combinations of pictorial publications. And so, on and on, leaders who never would have achieved through personal responsibility and attainment the opportunity to agitate before the Nation would suddenly come to influence the whole people and their constituent and conflicting parts. And many, irresponsible, in places of responsibility for the first time, found eager opportunity to blossom into new egoistic complexes, symbolic of frustration and aggression, in the upper brackets of the Nation's democratic government as in the lower brackets of its invisible movements.

Here, again, it was a picture of the influence of power and of the impact of technology and ideology upon the people and their cultural heritages. It was an epoch in the public life commensurate with the power of science and technology in the immeasurable achievements of war. And so the flood tide of artificial influences often exceeded and transcended the logical processes of educational effort and of the growth and exercise of public opinion and the determining of public policy.

Something of the measure of all this could be seen from an examination of the records of what was being done and what had been done within the short span of this cross section of the American picture. Samplings were available to review the source materials for study; the annals of publications; the record of a million newspaper clippings; the bibliographies of the new articulate writers; the meetings of groups and the listening-in of millions. All these constituted a powerful tributary stream to the total rising flood tide of change and crisis as well as to the challenge as to what was to be done about it. What was the way on?

PART III

THE WAY ON

XX

The Way It Was

On the assumption that the South and the Nation, exclusive of the crisis of world war and survival, were facing their greatest crisis since the period a hundred years earlier, which led to the War between the States, there was urgent need for a critical analysis of the whole situation and for such realistic facing of facts as might turn the drama into a happy ending. There was needed more, however, than either the careful, scientific inventory of the facts or the dramatic presentation of crisis and tragedy in the making. There was needed a new high morale on the part of all the people everywhere as the first essential to the exercise of a great wisdom, a careful planning, and a master strategy for the better ordering of race relations in the war and post-war period. Could the South and the American people come quickly to grips with reality in such way as to master the situation?

An examination of the specific facts and situation through which the crisis was reflected showed clearly that the heart of the problem and the crisis was found essentially in the complexity of the situation, in the power of conflicting forces, in the psychology and hysteria of war, and in the societal pressure which sought to integrate all peoples and all areas into a common culture. More specifically, the explanation of the situation was twofold. The first was in the understanding of the evolutionary process of change going on in the South, in the Nation, and in the world with inevitable consequent changes in the culture and economy of the people, and in the attitudes, aspirations, and behavior of minority and racial groups. The second was in the impact of war with its hastening of societal change, its specific widening opportunities for occupational and educational opportunity, and the consequent power of federal authority and coercion, alongside the power of accelerated public opinion and agitation.

There was no longer time or place for the immature blaming of somebody, here and there, hither and yon, or the calling of names and the exercise of bitter denunciation, white against Negro, Negro against white, South against North, North against South. The situation had gone far beyond the point where the mere placing of blame was of any essential merit in the larger crisis of meeting a great national need. As a matter of fact, it was possible to come to such agreement concerning the blame in the situation as to enable all forces to take the next step, namely, to remedy the situation regardless of who was to blame.

For certainly the white South, as the picture of the recent tensions showed, might be said to have done almost everything that might lead to tensions and conflict and had done very little to prevent it. Yes, that was true, so what? How was it possible then for the South to make good in next steps, "forgetting the things of the past"?

The catalogue of episodes and behavior patterns was such as to be almost unbelievable if it had not been shown actually to be true. Well, if this was true, as it was, what of it? What was the next step in the light of this and in the light of a fair recognition by the South of a responsibility?

Certainly there were great mistakes, as it appeared from all the evidence, on the part of many of the overenthusiastic agitators and intellectuals, as well as many of the earlier communistic radicals and some Axis forces, the results of which ignored the facts of reality and were either oblivious or careless of the cost of the tragedy which follows the road of racial revolution. Here, again, the catalogue of attitudes, actions, recommendations, epithets reflects a situation which again would be unbelievable if it had not actually been true. Well, what of it? What were the next steps to be taken, especially in the light of the Nation's recognition of its responsibility and of the organic nature of the situation involved?

So, too, there was no doubt that both Negro leaders and the common mass of Negro folk had made inevitable mistakes. They appeared to be least to blame in general, but often specifically in between the pressure of the other groups afforded concrete instance and occasions for much of the conflict and tension. There was no doubt that in the upper brackets of the distinguished Negro leadership there had been few mistakes, and there had been a magnificent morale and leadership. Yet the picture showed an extraordinary attitude and level of racial attack on the part of the most radical Negro leaders and many of the Negro newspapers, which again might have appeared unbelievable to those who calmly and intellectually looked at it in later years. For there was practically a universal and unanimous attack upon all white leaders, North or South. With all that they had done, the Roosevelts were characterized as words, words, words. No matter what a southern liberal leader might have done, there were always bases for attack and satire and cynicism, so that both in the North and the South many white leaders were in a mood to give up, not knowing what else could be done.

Well, again, all of this was self-evident and well known. It was logical and inevitable, and it would be of the essence of immaturity to blame the Negro race for this period of transition or to justify the South or the rest of the Nation in their undemocratic and uncivilized reaction. The question again was what to do about it. What were the next steps regardless of where the blame might lie?

It was important, however, to be sure that the facts were known and rightly presented and portrayed, on whatever levels of attitude or approach or in whatever areas of conduct and reality, for it was early quite clear that rumors and opinions and dogmatic assertions and accusations constituted the basis and the beginning of much that was tragic and of much more that threatened to be more tragic. Just as in the preview to the presentation of the story of rumors, tensions, and conflict it was urged that the importance of the truth be emphasized, so, again, in looking to the future it was fundamental to ask at every turn and every stage of the problem: "What are the facts? What is the truth? Is this or that or the other true, and what other truths must be examined in relation to them?" Here again the catalogue of inaccuracies and misrepresentations and subterfuges reflects an unbelievable immaturity on the part of American leadership, which was presumed to be competent to discover scientific facts and to check them in relation to the problems in hand. So great was the importance of facts, the number of conflicting situations, and the confusion throughout the Nation that even after many studies had been made and the story of race conflict presented there was question as to whether the Nation did not still need a new and more comprehensive inventory of what had happened and what was happening in all the regions.

The main story, however, and the major area of tension were the South and its biracial culture, which had grown rapidly into a national as well as a regional crisis. It was important both in the understanding of the situation and in the directing of planning to take into consideration the complexity of the southern evolutionary development and of the war crisis.

In the first place, the South was itself an example of complex culture, symbolic of how all cultures grow. The South was essentially a culture of the folk, close to nature and close to the land. The power of nature and its nurture, in river valleys and mountain places, in the piney woods and cut-over lands, in all the episodes of cold and heat, storm, rain, drouth, had created a folk culture of distinctive quality. More specifically, the culture of the South was the culture of a folk, conditioned in their historical setting, through the influence of slavery, the Civil War, and its reconstruction period. To the age-long accumulation of race prejudice the South had become so conditioned to race as class and caste as to reflect the racial situation as supreme over all others, a symbol of survival and of life and death. To this had been added the irresistible force of a people who had made their *folkways* of race coincide with their *stateways* and legislation of race segregation.

There was then the whole social complex resulting from the destruction of the South's earlier culture economy and the tragic consequence of its having been subjected by coercion for a short time to the political domination of its former slaves. It was beginning to be clearer to a larger number of people that the passing of laws and the writing of resolutions alone was a superficial approach to such an organic problem of universal culture. No matter what the verdict of right or wrong might be, the problem was one of universal folk culture.

There were other aspects of the evolutionary, cultural development which were more specifically pertinent to the racial crisis of the early forties. This was to be found in the natural cultural change and evolution which were taking place in the South and in the Nation in the wake of increasing technology, widening education and communication, and changing economy. There were some aspects of the changing economy which were reminiscent of what had happened a hundred years earlier in the 1840's. At that time it might have been shown that the plantation economy and slave culture were not only being outmoded in the development of world democracy, but that the plantation system itself was unsound economically and would break down of its own weight. Such a recognition, it has been pointed out often, if implemented into realistic action and wisdom might have avoided the tragedy of the war of brothers, stranger and more terrible than fiction.

In the early 1940's there were a number of aspects of the changing southern economy growing out of evolutionary development, which were later made the basis for a great deal of racial rumor, conflict, and tension in the South's protest against change. In the first place, a chief point of tension was in the radical undermining of the domestic economy of the southern family, where millions of Negro women, as domestic servants, were organically part and parcel of the way of life of the southern women and the southern family. Through the evolutionary development and through the peculiar incidents of war that economy had been practically completely destroyed. No longer were Negro women subject to the beck and call of the white family. No longer could help be had even at wages which seemed exorbitant to the southern housewife. And especially no longer was the Negro woman available at nominal wages supplemented by the left-overs of food and raiment. That economy was no longer tenable either on the basis of occupational opportunity for Negro women or on the basis of their own ideals of personality and family life. That was a major revolution, and there were no longer anywhere in the South any "niggers" to do the work. It never was customary for any people or culture to take lightly the breaking down of a long cherished tradition or way of life.

So, too, in the workaday world where the Negro man had so long been the pillar upon which rested the manual labor on farm and in city there had come about a similar revolution. No longer were Negroes available at will to do whatever work the white man wanted done at whatever price. Millions of those who had worked long and faithfully in the same positions were suddenly caught up in the floodtide of new opportunity and new dreams for a better world, which transcended the old ideals of loyalty to employer or the white man. Here, again, it was an occupational opportunity of a changing economy, and the attitude of the Negro towards his work and personality which combined to shake the foundations of the old labor economy of the South. The old southern acclaim that "to those who want to work we give work; those who do not we put on the chain gang or shoot them" was no longer valid, although sometimes it was still vociferously echoed by some southerners whose chorus was, "We never have any trouble with Negroes. They know what to do and do it."

Then there was another very important evolutionary change. The Negro himself had changed tremendously. It was not only that he had developed an important upper and middle class; it was not only that he had developed a magnificent leadership and thousands had received higher educational opportunities. It was not only that Negro youth, sensing the epochal spiritual change and racial attitudes and led by Negro leadership of the North and South was minded to experiment with every type of equal opportunity; it was all this and more. It was as if some universal message had come through to the great mass of Negroes, urging them to dream new dreams and to protest against the old order. It was as if there were pathos and tragedy in their misunderstanding of the main tenets of a bitter Negro leadership, and as if many of the Negro leaders of limited mentality had confused them with the idea that any sort of work or courtesy or cheerfulness was an index of subservience to the white man. In all of this, whether it was pathos and tragedy or admirable idealism and noble effort, the net result was the new Negro facing the old white man. The passing of laws and violence here could no more stem this tide than could the passing of laws and coercion change overnight the attitude and will of the white South. The facts were as they were.

In the years of evolution and change there was also a new type of behavior among the youth of the white South. Strangely enough, this was of a twofold kind, often trending in opposite directions. There were the college youth of the South, both men and women, often sensing the new responsibility for the South towards the Negro and frankly advocating new reaches in the economic and cultural opportunities of the Negro. Many of them, like the Negro youth, experimented with the broader approach to more nearly equal opportunities of the two races. If many of the Negro youth, men and women, interpreted the broader viewpoint of white youth and the social customs of using more familiar salutation in terms of given names as being a new invitation and new achievement on the level of social equality, it was but a logical conclusion which youth of any other race would have reached. But whatever the nature and cause, it was clear that there was a new behavior here and one that was almost inevitably bound to bring some tragedy in its wake. It was in reality symbol of evolutionary change.

On the other hand, there was evident, especially in the wake of rumors, tensions, and conflicts of the early forties, what appeared to be a trend in the opposite direction. Millions of young southern whites on farms and in factories, as they drove taxicabs and as they drove busses, and as they went to war and as they worked in munitions plants, appeared to revive the old symptoms of race dominance and perhaps hatred. Their chief refrain was perhaps: "These Negroes think they can act like white folks. Well, we'll show 'em." "No Negro, spoiled up North, can come down South and act like white folks." "As long as the 'nigger' stays in his place I am for him, but no law is going to keep me from making him stay in his place." One surprising fact was the large number of youth in community race riots or minor conflicts.

This seeming retrogressive behavior on the part of some southern white youth in conflict with the behavior of Negro youth, some of them more highly educated, was resulting in what appeared to be little short of real hatred between the two groups. This was a particularly tragic situation, because it had been customary for white leaders to place great faith in the new generation of southerners. "Just wait," they would say, "until the next generation comes along, and everything will work out." "But would it?" they were beginning to re-ask themselves. Here, again, the complexity of the situation was of the essence of the problem which demanded wise strategy.

Finally, in this evolutionary aspect of the problem, the world, and races in particular, had changed a great deal, this change becoming more articulate in the early 1940's. It was not only that the professions of world democracy which had grown out of a world war had brought to the surface the great problem of minority peoples and races. It was not only that the charters of freedom which were being advocated throughout the world had featured the liberation of minority and enslaved peoples. It was not only that the Negro leaders themselves had made great advance and were more articulate in their demand for complete equality of opportunity. It was all of these and more. It was as if a new epoch had reflected the results of science in the study of peoples and their environment. It was as if science and technology had suddenly offered to all the peoples of the world new reaches and equipment and opportunity. And it was as if the cumulative trend of education and religion throughout the world, exclusive of the racial and nationalistic reaction of the Axis powers, had suddenly liberated the minds and spirits of races everywhere. There was a new race consciousness which would be heard. This, too, was an inevitable product of evolution and was an essential part of the American scene.

There had been also great changes in the general economy and culture of the South, many of which affected the Negro. No longer primarily a farmer and rural dweller, he had migrated to the cities in great numbers. The industrialization of the South, on the other hand, had not provided him with his ratio of first-class employment, and there had developed consequent problems of unemployment, congested centers, and certain criminal tendencies. The cotton economy of the South was no longer so completely dominant in a better balanced economy, and the number and status of the tenant farmer had changed. Many Negroes had bought farms and the Negro tenant farmer, alongside the white tenant, had been made the special object of New Deal efforts. There had been important developments with reference to the Negro and labor unions, membership in which had become one of the points of issue and conflict, as well as one of the points of reported progress.

More specifically, the Negro had made great advances in education. This had not only multiplied many times the number of Negroes who were better educated, but the influence of the educated Negro and his educational leaders had been profound in the changing attitudes of Negro youth and of many of the Negro common folks. Thus, for instance, Negro college education had been growing nearly four times as fast as the total school enrollment. Since 1900 the children in American high schools had increased twelve times while Negro students had increased about forty times. Especially significant was the development of Negro colleges in the South and the extent to which they conformed to the standard requirements of American colleges. And it was noteworthy that the majority of the most distinguished Negro scholars and educators were in southern institutions. It was true also that the great mass of southern white folk was little aware of the great strides which the Negro had made in education and the resulting development of the Negro's estimate of his place in the scheme of things and of his new self-esteem.

Now these and other natural developments in an age of science, speed, technology, and change had, as logical and normal products of the evolutionary process, already set the stage for readjustments which would be unusually difficult. Then came the war with all its attendant circumstances to provide the specific incidence through which the sweep of rumors, tensions, and conflict was greatly accelerated. In the search for the answers to what had happened and what was best to be done, it was important to understand that the war was not the essential cause, but the incidence and the occasion for much of what happened. Post-war planning and procedures, therefore, would have to take all this into account.

Certain general conclusions with reference to the influence of the war seemed apparent. In the first place, there was the rise and contagion of rumors all over the country, long before the special flood tide of southern rumors arose. The Gallup Poll, the Boston Rumor Clinic, the Philadelphia Clinic, and other avenues of inquiry revealed not only thousands of rumors, but many of the same sort that later centered around the Negro were also told with other applications. Many of the rumors about the Eleanor Clubs and the ice picks, for instance, were heard in the East almost simultaneously with those in the South. So, too, the famous New England rumor about Negro soldiers' mutiny on the Normandie antedated many of the southern rumors about the Negro.

What rumors could do and did do in the atmosphere of war psychology was all too well illustrated in all parts of the country. In Washington, the rumor that there would be an uprising of Negroes set a whole city, capital of the world, as it were, agog with excitement. It was reported that all the offices of all government agencies had received word of the uprising and many of them advised their women employees to get along home early and keep out of the way of danger. Telephones rang, White House and congressional folk clamored to know what was to be done to avoid trouble, search was made for the basic facts of rumors, and, all told, the police and military as well as the civil public were ready for emergency which never developed.

The Detroit riots had at least a part of their momentum in the mere rumor that the white people had killed a Negro mother and her child. The Beaumont, Texas, riots were fanned by the story of a white woman being raped, which later proved to be rumor only. In New Orleans, the whole city, for the most part, including the police, was on the alert for perhaps nearly two days because of the rumor that the Negroes would rush the theatres, restaurants, streetcars, and other areas of segregation.

Then the war had a number of very specific influences upon the South and the Negro. It would have been difficult to list them in their priority of time or influence, and perhaps that was not necessary. Yet, in general, war did set the incidence for what was to come in many instances, samplings of which helped to tell the story.

First were the needs and demands of the war for all-out effort in the areas of work and the armed forces and their allied activities. Here was demand for all those who would work and were qualified either to do the work or train for it. The result was a new and widening opportunity for the Negro at new and higher wages. The rush of Negroes to meet this need and opportunity resulted in the disturbed economy which has already been portrayed as the basis of perhaps the largest number of rumors.

Then the same broad provisions for making available opportunity for Negro workers in governmental services also provided the government with its opportunity to supervise conditions, to impose standards of hours and pay, and to oppose segregation and differentials. This, then, was the basis for conflict, some of which had already been set up by the New Deal regulations against racial discrimination. The emergency of war and the desire of the South to stand by, together with the call of patriotism, for several months led the South to cooperate more fully than it would have done otherwise. The later reaction was perhaps for this reason more violent and subject to the demagogic appeal of certain southern forces and personalities.

Then there was the major factor of Negro troops being stationed in the South where provisions for their accommodation on the biracial level had not been adequate, even for southern Negro soldiers. More specifically then Negro soldiers from other regions were sent South where it was inevitable that they protest the segregation and discrimination to such effect as to cause conflict. War again was reflecting the spectacle of one American soldier fighting another American soldier with the consequent sweep of stories, rumors, and bitterness.

So, too, there were thousands and hundreds of thousands of the whites in the armed forces, and their wives, who came from other regions to experience the South's biracial culture with the resulting criticisms, antagonisms, and bitterness which were often basic to the spread of stories and rumors. All of these, again, became occasion for the new discovery of the South to which we have referred and the seeming utter incapacity of the folk from other regions to understand the South.

Then came the flood of criticisms and accusations and what the South was accustomed to characterize as unjustified interference and coercion. Prominent among those who irritated the South most were the earlier Communists, the later editorial writers and agitators, and the extremist Negro leaders who developed a crusade for equality which appeared as an epic sort of thing, with its chief level of attack an uncompromising denunciation and bitterness. One result was that the South misunderstood and mistrusted most of the great Negro leaders who tried to achieve the best possible results.

Then came the extraordinary sweep of rumors and bitterness against the First Lady, whose efforts throughout the Nation toward the amelioration of the lot of the unfortunate or the disinherited or the minorities led her into the main picture of the South and its biracial culture. Here, again, from the earlier days of her visit to the Southern Conference on Human Welfare to the famous Nashville incidents, and later, she had become symbol to the South of racial equality and of outside interference. Here again was occasion and incidence, not cause, of the extraordinary behavior of the South, forgetful of its chivalry and manners. The fact that Mrs. Roosevelt's interregional manners were beyond reproach did not change the situation, although as time went on more and more southern people became ashamed of their South's behavior here.

Finally, the concrete incidents of friction, violence, misunderstandings, and misbehavior provided, in the aggregate, a powerful cumulative basis for rumors, stories, denunciation, threats, and crisis. The story had been portrayed over and over again, in sufficient detail to make clear how the crisis arose and developed and the need for meeting it regardless of the cause. Yet, in order to be able to sense the total situation as it actually was, with a view to stable adjustment, it was necessary to review again and again something of the actual fact basis for many of the rumors. And here again was drama being enacted on a great cultural stage with powerful actors and extraordinary stage properties.

It was not possible to catalogue the total accumulation of tensions, conflict, and violence because no man counted them, no man could. Yet there had been ample recordings to lead to such conclusions as "the United States stands frozen and paralyzed before its Negro problem" and "As matters are developing . . . the attitude . . . whether intentionally or not . . . is tending to produce a race war." And again, "If it is not intentional and the war occurs as a sort of mass accident, the tragedy will be absolute."

The samplings which justified those conclusions and many others like them and which set the stage included, in addition to the great body of rumors recorded, also an extraordinary body of facts. Was it true that:

There were race riots of major proportions in the major regions of the Nation: North, East, South, West, and Far West. Yes, that was true.

There were conflicts and episodes of violence in camps and camp cities where Negro and white were in training. Yes, that was true, too.

There were uncounted incidents and episodes of individual violence to members of the armed services. Yes, including homicides.

There were numerous incidents of threatened revolt and riot on the part of Negro men in training in various parts of the Nation. Yes, almost wherever they were not accorded adequate facilities.

There were uncounted incidents of violence and conflict between white civilians and Negroes. Yes, regardless of who was to blame, a disgraceful record.

There were uncounted incidents of violence and brutality on the part of local and state law enforcement officers. Yes, a new pattern of "taking care of the Negro."

Did Negro soldiers sometimes attack white military police? Yes, they did.

Did Negroes sometimes attack white citizens and occasionally women? Yes, they did.

Did white civilians sometimes attack Negro soldiers? Yes, they did.

Did white soldiers sometimes attack Negro soldiers? Yes, they did.

Was it true that there were threats on both sides? Yes, that was true, too.

Was the long catalogue of rumors and stories that provided the basic materials for the crisis as portrayed an exception? No, the half had not been told.

There were then the resulting attitudes of the people in the South and in the Nation, adequate samplings of which were presented in the chronicles of rumors, stories, and tensions; in the story of what had been done or attempted; and in the portraiture of the rising tide of crisis. Yet it was important, in sensing the cultural drama of the South and the Nation, to reemphasize some of the resulting attitudes and status of the people everywhere.

There was extraordinary ignorance on the part of the white South concerning the culture, personalities, and general progress of the Negro.

Accordingly, there was extraordinary distance between the white South and the upper brackets of Negro leadership.

There was extraordinary ignorance on the part of the rest of the Nation concerning both the Negro and the South in most of its areas of life and work.

There was a considerable trend in the South for the policies and actions of law enforcement officers to coincide with the folkways to keep the Negro in his place.

The stateways and legislation were again being made to coincide with the powerful folkways of race in an irresistible solid front.

There was an increasing trend outside the South to alter the southern biracial culture.

There was an ever-increasing trend on the part of the Negro to resist the folkways and to get "out of his place."

And in this logical and laudable ambition, there was the chief pattern of impatience, of refusing to admit limitations, and of failure to assume the normal obligations that go with the striving for equality and fraternity.

There was then the resulting trend toward conflict and race war which had been portrayed and which had alarmed so many observers throughout the Nation.

In the aggregate of public opinion there were some who felt that irresponsible agitation of race conflict was approaching the point of treason. They felt that the results of irresponsible agitation, to see the fireworks, as it were, were the same as in the case when the trouble was Axis inspired.

Many felt that great unfairness to the Negro was involved in the fantastic demands for universal change by presidential edict, regardless of whether the way had been prepared.

To advocate special privilege for the Negro who was, without his being responsible, not expected to conform to the processes of growth and development essential for achievement and qualification, was, they thought, especially unfortunate for the Negro.

Many felt that the emphasis should be placed upon

realistic work: preparing the Negro for his great opportunity, insuring more nearly adequate facilities for the Negroes in camps and industrial cities, rather than upon talk and denunciation. More and better housing, better transportation facilities, and other accommodations, a greater participation in all cultural and economic life, they thought, would help a lot in avoiding race riots.

These and other conclusions, however, would be embodied in the story of what was being done about the total situation.

XXI

What Was Being Done About It

In the total portraiture of what was to be done there were two main pictures. One was the story of what had actually been undertaken and attempted. The other was the projection of conclusions, gained from total observations, somewhat into the future. Was it possible for the South and the Nation to achieve certain mastery over the situation? What was the most and the best that could be done? What was the way to enduring adjustments and progress? Was there any happy medium or any medium through which understanding and action might go hand in hand?

In the story of what had been done and what was being attempted, there were again two parts. One was the catalogue of what had been done and attempted in the years between the first World War and the second. The other was the story of special efforts which had been made during the period of crisis portrayed in this story of 1942–1943.

Once again, there were two aspects of the background picture which set the stage for later special activities. One was the experiences of the first World War and what happened then. The other was the experience of the depression period of the 1930's and of the multiple efforts toward social reconstruction. How those efforts affected the Negro and his relation to the South and the Nation was an essential part of the picture.

There was a crisis in race relations following the first World War which had many of the characteristics of the trend toward crisis in the first years of America's entrance into the second World War. That is, there were many rumors of Negro uprisings and much fear of what returning Negro soldiers would do. Some of the rumors were as unreasonable and fantastic as those of the second war. There were two chief differences. One was that the rumors in the first war were never so numerous and of such wide variety. The other was that the rumors were later in developing and tended to focus upon post-war dangers. Nevertheless, there was much of the same pattern of fear and of seeking ways to outflank the dangers that seemed to be gathering force. There was a third difference in that at that time the Negro and the Nation had not become so articulate in the demand for equal opportunity. The base of the rumor structure was, therefore, much narrower.

From this experience, however, there grew up the Commission on Interracial Cooperation, whose work stamped it as one of the most distinctive and effective movements in the annals of the Nation. Essentially its methods provided for interracial committees in all the southern states and in as many local communities as possible. The objectives were to promote better understanding and relationship through the meeting of members of both races on common grounds of mutual interest and welfare. Later there were studies and research into the chief points of tension, publication for educational purposes, and efforts for the protection of civil rights and the promotion of greater opportunity for the Negro in all aspects of life. As the years went by, the Commission, originally acclaimed "radical," came to be regarded by the great majority of Negroes as being too conservative to meet needs.

There had been, therefore, a number of attempts to broaden the Commission's work and organization into a region-wide council on southern development, in which the Negro's part was given its organic place in all aspects. Over against this attempt to build an over-all regional agency which would strive to achieve desired results in all aspects of the southern economy and culture, the Southern Conference on Human Welfare was set in motion, its genesis being outside the South and its methods following somewhat the patterns of many of the more emotional reform organizations.

During the year of this story there were, exclusive of governmental programs, several other major efforts. The first was a special study of the Interracial Commission and exploration of the possibilities of its strengthening its work and its influence. The results of those efforts still awaited the results of three other special efforts. The first of these was the Durham Conference of leading Negroes and their notable statement. The second was a similar Atlanta Conference. A third was a collaborating conference of both groups at Richmond. The findings of these were exhibits in the total picture to be supplemented by a continuing committee to meet in Atlanta in the effort to adopt a charter of race relations and seek ways to implement it in practical work.

The Durham Conference

The findings of the Durham Conference were published as a statement by southern Negroes, entitled "A Basis for Interracial Cooperation and Development in the South":

"The war has sharpened the issue of Negro-white relations in the United States, and particularly in the South. A result has been increased racial tensions, fears, and aggressions, and an opening up of the basic questions of racial segregation and discrimination, Negro minority rights, and democratic freedom, as they apply practically in Negro-white relations in the South. These issues are acute and threaten to become even more serious as they increasingly block, through the deeper fears aroused, common sense consideration for even elementary improvements in Negro status, and the welfare of the country as a whole.

"With these problems in mind, we, a group of southern Negroes, realizing that the situation calls for both candor and wisdom, and in the belief that we voice the sentiments of many of the Negroes of the Nation as well as the South, take this means of recording our considered views of the issues before us.

1. Our Nation is engaged in a world-wide struggle, the success of which, both in arms and ideals, is paramount and demands our first loyalty.

2. Our loyalty does not, in our view, preclude consideration now of problems and situations that handicap the working out of internal improvements in race relations essential to our full contribution to the war effort, and of the inevitable problems of post-war reconstruction, especially in the South where we reside.

3. The South, with its twenty-five million people, one-third of whom are Negroes, presents a unique situation, not only because of the size of the Negro population but because of the legal and customary patterns of race relations which are invariably and universally associated with racial discriminations. We recognize the strength and age of these patterns.

We are fundamentally opposed to the principle and practice of compulsory segregation in our American society, whether of races or classes or creeds; however, we regard it as both sensible and timely to address ourselves now to the current problems of racial discrimination and neglect, and to ways in which we may cooperate in the advancement of programs aimed at the sound improvement of race relations within the democratic framework.

4. We regard it as unfortunate that the simple efforts to correct obvious social and economic injustices continue, with such considerable popular support, to be interpreted as the predatory ambition of irresponsible Negroes to invade the privacy of family life.

5. We have the courage and faith to believe, however, that it is possible to evolve in the South a way of life, consistent with the principle for which we as a Nation are fighting throughout the world, that will free us all, white and Negro alike, from want, and from throttling fears.

POLITICAL AND CIVIL RIGHTS

"1. We regard the ballot as a safeguard of democracy. Any discrimination against citizens in the exercise of the voting privilege, on account of race or poverty, is detrimental to the freedom of these citizens and to the integrity of the State. We therefore record ourselves as urging now:

a. The abolition of the poll tax as a prerequisite to voting.

b. The abolition of the white primary.

c. The abolition of all forms of discriminatory practices, evasions of the law, and intimidations of citizens seeking to exercise their right of franchise.

2. Exclusion of Negroes from jury service because of race has been repeatedly declared unconstitutional. This practice we believe can and should be discontinued now.

3. a. Civil rights include personal security against abuses of police power by white officers of the law. These abuses, which include wanton killings, and almost routine beatings of Negroes, whether they be guilty or innocent of an offense, should be stopped now, not only out of regard for the safety of Negroes, but of common respect for the dignity and fundamental purpose of the law.

b. It is the opinion of this group that the employment of Negro police will enlist the full support of Negro citizens in control of lawless elements of their own group.

4. In the public carriers and terminals, where segregation of the races is currently made mandatory by law as well as by established custom, it is the duty of Negro and white citizens to insist that these provisions be equal in kind and quality and in character of maintenance.

5. Although there has been, over the years, a decline in lynchings, the practice is still current in some areas of the South, and substantially, even if indirectly, defended by resistance to Federal legislation designed to discourage the practice. We ask that the States discourage this fascistic expression by effective enforcement of present or of new laws against this crime by apprehending and punishing parties participating in this lawlessness.

If the States are unable, or unwilling to do this, we urge the support of all American citizens who believe in law and order in securing Federal legislation against lynching.

6. The interests and securities of Negroes are involved directly in many programs of social planning and administration; in the emergency rationing, wage and rent control programs. We urge the use of qualified Negroes on these boards, both as a means of intelligent representation and a realistic aid to the functioning of these bodies.

INDUSTRY AND LABOR

"Continuing opposition to the employment of Negroes in certain industries appears to proceed from (1) the outdated notions of an economy of scarcity, inherited from an industrial age when participation in the productive enterprises was a highly competitive privilege; (2) the effects of enemy propaganda designed to immobilize a large number of potentially productive workers in the American war effort; (3) the age-old prejudices from an era when the economic system required a labor surplus which competed bitterly within its own ranks for the privilege of work; (4) the established custom of reserving technical processes to certain racial groups; and (5) craft monopolies which have restricted many technical skills to a few workers.

"Our collective judgment regarding industrial opportunities for Negroes may be summarized as follows:

1. The only tenable basis of economic survival and development for Negroes is inclusion in unskilled, semi-skilled and skilled branches of work in the industries or occupations of the region to the extent that they are equally capable. Circumstances will vary so as to make impossible and impracticable any exact numerical balance, but the principles enunciated by the President's Fair Employment Practices Committee are regarded by us as sound and economically essential.

2. There should be the same pay for the same work.

3. Negro workers should seek opportunities for collective bargaining and security through membership in labor organizations. Since there can be no security for white workers if Negroes are unorganized and vice versa, labor unions of white workers should seek the organization of Negro workers, on a fair and equal basis.

4. We deplore the practice of those labor unions which bar Negroes from membership, or otherwise discriminate against them, since such unions are working against the best interest of the labor movement. We hold that only those labor unions which admit Negroes to membership and participation on a fair and democratic basis should be eligible for the benefits of the National Labor Relations Board, Railway Labor Act, State Labor Relations Acts and other protective labor legislation.

5. It is the duty of local, state and federal agencies to insist upon and enforce provisions for the industrial training of Negroes equal in quality and kind with that of other citizens. We believe, further, that Negroes should have equal opportunity in training programs carried on by industries and by labor organizations.

6. We urge Negro representation on regional organizations concerned with the welfare of workers.

7. We regard the wage-and-job-freezing order of the War Manpower Commission as holding the seeds of a distinct disadvantage to Negroes and other marginal workers. Most of these workers are now employed in the lowest-income job brackets. The 'freeze' order can remove the opportunity for economic advancement. There is as yet no assurance that under existing circumstances the War Manpower Commission can deal more equitably by the Negro in the future than it has in the past.

8. We are convinced that the South's economic and cultural development can be accelerated by increasing the purchasing power and skills of Negro workers.

SERVICE OCCUPATIONS

"Any realistic estimate of the occupational situation of Negroes supports the view that Negroes will be employed in greatest proportion for a long time in service occupations. We see, however, possibilities of making of these fields scientifically guided areas in which training and organization will play a greater part in bringing about results mutually beneficial to employer and employee. We believe that greater service will be rendered and greater good will be engendered in the service fields if the following principles are observed:

1. More thorough training should be provided workers who plan to enter the service field, but the reward of the job

and treatment on the job should be such as to make the workers feel that their training is justified. Opportunity should be given the service worker to advance through the opening up of additional opportunities.

2. A wholesome environment, living accommodations, food, uniforms and rest rooms, all of an approved standard, should be provided service workers.

3. Opportunity should be given the service worker to live, after his stipulated hours of work, as an individual undisturbed in his private life by the whims and caprices of his employers.

4. In view of the strides made by labor in general, while the service worker's lot has remained about the same, service workers should be organized into unions with recognized affiliations.

5. Service workers should be included in the provisions for old age insurance, unemployment compensation, workmen's compensation, the wage and hour act, and other benefits of Social Security legally provided to workers of other categories.

We believe that these provisions will help to insure some intelligent service and wholesome loyalty (which will improve both the quality of labor and personal relations) in service occupations.

EDUCATION

"As equal opportunity for all citizens is the very foundation of the democratic faith, and of the Christian ethic which gave birth to the ideal of democratic living, it is imperative that every measure possible be taken to insure an equality of education to Negroes, and, indeed to all underprivileged peoples.

1. Basic to improvement in Negro education is better

schools, which involves expenditures by States of considerably more funds for the Negro schools. This group believes that a minimum requirement now is (a) equalization of salaries of white and Negro teachers on the basis of equal preparation and experience; (b) an expanded school building program for Negro schools designed to overcome the present racial disparity in physical facilities; this program to begin as soon as building materials are available; (c) revision of the school program in terms of the social setting, vocational needs and marginal cultural characteristics of the Negro children; and (d) the same length of school term for all children in local communities. Our growing knowledge of the effect of environment upon the intelligence and social adjustment of children, in fact leads us to believe that to insure equality of educational opportunity it is not enough to provide for the underprivileged child, of whatever race, the same opportunities provided for those on superior levels of familial, social, and economic life. We feel it a function of Government to assure equalization far beyond the mere expenditure of equivalent funds for salaries and the like.

2. The education of Negroes in the South has reached the point at which there is increased demand for graduate and professional training. This group believes that this training should be made available equally for white and Negro eligible students in terms defined by the United States Supreme Court in the decision on the case of Gaines versus the University of Missouri.

3. Where it is established that States cannot sustain the added cost of equalization, Federal funds should be made available to overcome the differentials between white and Negro facilities and between southern and national standards.

4. It is the belief of this group that the special problems of Negro education make demands for intelligent and sym-

pathetic representation of these problems on school boards by qualified persons of the Negro race.

5. The education of Negro youth can be measurably aided by the use of Negro enforcement officers of truancy and compulsory education laws.

AGRICULTURE

"The South is the most rural section of the Nation, and Negroes, who constitute 33 per cent of its population, are responsible for an important share of the agricultural production on southern farms.

"We recognize that the South is economically handicapped and that many of its disabilities are deeply rooted in agricultural maladjustments. To win the war, there is need for increased production of food, fibre and fats. In the present organization of agriculture, Negroes are a large part of the sharecropper and tenant group and a great majority of the rural Negro workers are in this class. Circumstances deny the Negro farmer sufficient opportunity to make his full contribution as a citizen. We suggest the following measures as means of increasing the production of the area, raising the status and spirits of Negro farmers, and of improving the region's contribution to the total war effort.

1. Establishment of sufficient safeguards in the system of tenancy to promote the development of land and home ownership and more security on the land, by:

    a. Written contracts

    b. Longer lease terms

    c. Higher farm wages for day laborers

    d. Balanced farm programs, including food and feed crops for present tenants and day laborers.

2. Adequate Federal assistance to Negro farmers should be provided on an equitable basis. The war effort can be

materially aided if adequate provisions are made now for the interpretation of governmental policies to rural Negroes.

3. The equitable distribution of funds for teaching agriculture in the Negro land grant colleges to provide agricultural research and experimentation for Negro farmers.

4. The appointment of qualified Negroes to governmental planning and policy making bodies concerned with the common farmer, and the membership of Negro farmers in general farmers' organizations and economic cooperatives, to provide appropriate representation and to secure maximum benefits to our common wealth.

MILITARY SERVICE

"We recognize and welcome the obligation of every citizen to share in the military defense of the nation and we seek, along with the privilege of offering our lives, the opportunity of other citizens of full participation in all branches of the military service, and of advancement in responsibility and rank according to ability.

"Negro soldiers, in line of military duty and in training in the South, encounter particularly acute racial problems in transportation and in recreation and leave areas. They are frequently mistreated by the police. We regard these problems as unnecessary and destructive to morale.

SOCIAL WELFARE AND HEALTH

"1. We believe that some of the more acute problems of Negro health, family and personal disorganization are a reflection of deficiencies in economic opportunity, but that social and health services for Negroes will continue to be necessary in considerable amounts even with improvement of their economic status. As a means of reducing the mortality and public contagion resulting from inadequacies of medical attention and health knowledge, this group believes that minimum health measures for Negroes would include the following:

a. Mandatory provisions that a proportion of the facilities in all public hospitals be available for Negro patients;

b. That Negro doctors be either included on the staff for services to Negro patients, according to their special qualifications, or permitted as practitioners the same privilege and courtesy as other practitioners in the public hospitals;

c. That Negro public health nurses and social workers be more extensively used in both public and private organizations.

2. We advocate the extension of slum clearance and erection of low-cost housing as a general as well as special group advantage. The Federal government has set an excellent precedent here with results that offer much promise for the future.

"It is a wicked notion that the struggle of the Negro for citizenship is a struggle against the best interests of the Nation. To urge such a doctrine, as many are doing, is to preach disunity and to deny the most elementary principles of American life and government.

"The effect of the war has been to make the Negro, in a sense, the symbol and protagonist of every other minority in America and in the world at large. Local issues in the South, while admittedly holding many practical difficulties, must be met wisely and courageously if this Nation is to become a significant political entity in a new international world. The correction of these problems is not only a moral matter, but a practical necessity in winning the war and in winning the peace. Herein rests the chance to reveal our greatest weakness or our greatest strength."

THE ATLANTA CONFERENCE

The conclusions of the Atlanta Conference, composed of southern whites, tended to feature and approve the Durham statement:

"In October, 1942, a representative group of Southern Negro leaders met in Durham, N. C., and issued a statement in which they addressed themselves 'to the current problems of racial discrimination and neglect, and to ways in which we may cooperate in the advancement of programs aimed at the sound improvement of race relations, within the democratic framework.'

"Their statement is so frank and courageous, so free from any suggestion of threat and ultimatum, and at the same time shows such good will, that we gladly agree to cooperate.

"We do not attempt to make here anything like a complete reply to the questions raised nor to offer solutions for all the vexing problems. We hope, however, to point the pathway for future cooperative efforts and to give assurance of our sincere good will and desire to cooperate in any sound program aimed at the improvement of race relations.

"These Negro leaders rightly placed emphasis in their statement on discrimination in the administration of our laws on purely racial grounds. We are sensitive to this charge and admit that it is essentially just. From the Potomac to the Rio Grande there are some ten million Negroes. While all citizens are governed by the same laws, it is recognized that Negroes have little voice in the making and enforcement of the laws under which they must live. They are largely dependent upon the will of the majority group for the safety of life and property, education and health, and their general economic condition. This is a violation of the spirit of democracy. No Southerner can logically dispute the fact that the

Negro, as an American citizen, is entitled to his civil rights and economic opportunities.

"The race problem in any Southern community is complicated by our economic limitations. The factors which have kept the South a tributary section have also kept it poor and lacking in sufficient industry to develop and to provide enough jobs and enough public funds for every public need. Yet the only justification offered for those laws which have for their purpose the separation of the races is that they are intended to minister to the welfare and integrity of both races. There has been widespread and inexcusable discrimination in the administration of these laws. The white Southerner has an obligation to interest himself in the legitimate aspirations of the Negro. This means correcting the discrimination between the races in the allocation of school funds; in the number and quality of schools and in the salaries of teachers. In public travel where the law demands a separation of the races, primary justice and a simple sense of fair play demand the facilities for safety, comfort and health should be equal. The distribution of public utilities and public benefits, such as sewers, water, housing, street and sidewalk paving, playgrounds, public health and hospital facilities should come to the Negro upon the basis of population and need.

"It is recognized that there is often practical discrimination by some peace officers and in some courts in the treatment of Negro prisoners and in the abrogation of their civil rights. There is no such discrimination incorporated in the laws of any of the Southern states. False arrests, brutal beatings and other evils must be stopped.

"In the economic field, unquestionably procedures should be undertaken to establish fully the right to receive equal pay for equal work. To do otherwise works a wrong to our entire economic life and to our self respect. With so large a proportion of our wage-earning population belonging to the minority race, if we cannot plan for a well-trained, well-employed and prosperous Negro population, the economic future of the South is hopeless.

"Most of the Negroes in the South are on farms and in rural communities. Failure to provide for them all the facilities for improving agricultural practices through schools, county agents, and supervision holds back all of the South. Fair wages, longer tenures of leases and increased opportunities for farm ownership are also necessary.

"All men who believe in justice, who love peace and who believe in the meaning of this country are under the necessity of working together to draw off from the body of human society the poison of racial antagonism. This is one of the disruptive forces which unless checked will ultimately disturb and threaten the stability of the nation. Either to deny or to ignore the increased tension between the white and the colored races would be a gesture of insincerity.

"That there are acute and intricate problems associated with two races living side by side in the South cannot be denied. But these problems can be solved and will ultimately disappear if they are brought out into an atmosphere of justice and good will. If we approach them with contempt in one group and with resentment in the other group, then we work on hopeless terms. The solution of these problems can be found only in men of both races who are known to be men of determined good will. The ultimate solution will be found in evolutionary methods and not in ill-founded revolutionary movements which promise immediate solutions.

"We agree with the Durham Conference that it is 'unfortunate that the simple efforts to correct obvious social and economic injustices continue, with such considerable popular support, to be interpreted as the predatory ambition of irresponsible Negroes to invade the privacy of family life.' We agree also that 'it is a wicked notion that the struggle by the Negro for citizenship is a struggle against the best interests of the nation. To urge such a doctrine, as many are doing, is to preach disunity, and to deny the most elementary principles of American life and government.'

"It is futile to imagine or to assert that the problem will solve itself. The need is for a positive program arrived at in an atmosphere of understanding, cooperation and a mutual respect."

The Richmond Meeting

The results of the Richmond meeting were twofold. One was a joint resolution and the other was the appointment of a Continuing Committee. The resolution:

"This is a day of great differences, strong feelings, and epochal conflicts throughout the world. Yet the world's greatest need and hope is to find common ground for universal action and balanced harmony among all peoples. Manifestly, such a goal must be reached through cooperative approximation to the largest measure of agreement in line with the largest number of values and the largest number of people.

"We face, therefore, the double crisis of standing firm for the conservation and preservation of human rights; yet to seek these ends by the way of peace and planning rather than by conflict and revolution.

"In America, and particularly in the South, we face the problem of readjustments to meet the demands of present and post-war conditions with reference to the Negro and the future development of a great region of the Nation. This, exclusive of the war, is the greatest crisis of the South and Nation.

"This is the problem of two great peoples caught up in the midst of transition between the powerful heritage of the past and the mighty pull of the future. For here is the white

South, a *great* people often doing little things and good people often doing *bad* things. And here is the Negro South, caught as always between the upper and nether millstones of conflicting forces and also paying the price of extraordinary transition from level to level of cultural achievement, and needing plenty of understanding and cooperation. And here is the white South inexorably conditioned by cultural complexes, suffering terribly, too, and needing sympathy and help as few peoples have ever needed in the annals of man. And, even more important, the two, white South and black South, are part and parcel of the Nation, whose people need, scarcely less than the two regional peoples, the sense of time and wisdom.

"The war has sharpened the issue of Negro-white relations in the United States, and particularly in the South. A result has been increased racial tensions, fears, and aggressions, and an opening up of the basic questions of racial segregation and discrimination, Negro minority rights, and democratic freedom, as they apply practically in Negro-white relations in the South. These issues are acute and threaten to become even more serious as they increasingly block, through the deeper fears aroused, common sense consideration for even elementary improvements in Negro status, and the welfare of the country as a whole.

"This is a rare challenge to the leadership of the South: to the white leadership to find new ways of cooperation and to justify increased confidence of the Negro leadership in the white South; to the Negro leadership, to sense the difficulties involved and to meet increasing demands, without slowing down their essential efforts.

"As evidence of the promise of this leadership, two recent southern conferences on race relations, one at Durham under the auspices of Negro leadership, and one in Atlanta, under the auspices of white leadership, have blazed new trails. As a follow-up of these and with the above problems and backgrounds in mind, we, a group of southern whites and Negroes, representing both the Durham and Atlanta groups, meeting as a collaboration committee at Richmond, Virginia, June 16, 1943, and following the general trend of the Atlanta group, urge the general adaptation of the Durham statement entitled 'A Basis for Interracial Cooperation and Development in the South,' which has had extraordinary nation-wide endorsement.

"The framers of this covenant, realizing that the situation calls for both candor and wisdom, have included adequate and searching analysis of the principal issues involved, duly interpreted in their proper perspective. The problems so featured include political and civil rights, industry and labor, service occupations, education, agriculture, military service, social welfare and health.

"In the area of political and civil rights the essential problems featured were those of franchise and the ballot, jury service, personal security, services in public carriers, the elimination of violence, within and without the law, the elimination of lynching, and the employment of an increasingly larger number of Negroes in the public service.

"In the area of work opportunities: the increased training for all skilled, semi-skilled, and unskilled labor, and opportunity for employment; the readaptation of labor union policies both for the best interests of Negroes and labor unions; the problems of dual standards of pay; support of but guarding against discrimination in local, State, and federal procedures; special problems of service workers and standards of living.

"In the area of education: equalized opportunities in all aspects but especially including institutions of higher learning, professional training, and equal salaries.

"In the area of agriculture: adequate opportunity for the

Negro farmer, including a sound system of tenancy, adequate State and federal assistance, increased opportunity for farm ownership, fair farm wages, and the wider employment of Negro farm and home agents.

"In the area of military service: along with the obligation to serve, the opportunity for full participation and advancement in the war activities and a continuing better adjustment of unsatisfactory situations.

"In the area of social welfare and health: adequate provisions for safeguarding the public health, for training physicians and nurses, and for their employment. Also, the erection of low-cost housing and other facilities for improving community life.

"We recognize now the importance of affirmative action, without which we shall fall far short of our hopes and possibilities. To this end we direct that the continuing committee, as appointed by the two groups now consolidated in this larger collaboration committee, be charged with the responsibility for working out methods and practical means of approach.

"We urge especially that efforts be begun to prepare the post-war world for a wise and successful reception of our returning soldiers and to prepare both our soldiers and the people for attitudes and procedures adequate to carry the great load of post-war needs.

"In all these, we urge the public to a new sense of the meaning of these needs as in accord with our professed principles of Christianity and democracy."

The Continuing Committee in Atlanta

The Continuing Committee in Atlanta, to be composed of a score each of white and Negro members, would attempt to covenant together for better cooperation, more positive and specific action, and for enduring ways and means for carrying out the recommendations.

In the meantime, many national agencies and groups had become actively interested. Most important was the Rosenwald Fund's new Division of Race Relations set up as a major effort with its distinguished directors in charge of far-reaching programs. The American Missionary Association Division of the Board of Home Missions of the Congregational Christian Churches had created a special department on race relations with Dr. Charles S. Johnson as its Director. The Federal Council of the Churches of Christ in America had established a commission on democracy in racial and cultural relations. Many governmental agencies were directing special efforts toward both study and action. Newspapers and literary periodicals were giving special editorial and feature emphasis. The national Negro agencies and associations were accelerating their efforts. New national conferences and committees were being proposed.

Because of new conflicts and riots in a number of communities throughout the United States, there had followed many suggestions as to what was best to do. Chiefest among these were the requests for action on the part of the President of the United States. Many suggested that he make a special radio broadcast to the Nation. Others insisted that he appoint an official congressional investigating committee. Still others that he appoint a nationwide civic committee, composed of distinguished governmental officials and private citizens, whose function would be to make the most thorough inquiry possible, with the financial burden being borne by private agencies.

The record of work done over the years by the National Association for the Advancement of Colored People was not a part of the story of race rumors and tensions in the early years of the war. It was true that the N.A.A.C.P. was often considered one of the disturbing outside influences and it was generally thought by the relatively few southerners who knew about its work that its methods were often questionable. Its work in the South had generally been thought of as in radical contrast to the Commission on Interracial Cooperation. The bitterness of many southern editors and publicists against the N.A.A.C.P. had something to do with the new solid South alignment, but its total story was a separate one.

So, too, there were other Negro organizations hard at work, including the National Urban League, the National Negro Council, and others. There were many smaller groups and hundreds of Negro individuals working and writing and talking. So, too, no one had counted the white individuals and groups that kept the papers and the platforms, the radio and the wires busy with suggestions, remedies, and plans.

A monthly news summary of national events and trends in race relation reported as of July, 1943, by Charles S. Johnson, for the Rosenwald Fund, listed no less than fourteen citizen committees in eight states, nineteen instances of federal, state, and city action; and forty-eight special conferences in approximately twenty states. It was all a typical American phenomenon which required a separate story.

It was from that point, then, that the challenge came to point the way out of the present crisis and the way on to more stable and enduring race relationships through procedures worthy of American democracy. Was it possible to focus on conclusions in such a way as to point the way out and on?

XXII

The Way Out and the Way On

The final chapter of this story of race and rumors of race, as reflected in the drama of one short year, is perhaps necessarily couched more in terms of questions than of answers, of education more than action, of interpretation more than edict. For the portraiture reflects situations in which there was no one way out, but many ways; problems for which there was no one solution, but many solutions; questions for which there was no categorical answer in terms of yes or no, now or never, all or none, white or black, but for which there were many answers in terms of relationships and perspective such as would be inherent in the growth and development of any great cultural epoch.

This did not mean that there was not emerging at all times a clear-cut picture, a positive declaration of conclusions, a singleness of purpose toward major objectives, or a long road forward that knew no turning. On the contrary, the comprehensiveness of the task, the complexity of the situation, the universality of the need, and the clarity of the issue made all the more necessary a maturity of approach that guaranteed successful attainment in such perspective as would insure an enduring democracy in every single fundamental that was consistent with the new realism of the folk the world over. More specifically, however, it was necessary that there emerge something definite, positive, conclusive with reference to the exact situation in America and more particularly in the southern regions of the United States.

Yet the total situation with reference to the Negro required the long look ahead and the complete strategy, as well as an understanding of the past and the meeting of current crisis. It was as if there was need for a total victory to be won in such enduring ways as to insure also an abiding peace rather than the limited excitement of one or two successful battles that would defeat the greater cause. It was as if the welfare, the growth, and development of the millions of black folk were more important than the winning of a point of conflict or the display of smartness. It was as if a great affection for the Negro people and a great understanding of their case were more important than the ambition of a few.

Or again it was as if there were the new global sense of world democracy which sought to give opportunity and freedom to all folk without destroying other folk of different cultural and physical heritage; or as if the elemental principles of the great freedoms must not be overlooked in the narrow intellectualism of abstract logic or in the use of force to coerce all peoples in the way of specific, unexamined moral principles. Or still again it was as if there were a new and powerful sense of human progress in which no group or people could enslave another group or could isolate either itself or other groups, but that instead there must be the greater good of attaining strength and unity and equality through diversity and integration. In all of this it was very difficult for the observer not to exhort and advise and preach, substituting immature moralisms for the reality of analysis and strategy for enduring progress.

As in some great drama there are plot and powerful moments of crisis and action; as in some great symphony, there are recurring motifs and rising crescendo swelling through a central inviolable theme; as in some great scientific effort there are fundamental hypotheses and adequate observations many times repeated, so in the American story of race, revivified through new tensions in the early war years, there were certain uniformities and constants set in the framework of organic and practical democracy, the clear observation and repetition of which were basic to understanding and directing next steps in the way out of current dilemma and the way on toward enduring democracy.

Inasmuch as the first conclusions of the story were often couched in terms of questions it was important to determine what might be the main questions, what would be the nature of their answers and how the right answers could be found. Was it possible, in order to discover these questions and their answers, first to declare a moratorium on all emotional and violent reactions and tempers; to ascertain first the facts and the truths involved in their perspective? To have done with closed minds and immature dogmatism, wherever found? To declare a moratorium on all acts of violence as the over-simplified answer to complex problems; on all exhibitions of demagoguery whether political, intellectual, or personal; on the calling of names, the substitution of blame-placing for intelligent thinking and acting? Was it possible, on the one hand, to forget, for the time being, who was to blame, in order to focus all attention upon the facts and what was to be done and how? Or, on the other hand, frankly to acknowledge common errors on all sides, and to proceed from that point forward without repeating those errors over again?

Without minimizing the larger aspects of the problem, was it possible nevertheless to focus attention on the specific aspects which related primarily to the South and then to follow with equal definiteness the major implications to the rest of the Nation? Without in any way minimizing the importance of the basic theoretical and philosophical principles involved, was it possible nevertheless to focus upon very specific and practical things to do? Without in any way minimizing the importance of clear-cut conclusions and policies, was it possible nevertheless to focus upon the realism of cultural differences and diversities in order that the best answers to many questions could be found?

Sometimes a simple but vivid experience or a dramatic incident illustrated the living reality of the problem better than the attempt to describe it. Thus, there was a private, writing from a camp in the Deep South, whose name was identical with that of a southern senator from the same state: "We work and drill pretty damn hard . . . preparing for the time . . . when we are going across to fight the enemies of democracy . . . makes us begin to wonder whether we should be shipped to Africa or Detroit . . . I for one would just as soon run my bayonet through the foremost young man in your race riot photo as I would through any other enemy of democracy. And I think there are plenty of other bayonets down here to back me up."

Now if this young private was a southern boy, what did he mean? If he were from other parts of the Nation, what did he mean? If he were a Negro soldier, what did he mean? Thousands of soldiers from the South had begged that while they were willing to give their lives for America's fight for democracy, they were not willing to come back and have their southern biracial culture changed by government power without their consent. Other thousands from other parts of the Nation had expressed a similar unwillingness to slave and die for democracy if America was to deprive the Negro of his rights, as symbolized in riots and violence of the early 1940's. Now the questions continued, both in the search for the answers and to illustrate the extraordinary difficulty of the occasion: Was there no way to settle this thing except to have the two segments of American soldiers fight it out? What of America's way of democracy, Christianity, patriotism, science, education, fellowship, humanity, common sense —did these count for anything?

Now since the burden of the problem was first a southern concern, and then a national dilemma, was it possible for the southern people, sensing the crisis involved, to take stock of themselves and to ascertain to what extent they were wrong, both in certain fundamental assumptions and in the tragedies of race conflict and exploitation?

Could the South follow the preachings of their revivalists, whose pattern of religion they had so often adopted? In their campaigns to save the people, they undoubtedly had evolved an effective psychology. In their powerful appeals for repentance there were two elemental prerequisites for salvation. First, "the conviction of sin," the recognition of error and confession before the public; and second, the "surrender" of a stubborn heart or will to the end that change could take place. After that, "conversion" was relatively easy with the process not nearly as painful as had been anticipated.

Could the South take some of its own medicine here? Would the South admit for once that it was wrong? Would the South be willing to give up some of its fears and folkways of exploitation, and at least consider a new approach? Would the South confess an error before the public without feeling that it was faithless to its people? Would the South quit "getting mad" because honest questions were raised? Would the South be willing to try out certain new ways of doing things and certain broader understanding of fellowship?

Now these specific questions, applied to the here and now, seemed a far cry from the earlier ones about the world nature of the problem of race and its essence of cultural progress. Yet since the situation was after all a specific southern problem of cultural heritage, attitudes, and change, such questions were in the nature of "first things first." And in the search for the truth in its best perspective, there were many other questions which southerners were beginning to ask themselves.

To what extent was it possible that the South had been wrong in many of its attitudes and policies? Was the South wrong in assuming that it could insist that all other parts of the Nation would accept and adopt its policies and principles of segregation? Or that as a minority in politics it could insist that a minority people, the Negro, should not be given the vote in other regions if the majority of the people assumed as a matter of fact that this should be the case? Was the South trying to do exactly what it protested the Nation was trying to do to it? Was the South wrong more specifically in depriving the Negro of his vote because of race?

Was the distinguished southern senator, eminent in experience and legislation, eloquent in debate, prominent in fiscal planning and legislation, wrong when he said: "Of course anybody knows that no self-respecting white southerner would advocate the Negro's voting"? Was the South wrong in insisting that it always had been and always would be different from the rest of the world with reference to the Negro? Was the South wrong in always being on the defensive and in devoting more of its energies and abilities to negative protest and denunciation than to positive work and creative effort? Was the South wrong in justifying its own behavior on the grounds that the rest of the Nation discriminated against the Negro and that other regions treated the Chinese and the Japanese similarly?

Was the South wrong in its insistence that "social equality" must always be the symbol of fear and crisis? Was the South's whole concept of social equality wrong in many ways? In the first place, was social equality involved at all in the working together, side by side, of Negroes and whites? Was there any more social equality in riding together in the streetcars, busses, and trains, than coming together in banks or post offices, or in stores? Was social equality implied in sitting together in railway stations? Was it a mistake to base all this unnecessary fear upon the logic of unexamined traditional attitudes?

Was the South wrong in assuming that opportunity for equality meant coercive or compulsory association together in terms of social equality? Did the people of other regions of the Nation or world assume that because the Negro may achieve equal opportunity that, therefore, all whites must associate with all Negroes? Was there any relationship between justice and opportunity freely provided for all citizens and compulsory, personal association? Was the South wrong in assuming that this was what the Negroes wanted?

Was the South wrong in being unwilling to examine its traditional heritage and behavior? Was it wrong in assuming that any facing of facts unfavorable to the South and their publication must be considered as acts of disloyalty and evidence of joining the defamers of the region? Was the South wrong in taking the attitude that criticism of its limitations and deficiencies ignored its capacities and excellence or that criticism of the South assured the rightness of its critics? Was the South wrong in ostracizing those of its own inquirers who appeared to go too far and in denouncing those from other regions?

Was the South wrong finally in assuming that nothing could be done about the race situation except to let it alone; and were its leaders wrong in assuming that since they could do nothing that was not attacked and ridiculed by the extremists, therefore, they might just as well quit? That is, when the last "liberal" had been unreasonably assailed and when the last governor who stood out against the southern reaction had been ridiculed, was the South wrong in forgetting that the same needs and values were there as before? Or when the immaturity of the intelligentsia, white and

black, had made such fantastic demands and when ignorance
and limitations had so muddled the situation as to make
immediate solutions appear impossible, was the South wrong
in forgetting that its needs for statesmanship and mature
attitudes were all the more important?

Now it was emphasized that in all these questions the
implications of being wrong were not based primarily upon
moral principles. Rather, there were perhaps three measures
of what was meant by asking to what extent the South was
wrong. There was in the first place, the meaning of the word
in terms of personal morality and responsibility of the citizen
and the general moral principles involved in American ideology of freedom and opportunity. More important, however,
was a second meaning as measured by a superior wisdom
through which survival and progress would be assured. And
there was a third measure, namely, a strategy which would
insure the best results. Was the South, for instance, constantly using the wrong strategy and methods?

In the application of the term wrong as the negation of
superior wisdom and strategy there were several standard
measures which strangely enough were fundamentals in the
American philosophy. There were science, government, religion, patriotism, humanity. To ascertain the truth, science
and research were available as substitutes for ignorance and
dogma. For religion there was the measure of Christianity
and its brotherhood of men. For government, there was democracy with its guarantee of equality of opportunity. For
patriotism there was loyalty to the American Dream. And for
humanity there was the measure of human society as opposed to the biological survival of the animal world.

Now these were hard questions and difficult measures
which clearly placed upon the South the unequal burden of
the crisis. Yet if such questions and their answers would result in preparing the South better for next steps, the severity

of their implications would then be softened. For it was necessary for the South to make for itself plans for next steps, including ways and means of answering its own questions and of procedures for an increasingly effective regional direction at the same time that the regional and national culture and economy were better integrated. Was it possible to set forth certain clear-cut objectives which would provide that whatever was done in the future would be done within a framework through which the best efforts of all would be utilized most effectively?

Yet, before measures could be explored for the South's best next steps it was necessary to ask similar questions about the other two great groups of people involved, namely, the Negro and the Nation at large. In the case of the ablest Negro leadership, it was apparent that the capacity and record of the new Negro leaders at their best represented the best that America had produced at any time in its history. It was repeated often that of the three great groups the Negroes appeared least to blame for crisis and conflict.

Nevertheless, was it possible that their leaders were wrong in somewhat the same way as white leaders in being afraid to call attention to limitations and mistakes for fear they would be accused of testifying against the race and, therefore, of joining its critics? Was it possible that many prominent southern Negro leaders were wrong in being afraid of northern leaders who would accuse them of being subservient to the whites? Yet, right or wrong, their case was not as marked as was that of many leaders of labor, let us say, who were afraid to call attention to weaknesses lest they be termed anti-labor or labor-haters.

Again, was it possible that Negro leaders were wrong in being so sensitive to criticism or to the honest facing of facts? That is, was there anything wrong in saying that the Negro needs sympathy and understanding, even as other

folk need sympathy and understanding? Yet always the
Negro leaders felt that that connoted a certain condescen-
sion or pity. Was it possible that they were wrong in being
on the lookout constantly for mistakes of the white leaders
which, it might be presumed, could be foretold? That is,
since, as had been acknowledged by the white leadership,
no southern white man was adequately equipped to understand and to implement this understanding in satisfactory reality, would it be better to study the best that was
being done and move on toward something better? Was it
likely that many of the Negro leaders of the upper brackets
of cultural achievement were wrong in the assumption that
every white leader must be smeared, and that the smart attitude was to look down on all white leaders as essentially
backward?

Was it possible that many Negro leaders could develop
their own strategy far superior to the irresponsible extremists
of the Nation, who, professing to base their demands on
facts, ignored the great body of facts as measured by tradition, race prejudice, the ill-equipped but not-to-blame mass
of Negro people? Was it possible that the best way to change
facts was to face them first in all their complexity and perspective? Was it possible that many Negroes were wrong in
following an earlier vogue of the white intelligentsia who
substituted smartness and intellectualism for wisdom and
learning, the unfortunate results of which were everywhere
apparent?

Was it possible that Negro leaders were losing a strategic
position in not making a bold and forthright appeal to the
great body of loyal Negroes to face the extraordinary obligation that went with new opportunity? Was it possible that
they were unnecessarily alienating millions of their friends
throughout the Nation by demanding the impossible, or else?

In a similar way there were questions which the rest of the white Nation was asking about itself and which the South was asking about the Nation at large. Was it possible that many of the Nation's extremists were making the same mistakes as were made during the pre-Civil War days?

Was it possible that both the North and the South were wrong in continuing the fear of the earlier periods that each would be dominated by the other? Was it possible that many leaders of the Nation were unwilling to examine their traditional heritage, on the assumption that the South was always wrong and to blame? Was it likely that these leaders were wrong in their policy of always *criticizing the South* rather than reporting events as they did in other regions? Was it possible that the Nation had learned nothing from that tragic war of brothers?

Was it possible that many leaders were wrong in assuming that the only way to eliminate segregation was through coercion to enforce new regulations in the South rather than through national planning, through which opportunities might be offered to the Negro on a voluntary basis, in all the regions? Or was it possible that leaders in the Nation might find a better strategy by moving into the South and working side by side with the southern folk in a participating realistic service?

Was it possible that a Nation with ideals and force enough to undertake the conquest of a region could do the job better at less cost and sacrifice and in accordance with constitutional measures by providing facilities for the migration and education of Negroes, for their training and employment in areas where the people had constitutional provisions and the will to do the job? Would it be possible that the careful planning for the diffusion of those Negro people who wanted to move, and for training them and creating work further to do would also influence the South to do the same thing through gradual reconstructive measures of its own calculated to do best for its greater development?

Was it possible that some leaders were wrong who held that one of their chief purposes in life was to set the South in conflict and revolution? And that the South through revolutionary slaughter, could afford to lose some of its too many people? But that the leadership of the revolution should stay afar off from the conflict? Was it possible that most national leaders were not aware of the extremists?

Was it possible that the other regions of the Nation were wrong in ascribing most of their race conflicts between whites and Negroes to southern influence in the Nation? Granted that such an influence was in reality very great, was it possible that a large part of the responsibility lay elsewhere? Was it possible that many national leaders were wrong in being afraid to face the facts, even as the South was afraid and as the Negro was afraid?

Now in the light of the total situation, in time and space, or in the light of some great cultural epoch, these questions appeared futile and unnecessary, on the one hand, or commonplace and provincial, on the other. Of course, all the facts were true and were the inevitable, logical consequences of cultural epochs. Why, then, ask all these questions? Certainly they were unsatisfactory to all those Americans who wanted action and action now or who wanted no action and no action now? They were unsatisfactory to all those who refused to face the facts or to re-examine the traditional heritage.

Yet the answer to all these questions constituted a framework upon which a continuing better understanding could be built and upon which next steps could be based. Indeed, it seemed likely that only through the asking and answering of such questions could the way be cleared for realistic adjustment. Such questions also reflected the complexity and time quality of the situation as a cultural symbol and as a laboratory of cultural development.

In so far as the answers were in the affirmative, namely, that each of the three great groups had been wrong in much of their strategy and in many of their attitudes and action, the answer again would be, "Sure, what of it? Who said they were not wrong? Most peoples under similar circumstances have made the same mistakes. Now, what are the next steps from this point on?"

In so far as the answers to those questions were in the negative, namely, that the three great groups were not "wrong" in their major premises, even if wrong in points of strategy and understanding, then the answers were to be found in the best ways of harmonizing conflicting forces and of finding common grounds upon which to proceed. The problem would then become one of freedom and representative action of, for, and by all of the groups under the framework of American democracy. It was as if the great voice of America was saying, "I'm sorry, terribly sorry, that there are such fundamental differences among the peoples and cultures of this great Nation. We must get together."

In so far as the answers were both positive and negative, namely, that all three of the major groups were "right" in some and "wrong" in other aspects, it was clearly a normal problem for all the forces at work in a changing culture which was testing the enduring qualities of American democracy. Even so, it was a natural problem inherent in the new world. Manifestly the problem was one of planning in the best sense of the word to the end that practical ways and means might be worked out through all possible procedures of public and private agencies.

There was yet one other strategic problem of great importance, namely, the re-interpretation of the issues to the folk, to the common man everywhere, in the South, in the Nation at large, white man and black man. For here was the key, not only to the crisis of race and the Negro but to the future of the South and the Nation. Was it possible so to get the attention of the common man as he lived and moved and had his being in the framework of a great tradition and of a great loyalty and of a great love of life under these conditions that the total situation could be interpreted to him?

There were powerful doctrines and beliefs of the common man in all America and especially in the South which motivated his life. His religion, his democracy, his patriotism and loyalty, his love of family, and his sense of decency were levels of life upon which most of his conduct was based. Could these be applied now to the crisis of race and the understanding of peoples? The common man would never substitute riots and bloodshed and Hitlerism for them if he ever really sensed their meaning and beauty in the picture of America's leadership and of his own articulate role in a new world.

It was as if once again the people of the South were gathered together in solemn assembly, as, indeed, the Continuing Committee was to do in Atlanta, conscious of their heritage and opportunity. It was as if again, in the name and spirit of America and of all her resources and institutions, they covenanted together in harmony and unanimity to achieve something epochal in a new purpose, a new understanding, and a new fellowship.

It was as if in the name and spirit of America's science and education they could seek to find and to tell the truth. In the name and spirit of America's democracy would they seek the way of equal opportunity? In the name of America's patriotism, would they strive for loyalty to the American Dream, for leadership to guide, and for statesmanship adequate to carry the burden of the New America? In the name and spirit of America's Christianity, would they search for the new faith of fellowship? In the name of humanity, would they substitute the measures of the good society for the old biological struggle for physical survival? It was as if, in the name and spirit of all these and the living reality of a complex world, these people were asking whether they could dedicate themselves to the task of doing the most and the best that could be done here and now.

Could they, therefore, agree upon a new declaration of American principles and a new dedication to the task of covenanting together with all regions and all races for the continued better ordering of our society? Could they recognize fully that in the current crisis this covenant was as important as the earlier compacts of their forefathers? And that the framework within which they covenanted together must comprehend a concept and a charter which guaranteed equality of opportunity for all peoples? This meant more specifically that the Negro in the United States and in every region was entitled to and should have every guarantee of equal opportunity that every other citizen of the United States had within the framework of the American democratic system of government.

Yet there was the need of adequate adaptation of all means for the successful achievement of this task. Since in the order of all nature and creation and of the growth and development of the people and society, there were always certain features peculiar to each society; since in the order of democracy there were certain elemental principles of self-government that are inherent in each folk and regional society; and since in both the physical and cultural heritage of the South there were certain cumulative and tragic handicaps that represent powerful factors in the situation, could the Nation, in covenant with the South, exercise a wisdom and maturity through which methods, procedures, and rates of change might be worked out by the folk and the region itself in the spirit of and in conformity with the principles of American democracy?

And yet there was always a first problem of the common man and how to achieve with him an understanding, not only of his special problem, but of the broader and bigger problem of the South and of the Nation as a whole. Meetings and conferences often irritated him. They more often touched him not at all. He was more and more skeptical of what the professional leaders had to say. His schools and his churches no longer offered authentic standards, and he was forever wanting to set his own standards within the framework of his southern cultural conditioning, intensified through emotional loyalties and new confusions wrought by war and the new world revolution. Yet, too, he was eager to become a participating part in the new world and he was eager for words of approval and for wise guidance.

This "common man" was first of all the white South. He was, then, secondly, and no less concretely, the Negro South. There was excellent prospect of getting the main leaders of both groups together. There was little prospect of getting together the two groups of common folk and of interpreting the problem and of attaining the desired ends. Here were problem and pathos adequate to challenge the best that the South and the Nation could do.

One of the first essentials, therefore, was clearly the need for some sort of a new leadership or for some sort of articulation of the present leadership which had changed greatly in the last few decades. There was less influence of the professional folk, the college president, the professor, the school folk, the lawyer, and more influence on the part of the business man, the industrialist, the labor leader, the politician. These leaders appeared to be rather the spokesmen and the representatives of the common man than leaders as such.

There was great need of success in getting these leaders to face the problem of race relations in company with such professional leaders as commonly constituted the membership of conferences on race relations. The two groups were far apart and needed a common integrated leadership and a common responsibility.

The sweep and power of the emotions in time of war and crisis were recognized and the rights and tendencies in the democratic way of life for thousands of individuals and groups to agitate, organize, and promote their own peculiar programs were acknowledged. This was and must be the essence of a democracy. But it was also the way of democracy to focus upon fundamentals and to give opportunity to responsible leadership through the orderly agencies of government and of private citizens. To this end would the Nation covenant together in responsible organizations, to provide leadership and clearing house, and to avoid conflicts, waste, and overlapping, on the one hand, and, on the other, to minimize the harmful influence of irresponsible forces in the great hour of need for good will and for effective ways of doing what was needed?

In connection with this need for special leadership, it was urged also that the Nation was committed to what was generally called, both in private business and in public life, post-war planning to the end that we might be ready for the demobilization and reintegration of our millions of returning soldiers into the best possible American way of life. This was of peculiar importance in the case of returning Negro soldiers and the resulting morale of the post-war period. Recognizing that the problems of the folk and of race constituted a more difficult problem than that of physical planning, by the same token it was urged that there was all the more obligation to apply to this great area of democracy, in realistic planning, the best the sciences, social sciences, the humanities, and religion could do in the realistic working out of next steps.

The next great general need, therefore, was for planning in the genuine sense of taking into account all the factors involved, resolving them into their component parts, and then working them into a realistic program of participation and direction. This meant not only the usual specific ways of getting things done, but also the wider program of substituting actual work for arguments on beliefs, folkways, and mores. It meant the substitution of things to be done, manifestly good for all the people, for the old ideologies, and complexes of race conflict.

Manifestly, therefore, the supreme approach was the substitution of ways and means coming within the framework of realistic planning, in which men everywhere assume that in the world the Negro has an increasingly complete participation; in the new transportation the Negro must have his right part; in the new redistribution of opportunity, of course, the Negro must have his part; in the new agriculture and economic arrangements, of course, provision must be made for his adequate participation. And so for the newly equipped Negro citizen and leader in cultural opportunities, in political opportunities, and in all others, of course, any plans that were made would assume that he must have his pro-rata position in the social order.

The story of race in the South and the rest of the Nation in the early 1940's reflected more than ever a twofold need. On the one hand, there was need of powerful purpose and good will set in the midst of such action programs as characterized the American principle of joint civic and voluntary effort working with the agencies of government. There could be no substitute for this. But there was also needed the scientific base of physical facts and social relationships set in the framework of a comprehensive understanding of the living reality of the situation. There could be no substitute for this. The need was then that from these two there might emerge such realistic understanding and planning as would result in enduring racial relationships and development commensurate with the ideals and goals of American democracy set in the framework of whatever new world order was to emerge.

Nor could there be any substitute for the conscientious self-examination of the people in all regions and on all levels of leadership and the folk. It seemed easily possible that the South might remake and enrich itself and its place in the Nation as an increasingly powerful and indispensable contribution to the greater American culture. It seemed possible also that the South might possibly weaken itself and destroy much of its potentialities by devoting most of its energies and emotions to negative and untenable programs rather than to the positive development of its resources, its people, and its institutions. It seemed easily possible that the rest of the Nation might so cooperate and work with the southern regions as to bring about the full fruition of the national enrichment and unity. It seemed also possible that the hazards and dangers of not doing this constituted a part of the national crisis.

As when some youth faces crisis in battle above the clouds with a thousand hazards engulfing him and his companions, there emerges something greater than physical combat, something in the unconquerable spirit, which transcends the ordinary routine of mortals, so, hidden in crisis of folk and race, are elements of the spiritual world that transcend the ways and means of ordinary routine. The story of race, in emphasizing the spiritual qualities and the difficulties of the situation, pointed to another conclusion. It was that perhaps the most and the least that could be done, in conformity with all the ideals and realities involved, was not only to interpret the situation as adequately and widely as possible, but to provide arrangements whereby there would always be available the best possible leadership and the best possible spirit and good will to meet the changing situations in ways commensurate with their meaning to the life and work of a great region and Nation.

There was the old saying about the "saddest words of tongue or pen" recording that which might have been. In terms of region and race and Nation, the story of race and crisis recalled an earlier and more powerful characterization that made possible an appeal to the future as well as to that which was past. "How oft would I and ye would not" reflected a powerful measure of promise and prospect for the South and the Nation. By the same token, here was measure of crisis and of leadership.

PART IV

QUESTIONS AND ANSWERS

XXIII

Questions and Answers about this Work

We come now to answer some of the questions about this story of *Race and Rumors of Race*. What were the sources of the rumors and who helped collect them? When and how was the study made? What was the basis of difference between rumor, story, incident? What was the relation between rumor and fact in illustrative cases? How much of "what they say" was true? What individuals were consulted? What printed materials were utilized? Why were no names mentioned in the text? Why was no special statistical or psychological study of rumors made?

Who examined the story of rumors before publication and what were their verdicts as to how the materials might best be utilized? Why were rumors and stories from other regions than the South not included? Why were so few rumors among the Negroes included? To what extent were there similar rumors in the Far West about the Japanese?

Who read the manuscript of the present book before publication? What were their chief criticisms? What changes were recommended? What changes were made? Why was the story presented in the past tense? What were the main reasons for publishing it? Why was it published by a southern press? What appear to be the chief criticisms of the volume from the viewpoint of the southern public? from the viewpoint of the national critics outside the South?

Beginning with persons, in the first place, it must be clear that complete responsibility for all final statements must be assumed by the author. It must be repeated again and again that no one who cooperated in the gathering of materials or in the reading of the manuscript could be responsible in any way for the number and nature of materials included or the nature of conclusions presented or the level of treatment featured. Nor were the collaborators throughout the colleges and universities of the South responsible in any way for the use made of their materials which were obtained on the assurance that there would be no identification except by special permission.

To begin with the last first, the manuscript was read by Louis R. Wilson, former dean of the Library School of the University of Chicago; W. W. Alexander, chief, Minority Group Service of the War Manpower Commission; R. D. W. Connor, former archivist at Washington; W. T. Couch, director of the University of North Carolina Press; Virginius Dabney, editor of the *Richmond Times-Dispatch;* Edwin R. Embree, president of the Julius Rosenwald Fund; Gordon B. Hancock, professor of Sociology at Virginia Union University; Katharine Jocher, assistant director of the Institute for Research in Social Science, University of North Carolina; Charles S. Johnson, director of the Social Sciences, Fisk University; Guy B. Johnson, research professor at the University of North Carolina; Sturgis Leavitt, director of the South American Summer School, University of North Carolina; Mildred Mell, head of the Department of Economics and Sociology at Agnes Scott College; N. C. Newbold, director of the Division of Cooperation in Education and Race Relations; President Homer P. Rainey of the University of Texas; Rupert B. Vance, research professor at the University of North Carolina; P. B. Young, editor-publisher of *The Journal and Guide*, Norfolk, Virginia. H. C. Brearley, professor of Sociology at George Peabody College for Teachers, read parts of the manuscript.

Among the criticisms of the first manuscript, the following seemed most important. The credo of the South appeared a little too hard on the South; there was need of a clearer statement of the attitudes in other regions; there must be clear differentiation between rumors and facts; not enough emphasis was given to the "good" white leaders in both the South and the rest of the Nation; not enough emphasis was placed upon the factor of hatred for the Roosevelts as cause for racial rumors; not enough emphasis was placed upon the Negro newspapers; criticism of the South was too severe in comparison with that of the rest of the Nation; and many suggestions as to minor details and as to facts were made. In all of these aspects revisions were attempted to meet the criticisms in a way consistent with the realities of the work.

There was at first a general questioning of the use of the past tense throughout the work. There were two objections offered. One was that the story loses some of its vividness and the other was that it was confusing until the reader was adjusted to the style. In general, most of the readers agreed to this arrangement in deference to the wish to make the book as objective as possible and to date it as a cross section of American life with which comparisons could be made at later intervals. It was hoped that the southern critics would interpret the story thus told, not as an attack upon the South but as portraiture which many observers could see at that time. And the story necessarily would still be out of date as soon as published and need a time schedule to make it authentic.

There was a University Committee on the Study of Rumors cooperating in the plans for collecting materials. It is hoped that it will continue to study both these rumors and the general phenomena of rumors everywhere. This Committee was composed of Russell Grumman, director of the Extension Division; John Frederick Dashiell, professor of Psychology; Louis O. Kattsoff of the Department of Philosophy; L. R. Wilson, professor of library science; Guy B. Johnson, research professor, Katharine Jocher, assistant director, and Howard W. Odum, director, the Institute for Research in Social Science. Special acknowledgment is expressed to Mr. Grumman for his very great contribution through the Extension Division of North Carolina and other States and to Professor Kattsoff for his help through other departments of philosophy in a number of colleges and universities.

There was no attempt to make a scientific study of rumors, although this task is of great importance. There was no statistical analysis of rumors and no study of their special psychological meanings except as they reflected the folkways and mores of the people.

On the other hand, some two thousand rumors constituted the basis upon which the inquiry into the nature of this crisis was made, although apparently there was no limit to the rumors that might have been collected. They still accumulate. The rumors constituted a sort of living background upon which was reflected the picture of race conflict and crisis. The rumors, gathered authentically from all the States in the Southeast, were then supplemented with stories and happenings, to which there were added personal discussions and criticisms, and all these then checked with fact and with publications and printed evidences. The final story then was written and rewritten after being read by a substantial number of those well adapted to the task.

The rumors were gathered, first of all, from whatever sources were available in the first steps of the inquiry, and subsequently in checking and rechecking. The majority of the rumors and stories were collected by members of the faculties of sociology and philosophy in the leading southern colleges and universities. Of very special assistance were the reportings which came in from the cooperation of the extension teachings of several universities. In addition to special catalogues provided by members of the faculties, there was also the bulk of the stories and rumors provided by students who reported them from the hinterlands of their own communities. Thus, not only the States but many communities in each State were represented. The first cataloguing was submitted to those who had cooperated with the view to checking and to adding others and newer ones. The lists were also submitted to these and other students with the request to appraise: Were they exaggerated? Were there other rumors omitted? What use could be made of them? Should they be published?

It was interesting to note that almost one-half of the original cooperators in the Deep South thought that perhaps they should not be published. Others, however, recommended strongly that they be published to the end that they might help interpret the seriousness of the situation and perhaps get the South to look at itself in a sobering way. Another index of the complexity of the situation was the decision of the Associated Press not to publish two stories written by their chief science reporter. It was thought that the stories might do more harm than good. There were also publications and publishing houses in New York who were not willing to publish many such stories after their representative had made exhaustive studies.

In asking for the cooperation of colleagues in the colleges and universities, assurance was given that no use of names or colleges would be made in any publication. General acknowledgment is, therefore, made for the extraordinarily effective and cordial cooperation which was practically unanimous. Some members of the faculties set students to work as special study groups or committees, some of them exploring the field during the Christmas holidays and on other special visits home. In the order of the number of rumors catalogued, the States ranked about as follows: South Carolina, North Carolina, Louisiana, Florida, Georgia, Virginia, Tennessee, Alabama, Mississippi, Kentucky, and Arkansas.

Among those invited to cooperate, of whom approximately two-thirds responded, but who are in no way responsible for anything in the book as such are: Myrtle Brooke, Alabama College; E. T. Gregory, Jr., University of Alabama; J. Herman Johnson, Auburn, Alabama; Durell Ruffin, Birmingham-Southern College; J. L. Charlton, University of Arkansas; Richard E. Clark, De Land, Florida; Edwin L. Clark, Rollins College; Coyle E. Moore, Florida State College for Women; J. Paul Reed, University of Miami; David L. Zielenka, Tampa, Florida; J. W. W. Daniel, Wesleyan College; J. A. Durrenberger, Georgia State Woman's College, Valdosta; Hugh N. Fuller, Emory University; Herbert N. Massey, Georgia State College for Women, Milledgeville; Mildred R. Mell, Agnes Scott College; W. L. Murray, La Grange College; Olive M. Stone, Georgia State Woman's College, Valdosta; B. O. Williams, University of Georgia; Harry Best, University of Kentucky; Wayne T. Gray, Union College; H. H. Groves, Transylvania College; J. Wesley Hatcher, Berea College; Robert I. Kutak, University of Louisville; N. O. Taff, Western State Teachers' College, Kentucky; R. F. Terrell, Morehead State Teachers' College; J. B. Weatherspoon, Southern Baptist Theological Seminary; E. H. Lott, Louisiana State University; Logan Wilson, Tulane University; Carl S. Joslyn, University of Maryland; Dorothy Dickins, Mississippi State College; A. D. Beittel, Guilford College; Allen K. Faust, Catawba College; P. H. Gwynn, Jr., David son College; Howard E. Jensen, Duke University; Glenn R Johnson, Woman's College of the University of North Carolina; Harriet Tynes, Queens College; Francis S. Wilder, Bilt

more College; Ellen Winston, Meredith College; Sanford
Winston, North Carolina State College; Allen D. Edwards,
Clemson College; Laura Smith Ebaugh, Furman University;
Eugene P. Link, Winthrop College; C. C. Norton, Wofford
College; Charles L. Trabert, Newberry College; E. J. True-
blood, Limestone College; H. C. Brearley, George Peabody
College; Ralph T. Case, Maryville College; William E. Cole,
University of Tennessee; H. J. Kloepfer, Knoxville College;
E. T. Krueger, Vanderbilt University; Winifred Lipscomb,
Tusculum College; Virgil E. Long, University of Chattanooga;
Margaret Townsend, Southwestern College; G. A. Yates,
Tennessee Wesleyan; Louise Young, Scarritt College; Belle
Boone Beard, Sweet Briar College; Alice Davis, College of
William and Mary; W. E. Garnett, Agricultural Experiment
Station, Blacksburg, Virginia; Wilson Gee, University of
Virginia; Thomas H. Grafton, Mary Baldwin College; Floyd
N. House, University of Virginia; Mattie Kean Keeter, State
Teachers' College, Radford, Virginia; Mary Phlegar Smith,
Hollins College.

In contrast to the sociologists, a relatively small number
of philosophy faculty members participated. The list of those
invited included: Samuel Luttrell Akers, Wesleyan College;
D. Maurice Allen, Hampden-Sydney College; Albert G. A.
Balz, University of Virginia; Lewis W. Beck, Emory Uni-
versity; John Keith Benton, Vanderbilt University; Kenneth
K. Berry, University of Tampa; Daniel J. Bowden, Elon
College; Scott Buchanan, St. Johns College; Eugene G.
Bugg, Vanderbilt University; Connie J. Burwell, Queens
College; Gertrude C. Bussey, Goucher College; Peter Car-
michael, Louisiana State University; John Reginald Cress-
well, West Virginia University; Charles Kidder Davenport,
University of Virginia; Homer H. Dubs, Duke University;
H. Octavius Enwall, University of Florida; Leonard J.
Eslick, Drake University; William Edwards Fort, Jr., Win-

throp College; Christopher Browne Garnett, Jr., George Washington University; Marjorie Silliman Harris, Randolph-Macon Woman's College; Francis Samuel Haserot, College of William and Mary; Raymond Preston Hawes, Goucher College; Louise R. Heath, Hood College; Benjamin Clark Holtzclaw, University of Richmond; Alexander Kohanski, Memphis, Tennessee; John Kuiper, University of Kentucky; Harold N. Lee, Newcomb College, Tulane University; Anna Forbes Liddell, Florida State College for Women; Leroy E. Loemaker, Emory University; Fritz Marti, University of Maryland; Frederick W. Meier, Louisiana State University; Donald Meiklejohn, College of William and Mary; Charles B. McMullen, Centre College; Harold Ralston, Erskine College; Edward Thomas Ramsdell, Vanderbilt University; Marten ten Hoor, Tulane University; Andrea Radoslav Tsanoff, Rice Institute; Mrs. Merle G. Walker, Atlanta Evening College; Bruce A. Wentz, Catawba College.

Special acknowledgment is due the three extension divisions of the universities of Florida, Virginia, and North Carolina; and also the Bulletin of the National University Extension Association for its announcement of the study.

Among others to whom special acknowledgments are due are Katharine Jocher for her great assistance in editing the manuscript, for reading the proof, and for special assistance in stating the "northern credo"; W. T. Couch for help in many ways; the staff of the University of North Carolina Press for editing the manuscript; Anna Green Smith for help in cataloguing the source materials; Hope Tisdale for preliminary classification of rumors; William H. Peacock for help in stating the "northern credo"; Leslie W. Syron for cataloguing rumors; Treva Williams Bevacqua for special help in the Institute office; and Belle Mooring for her extraordinary skill and patience in reworking constant revisions and checkings.

Special acknowledgment is due the Rosenwald Fund for assistance in gathering materials and publication of results, and to Dr. Will W. Alexander and Dr. Charles S. Johnson for their cooperation.

Nowhere in the story are names identified, either of those cooperating or of those whose conclusions might be quoted. Special references are noted in this chapter where identification of names and places are deemed necessary. The reasons for not identifying names would be self-evident in the usual cases. On the other hand, if the attempt had been made to name all those leaders, Negro and white, whose influence was significant, the list would be too long and too monotonous; to list some and not others would be out of perspective.

The names of all those who signed the findings of the Durham, the two Atlanta, and the Richmond meetings have been published in brochures by the Commission on Interracial Cooperation at Atlanta. Especially vivid was the revised edition of *Understanding Our Neighbors*.

The reference to the oft-quoted statement about the South's resistance to efforts to enforce the abandonment of segregation was to Mark Ethridge, whose address was reprinted by the Commission on Interracial Cooperation.

The principal Negro newspapers from which adequate checking can be made are: *Afro-American, Amsterdam News, Carolina Times, Chicago Defender, Daily World, Houston Informer, Journal and Guide,* and *Pittsburgh Courier*. Important Negro periodicals include: *The Crisis, Opportunity, Journal of Negro Education, Journal of Negro History,* and *Phylon*. Of special value were the columnists who wrote in these papers, in particular, in the *Chicago Defender*, Walter White, Langston Hughes, Harold Preece, and Charley Cherokee.

Among the periodicals whose whole year's volumes must

be consulted are *Negro Digest, PM, The Nation, The New Republic, Crisis, Opportunity, The Survey Graphic, The New Masses, Common Ground, The Southern Frontier.*

The simplest way for the reader to get a complete picture is to examine all of the articles in the *Negro Digest*. Since these are quoted from all of the above mentioned periodicals and many others, it is not necessary to list the many special articles in *The Nation, The New Republic*, etc. It is often important, however, to examine certain articles printed by *The Nation*, which frankly offer contrast, such as James Boyd's "Strategy for Negroes," June 26, 1943, contrasted with the several articles by Thomas Sancton. Of special interest also were the contrasting articles in *The Atlantic Monthly*, such as Virginius Dabney's.

There is also a fine list of new books interpreting both the present situation and the new Negro. Among these are the following: Armstrong, Byron K., *Factors in the Formulation of Collegiate Programs for Negroes* (Edwards, Inc., 1939); Atwood, Howell J., Wyatt, Donald W., Davis, Vincent J., and Ira D. Walker, *Thus Be Their Destiny; the Personality Development of Negro Youth in Three Communities* (American Council on Education, 1941); Benedict, Ruth, *Race and Racism* (Nusson Publishers Co., 1942); Benedict, Ruth, *Race; Science and Politics* (Modern Age Books, 1940); Benedict, Ruth, and Mildred Ellis, *Race and Cultural Relations. America's Answer to the Myth of a Master Race* (National Education Association, 1942); Brown, Earl, and George R. Leighton, *The Negro and the War* (Public Affairs Committee, Inc., 1942); Brown, Sterling, Davis, Arthur P., and Ulysses Lee, eds., *The Negro Caravan. Writings by American Negroes* (The Dryden Press, Inc., 1941); *Cavalcade of the American Negro*. Compiled by the Federal Writers' Project of the Works Progress Administration in the State of Illinois (Diamond Jubilee Exposition Authority,

1940); Cayton, Horace R., and George S. Mitchell, *Black Workers and the New Unions* (The University of North Carolina Press, 1939); Cuthbert, Marion Vera, *Education and Marginality: A Study of the Negro Woman College Graduate* (Columbia University Press, 1942); Dabney, Virginius, *Below the Potomac. A Book About the New South* (D. Appleton-Century Co., 1942); Dahlberg, Gunnar, *Race, Reason & Rubbish* (Columbia University Press, 1942); Daniel, Vattell Elbert, *Ritual Stratification in Chicago Negro Churches* (University of Chicago, 1940); Davis, Allison, and John Dollard, *Children of Bondage. The Personality Development of Negro Youth in the Urban South* (American Council on Education, 1940); Davis, Allison, Gardner, Burleigh B., and Mary R. Gardner, *Deep South. A Social Anthropological Study of Caste and Class* (The University of Chicago Press, 1941); Davis, Allison, *The Relation between Color, Caste and Economic Stratification in Two 'Black' Plantation Counties* (University of Chicago Press, 1942); Dollard, John, *Caste and Class in a Southern Town* (Yale University Press, 1937); Dollard, John, Doob, Leonard W., Miller, Neal E., Mowrer, O. H., Sears, Robert R. and others, *Frustration and Aggression* (Yale University Press, 1939); *Drums and Shadows. Survival Studies Among the Georgia Coastal Negroes.* Savannah Unit of Georgia Writers' Project of the Works Progress Administration (University of Georgia Press, 1940); DuBois, W. E. B., *Dusk of Dawn; An Essay Toward an Autobiography of a Race Concept* (Harcourt, Brace and Co., 1940); DuBois, W. E. B., *Black Folk: Then and Now. An Essay in the History and Sociology of the Negro Race* (Henry Holt and Co., 1939).

Embree, Edwin R., *American Negroes, A Handbook* (The John Day Co., 1942); Ford, James W., *The Negro People and the New World Situation* (Workers Library Publishers, Inc., 1941); Frazier, E. Franklin, *The Negro Family in*

the United States (The University of Chicago Press, 1939);
Frazier, E. Franklin, *Negro Youth at the Crossways. Their
Personality Development in the Middle States* (American
Council on Education, 1940); Gallagher, Buell G., *American Caste and the Negro College* (Columbia University
Press, 1938); Gleason, Elizabeth Atkins, *The Southern
Negro and the Public Library. A Study of the Government
and Administration of Public Library Service to Negroes in
the South* (University of Chicago Press, 1941); Graves, John
Temple, *The Fighting South* (G. P. Putnam's Sons, 1943);
Hayes, Lawrence, J. W., *The Negro Federal Government
Worker. A Study of His Classification Status in the District of
Columbia, 1883–1938* (The Graduate School, Howard University, 1941); Hullinger, Edwin Ware, *Plowing Through.
The Story of the Negro in Agriculture* (William Morrow and
Co., 1940); Hurston, Zora Neale, *Dust Tracks on a Road: An
Autobiography* (Lippincott, 1942); Johnson, Charles S.,
*Growing up in the Black Belt. Negro Youth in the Rural
South* (American Council on Education, 1941); Johnson,
Charles S., *Patterns of Negro Segregation* (Harper and
Brothers, 1943); Jones, Henry L., *The Negro's Opportunity*
(H. L. Jones and Co., 1940); Kiplinger, W. M., *Washington
Is Like That* (Harper, 1942); Laidler, Harry W., ed., *The Role
of the Races in our Future Civilization* (League for Industrial
Democracy, 1942); Locke, Alain Le Roy, and Bernhard J.
Stern, eds., *When Peoples Meet. A Study in Race and Culture Contacts* (Progressive Education Association, 1942);
Logan, Rayford W., ed., *The Attitude of the Southern White
Press Toward Negro Suffrage, 1932–1940* (The Foundation
Publishers, 1940); Lumpkin, Katharine D., *The South in
Progress* (International Publishers, 1940); Mabry, William
Alexander, *The Negro in North Carolina Politics since Reconstruction* (Duke University Press, 1940); MacCracken,
Henry N., and Charles Gorden Post, *Fair Play: An Introduc-*

tion to Race and Group Relations (Vassar College, 1942);
Mangum, Charles S., *The Legal Status of the Negro* (The
University of North Carolina Press, 1940); *Manpower and
Minorities.* Annual Report of the Bureau on Jewish Employ-
ment Problems (Chicago, Illinois); McCuistion, Fred, *Gradu-
ate Instruction for Negroes in the United States* (George Pea-
body College for Teachers, 1939); McGinn, Henry Jared,
The Courts and the Changing Status of Negroes in Maryland
(Ph.D. thesis, Columbia University, 1940); McKay, Claude,
Harlem: Negro Metropolis (E. P. Dutton and Co., Inc., 1940);
McWilliams, Carey, *Brothers under the Skin* (Little, Brown
and Co., 1943); Michie, Allan, and Frank Ryhlick, *Dixie
Demagogues;* Montagu, M. F. Ashley, *Man's Most Danger-
ous Myth: The Fallacy of Race* (Columbia University Press,
1942); Morgan, John William, *The Origin and Distribution
of the Graduates of the Negro Colleges of Georgia* (Mil-
ledgeville, Georgia: Privately printed, 1940); Morgan,
Ernest West, *A Racial Comparison of Education in Robeson
County* (Chapel Hill, N. C.: M.A. thesis, 1940); Murphy,
John C., *An Analysis of the Attitudes of American Catholics
toward the Immigrant and the Negro, 1825–1925* (The
Catholic University of America Press, 1940); Murray, Flor-
ence, ed., *The Negro Handbook. A Manual of Current Facts,
Statistics and General Information Concerning the Negro in
the United States* (Wendell Malliet and Co., 1942); *The
Negro and Defense. A Test of Democracy* (New York:
Council for Democracy, 1941); *The Negroes of Nebraska.*
Federal Writers' Project (Woodruff Printing Co., 1940);
The Negro in Virginia. Compiled by the Federal
Writers' Project of the Works Progress Administration in
Virginia (Hastings House, 1940); Newbold, N. C., *Five
North Carolina Negro Educators* (The University of North
Carolina Press, 1939); Ottley, Roi, *New World A-Coming*
(Houghton Mifflin Co., 1943); Parker, Albert, *Negroes in the*

Post-War World (Pioneer Publishers, 1943); Pierson, Donald, *Negroes in Brazil: A Study of Race Contact at Bahia* (The University of Chicago Press, 1942); Powdermaker, Hortense, *After Freedom; A Cultural Study in the Deep South* (The Viking Press, 1939); Ramos, Arthur, *The Negro in Brazil* (The Associated Publishers, Inc., 1939); Raper, Arthur F., and Ira De A. Reid, *Sharecroppers All* (University of North Carolina Press, 1941); Raper, Arthur F., *Tenants of the Almighty*, 1943; Raynor, William R., *Educational Discrimination between Whites and Negroes in the South* (University of North Carolina M.A. thesis, 1940); Redding, J. Saunders, *No Day of Triumph* (Harper and Brothers, 1942); Reid, Ira De A., *In A Minor Key: Negro Youth in Story and Fact* (American Council on Education, 1940); Reid, Ira De A., *The Negro Immigrant: His Background, Characteristics and Social Adjustment, 1899–1937* (Columbia University Press, 1939); Schapera, I., *Married Life in an African Tribe* (Sheridan House, 1941); Scott, Estelle Hill, *Occupational Changes Among Negroes in Chicago.* (Sponsored by Institute for Juvenile Research, University of Chicago, 1939); Shell, William H., *Negro Youth in Georgia Study Their Problems* (National Youth Administration for Georgia, 1941); Spirer, Jess, *Negro Crime* (The Johns Hopkins Press, 1940); Sterner, Richard, in collaboration with Lenore A. Epstein, Ellen Winston, and others, *The Negro's Share; A Study of Income, Consumption, Housing and Public Assistance* (Harper and Brothers, 1943); Stimons, James Samuel, *As Victim to Victims: An American Negro Laments with Jews* (Fortuny's, 1941); Stuart, M. S., *An Economic Detour; A History of Insurance in the Lives of American Negroes* (W. Malliet and Co., 1940); Styles, Fitzhugh Lee, *How to Be Successful Negro Americans* (The Christopher Publishing House, 1941); *Survey of Negroes in Little Rock and North Little Rock.* Federal Writers' Project of Works Progress Administration

(Sponsored by the Urban League of Greater Little Rock, 1941); Sutherland, Robert L., *Color, Class and Personality* (American Council on Education, 1942); *Teachers Salaries in Black and White* (Prepared by N.A.A.C.P., 1942); Terrell, Mary, *A Colored Woman in a White World* (Ransdell, Inc., 1940); *These Are Our Lives* (The University of North Carolina Press, 1939); Thompson, Edgar T., ed., *Race Relations and the Race Problem: A Symposium on a Growing National and International Problem with Special Reference to the South* (Duke University Press, 1939); Warner, Robert Austin, *New Haven Negroes. A Social History* (Yale University Press, 1940); Warner, W. Lloyd, Junker, Buford H., and Walter A. Adams, *Color and Human Nature; Negro Personality Development in a Northern City* (American Council on Education, 1941); Webster, Hutton, *Taboo: A Sociological Study* (Stanford University Press, 1942); Wesley, Charles W., ed., *The Negro in the Americas* (The Graduate School, Howard University, 1940); Wilkerson, Doxey A., *Special Problems of Negro Education* (U. S. Printing Office, 1939); Williams, Eric, *The Negroes in the Caribbean* (The Associates in Negro Folk Education, 1942); Woofter, T. J., and Ellen Winston, *Seven Lean Years* (University of North Carolina Press, 1939); Wright, Marion M., *The Education of Negroes in New Jersey* (Teachers College, Columbia University, 1941); Wright, Richard, *12 Million Black Voices. A Folk History of the Negro in the United States* (The Viking Press, 1941).

Of special importance is The Negro in American Life Series, published by Harper and Brothers, under the general direction of Dr. Gunnar Myrdal and sponsored by the Carnegie Corporation. Among the books that have appeared are: *Patterns of Negro Segregation*, by Charles S. Johnson, and *The Negro's Share*, by Richard Sterner. Of special value will be Dr. Myrdal's own book, *An American Dilemma: The*

Negro Problem and American Democracy which is an over-all summary of the entire Carnegie study.

In the time between the conclusion of this story and its going to press, there were continued inquiries and observations into the field, seeking to test the reliability and range of observations, the wisest use of materials, the hazards and dangers of misunderstandings, and the trends that apparently continued.

With reference to the number and range of rumors, it would appear that the catalogue might be continued on and on, adding more of the same and still other new ones. There were rumors of such clubs as the Disappointment Club, in which Negroes were required to reply by telephone to all advertisements wanting help, promising to report immediately, but always failing to show up. There were literally hundreds of communities in which rumors *almost,* according to still other rumors, led to open conflict. Town after town reported that they almost had one of the riots so much dreaded, but that a clearing up of the rumors and watchfulness of the officials prevented outbreaks.

In hundreds of other towns there were reported actual outbreaks of violence and what appeared to be unreasonable acts of brutality on the part of the whites against Negroes. These have multiplied and have added to the hazards which are inherent in a large catalogue of rumors.

This has led to the conclusion, in reply to certain objections to publishing a mass of rumors, that altogether the presentation of rumors with the implication of all their possibilities and dangers would do more good than harm in the avoiding of tensions and conflicts. Ben McKelway, in *The Bulletin* of the American Society of Newspaper Editors of September 1, 1943, states a clear case of how the effective exposure of rumors may avoid the dangers and reality of conflict:

"Last May Washington was seething with rumors of impending racial strife. Exposure by the newspapers and radio stations of these rumors clarified the atmosphere immediately and may have prevented an ugly outbreak. It is possible that our experience here may be helpful in some other city. At the same time, it would be a superficial conclusion to say that rumors start race riots and exposure can prevent them.

"It is probably true that if enough people in a community believe racial tension has reached the breaking point and if this belief is fostered by outlandish rumors of impending riots, any incident may start disorder that will substantiate the worst fears. In such circumstances, the newspapers have an opportunity to perform a public service by acting in time to bring the whole business out on Page One and discuss in absolute frankness the rumors, along with the facts which gave them currency.

"Early in May, and almost overnight, there was a repetition of a phenomenon in Washington which has been noted in less dramatic proportions in the past. Newspaper and radio switchboards were deluged with a swelling volume of calls asking about reported clashes between Negroes and whites. Circumstantial stories were passed around by respectable people concerning incidents which never really occurred. Men and women seemed to believe they heard things on the radio that never had gone on the air. A bank president assured his board that the police were giving him fine cooperation by stationing extra patrolmen around the building, and some of the city's most prominent citizens were telling each other that the newspapers were suppressing stories of street battles in which whites and Negroes were being killed. Soldiers were being held on the alert at nearby Army posts.

"The newspapers did not print anything about what most of the people were talking. They were even killing if not playing down some inconsequential police stories which might have been regarded by readers as significant. They were guided in this policy by the belief, which may have substantial foundation, that the less said the better about racial tension.

"But this situation required different handling. The Washington *Star* assigned reporters to gather all the fantastic rumors about racial disturbances then current and printed everything that could be dug up about them on the First Page in a semi-editorial news story urging people to stop spreading rumors and going to the bottom of as many of them as could be traced. Interviews with some of the Negro leaders, police officials, etc., were contained in the same story. All the radio stations and the other newspapers immediately joined in and there was a concentrated blast against rumor-mongering. A few days later the *Star* printed a detailed and factual story about the local street car issue (created by the efforts of the President's Committee on Fair Employment Practice to require the company to hire Negro platform men), tracing each development and divesting it of the mystery with which it had been clothed by lack of full and candid discussion in the past.

"The effect was instantaneous and, I believe, wholesome. The rumors dissipated in the thin air of which they were made. The talk stopped, at least, and the tension was relieved."

Similar examples have been noted in various communities. It must be clear, therefore, that an understanding of how rumors multiply and how they tend to increase tension will contribute a great deal to the improvement of the situation. Likewise, the pointing up of absurd features of many rumors, new emphasis upon the dangers of repeating them, new emphasis upon dangers which come from unnecessary talk about rumors and tensions will constitute another important step in minimizing present dangers. There is incontrovertible evidence to be found that a frank and realistic examination of these rumors has helped materially in changing attitudes. In many instances where the rumors and stories have been repeated there has been frank determination of individuals and groups to promote better attitudes and to insist upon fairer practices. Hundreds of southern white soldiers have not only expressed themselves in favor of going "all out" to salute Negro officers, but they have done it when it was called to their attention. There has been also, to use another illustration, an increasing number of southern folk who have expressed themselves in vigorous denunciation of the idle rumors that have been spread about the Eleanor Clubs and the work of Mrs. Roosevelt. There has been a great increase in the serious inquiries from business men, professional men, chambers of commerce, community organizations as to how they can help in stemming the tide of irresponsible talk and action. Admirable editorials have been written and repeated to emphasize the dangers of rumor-mongering and to point to the positive opportunity and duty of all citizens to discourage all such activities. In addition to this, there has grown up a new appreciation of the seriousness of the situation and among an increasingly larger number of southern folk the habit of self-examination. It is as if they were asking, "Are these things which we are doing under war pressure truly characteristic of the spirit and character of the South?"